TREASURES
FROM
UCL

OTUS BENGALENSIS.

Drawn from Nature and on Stone by E. Gould.

Printed by C. Hullmandel.

TREASURES
FROM
UCL

Gillian Furlong

UCLPRESS

First published in 2015 by
UCL Press
University College London
Gower Street
London WC1E 6BT

A CIP catalogue record for this book is available
from The British Library.

ISBN: 978-1-910634-00-4 (Hbk.)
ISBN: 978-1-910634-01-1 (Pbk.)

DOI: 10.14324/111.9781910634011

Designed by Andrew Shoolbred
Printed in Hong Kong by Great Wall Printing Co. Ltd

FRONT IMAGE: The Trevelyon Manuscript; the Tudor rose,
prominently featured (fol. 53r).

BACK IMAGE: Hand-coloured lithographic plate from
A monograph of the Ramphastidae: or family of toucans by
John Gould and Edward Lear, dated 1833. It shows the
species Ramphastos Toco (the Toco Toucan).

FRONTISPIECE: Hand-coloured lithographic plate of the
Otus Bengalensis (Bengal Owl), from John Gould's *A century
of birds from the Himalaya Mountains*, 1831.

Contents

Contributors

The publishers would like to thank the following for contributing entries to this book (numbers in brackets refer to contributed entries):

Rosemary Ashton
Emeritus Quain Professor of English Language and Literature and Honorary Fellow of UCL (no.50)

Paul Ayris
Chief Executive, UCL Press, Director of UCL Library Services and UCL Copyright Officer (no.11)

Frederick Bearman
Preservation Librarian, UCL Library Services (nos.4 and 37)

Mary Collins
Professor and Dean of Faculty of Life Sciences, UCL (no.55)

David D'Avray
Professor of History, UCL (no.6)

Adrian Forty
Professor of Architectural History, UCL (no.19)

Nicola Miller
Professor of Latin American History, UCL (no.49)

David Price
Professor of Mineral Physics and UCL Vice Provost (Research) (no.34)

René Weis
Professor of English, UCL (no.56)

Concordance

100 NOT OUT

G. DUDLEY PAGE.

1827 UNIVERSITY COLLEGE. LONDON 1927

Foreword

The holdings in UCL Special Collections form one of the hidden treasures of UCL (University College London). These materials, their content and their provenance have a great deal to say about the history of the university. UCL is the third oldest university in England after Oxford and Cambridge. As such the collections of rare books, manuscripts and archives which UCL holds have a lot to tell us about the way modern universities and their syllabi developed from the beginning of the nineteenth century. The history of education in Bloomsbury has been brilliantly captured by Professor Rosemary Ashton in her book on *Victorian Bloomsbury*. Professor Ashton is Emeritus Quain Professor of English Language and Literature and an Honorary Fellow of UCL. *Treasures from UCL* complements this work by explaining in some detail how the Library's collecting activities have contributed to the promotion of learning.

The book has selected a number of Treasures and looks at their importance to scholarship. Most of the entries have been written by Gill Furlong, who has a lifetime's familiarity with the materials in her care. Some of the entries have been written by leading academics in UCL with an interest in a particular subject. These collections are not nearly as well known as they deserve to be, and I welcome this book (in both paper and enhanced digital versions) to underline UCL's work in public engagement.

The breadth of the collecting in UCL Library Services over the decades is inspiring. Newton's *Principia* (entry **31**), for example, is one of the seminal works in the foundation of modern science. UCL's copy not only sits in UCL Special Collections, but it also goes out to undergraduate lectures. Students can then interact with the original of this great work, having just heard it described in their lecture. This is research-based teaching, one of the cornerstones of the educational experience in UCL.

As research on the holdings in UCL gathers pace, amazing new discoveries are constantly being made. The Trevelyon MS. (entry **27**) is now known to be a previously-unknown third copy of a compilation by Thomas Trevelyon (born *c.* 1548). Equally important is the recent discovery of the manuscript of a poem by Byron (entry **41**) inscribed into Samuel Rogers' *The Pleasures of Memory* (London, 1810).

Treasures from UCL is also another first, being published by UCL Press, a newly formed publishing activity which has as its aim to promote scholarly outputs across the globe, with a business model grounded in Open Access. UCL is London's Global University and we expect that UCL's scholarship will be well represented in the list of publications going forward, using a 21st century approach to the dissemination of knowledge and wisdom.

Professor Michael Arthur
Provost and President of UCL

OPPOSITE: The Centenary edition of the *College Magazine*, June 1927.

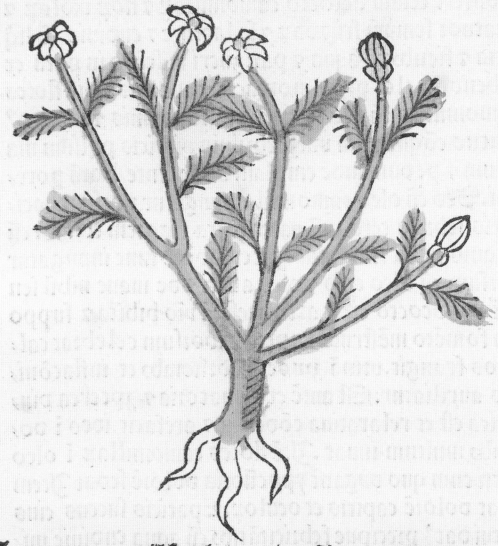

Camomilla   Camillen

Camomilla est calida z sicca in primo.haber virtutē
mollificandi et dissoluendi.frondes et flores sunt eq̄
lis virtutis.Et aqua decoctōnis ei⁹ cū arthimesia cū
qua fomentetur matrix valz puocando menstruum
Jdem valet mulieribus difficulter parientibz.Deco
ctio floz camomillaz et extremitatū absinthei z ra
dicū feniculi petrosilini z quatuoz seminum frigidoz
in vino cū zucro albo dulcorando de quo bibař valz
vunam puocādo ·lapidē expellēdo. inflatōz splenis

UCL Library Services and its Collections – a history

Founded in 1826, as the original University of London, UCL has acquired magnificent collections of manuscripts, rare books and archives dating back to the 4th century AD. These collections form an important international resource for teaching, learning and research.

Special Collections in UCL Library Services reflect not only the traditions and history of the institution. They also reveal the changing interests and innovations of its teaching and research, both areas for which UCL is renowned. Many of the most important early collections were donated or bequeathed by ex-students or professors, a practice that continues into the present digital age. The collections also offer many surprises, covering material not immediately associated with UCL. All contribute to the impressive wealth of its holdings, highlights of which are included in this volume.

Foundations

The Library was officially opened in 1829, and its first major bequests and donations came from UCL's professors and those involved with its foundation. Earliest donations include the 4,000 books given by Jeremy Bentham in 1833, while the first major manuscript gift, a magnificent 13th-century illuminated Latin Bible, was presented by William Steere in 1859 (p.22).

Ten science collections entered the Library between 1870 and 1894, including three of the most important: the medical collections of William Sharpey and Robert Grant (which contains the first edition of William Harvey's *De Motu Cordis*, 1628) (p.102), and the world-class early history of science collection bequeathed by John T Graves, Professor of Jurisprudence 1838 to 1843. Consisting of over 14,000 items, this includes early treatises of Sacrobosco (including eight incunabula) and 51 outstanding manuscripts, of which 11 early items on astronomy, astrology, mathematics and 'materia medica' are much rarer than theological or liturgical manuscripts of the same period. The most notable of these are an early 14th-century *Tractatus de sphera* (p.62), and a

OPPOSITE: An entry for *Camomilla* (the chamomile plant) from a Latin herbal, the *Herbarius Latinus*, printed in 1485. The text describes the beneficial uses of the '*frondes et flores*' (leaves and flowers).

15th-century illuminated calendar. Early editions of all the major landmarks in science are represented, the Euclid collection alone containing 83 printed editions before 1640. Other first editions include Newton's *Principia* (p.108) and *Opticks*, as well as those of Copernicus (p.80), Priestley, Boyle, Kepler, Galileo and Napier, just to name a few.

The first major collection of private papers to come to UCL was that of Jeremy Bentham in 1849, given by Sir John Bowring, who had inherited them. Numbering over 60,000 manuscript sheets, this collection is arguably UCL's most important manuscript collection, at the heart of one of the major research strengths in UCL Special Collections.

The social, educational and political reform movements of the 19th century are strongly represented in over half of the collections. The letters and papers of Sir Edwin Chadwick, variously Secretary to the Poor Law Commission 1834–48 and Commissioner of General Board of Health 1848–54, were given in 1898, while the archives of the Society for the Diffusion of Useful Knowledge, a noted educational publisher, were acquired in 1848. Most voluminous of all, comprising over 100,000 items, are the papers of Henry Peter Brougham, 1st Baron Brougham & Vaux; he was Lord Chancellor 1830–34, and one of London University's, and hence UCL's, founders. The Brougham papers were acquired in 1953 as part of the C K Ogden Collection, purchased with the help of the Nuffield Foundation, and of which more will be said later.

Among the other major bequests of the 19th century are the books and papers of the Dante scholar Henry Clark Barlow. These include 36 editions of *La Divina Commedia* printed before 1600, notably three incunabula and two copies of the first Aldine edition of 1502 (p.90).

The first of the several learned society libraries that have either deposited or donated their archives over the years came in 1887, when the Philological Society presented their collection. Amelia Edwards left her Egyptological Library in 1892 to complement her earlier endowment of the first Chair of Egyptology to Flinders Petrie (UCL's first Professor of Egyptology).

1900 to 1930s

The first librarian, Francis Cox, was appointed in 1827, but his services were terminated four years later due to funding constraints. Adrian Wheeler, appointed in 1871, made a series of catalogues for the general library, but the Library had no regular staff to speak of until the appointment of Raymond Wilson Chambers in 1901.

For the first half of the 20th century acquisitions continued to flow in, extending an already rich accumulation of special collections over an even wider variety of subjects. During this period UCL Library Services acquired its first major separate group of medieval manuscripts, its first seven major modern manuscript collections and its first important body of archives. Between 1906 and 1910 came the Mocatta Library of Jewish history, the Geologists' Association library and the Whitley Stokes library of Celtic and folk literature, and comparative philology, the last containing many limited editions and individual letters. The collection belonging to Frederic Mocatta contains two of the most valuable illuminated manuscripts in the Library, a 14th-century Castilian Haggadah (p.26) and a 16th-century *Mahzor* (p.58), both included in this selection.

1911 marked the beginning of a highly proactive stage in the Library's collecting activities, epitomised by the first purchases of medieval manuscripts. The development was initiated by Robert Priebsch, Professor of German from 1898 to 1931, to promote the study of palaeography at UCL. With the help of the then Librarian, R W Chambers (later Professor of English Language and Literature 1922–41), and Dr Walter Seton, College Secretary, Priebsch succeeded in persuading friends of the College to set up a fund to make purchases of manuscripts, notably the medieval German manuscripts bought at the famous Phillipps sale of manuscripts in April 1911. A collection of 18 German charters of the 14th to 16th centuries was also presented to the College in 1912 by Kaiser Wilhelm II. A small collection of charters was also started at this time. The earliest, Roger Mortimer's charter of 1199 to the Abbey of Cwmhir in Radnorshire, was given to the Library later, in 1957.

Among the second wave of major manuscript fragments bought at Bonn in 1921 is one of the earliest manuscripts in the Library. It is a part of one folio of a 7th-century uncial manuscript of St Mark's Gospel. Further purchases, most notably from the Sotheby's sale of the manuscripts of the British Society for Franciscan Studies and of Walter Seton in July 1927, increased the total to 213 individual manuscripts and fragments (66 dated before 1600). Among them are some of the most splendid the Library owns: a 13th-century lectionary with illuminated miniatures (p.30); a 13th-century manuscript of Rabanus Maurus's commentary on St Matthew's Gospel, from Pontigny (p.36); and a lovely 15th-century Book of Hours containing 19th-century forgeries (p.42). All are featured in this selection, and discussed in detail in both N R Ker's *Medieval Manuscripts in British Libraries* (1969) and Dorothy Coveney's *A Descriptive Catalogue of Manuscripts in the Library of University College, London* (1935). Much work remains to be done on the fragments, which include musical annotations covering several languages, and are thought to have derived from the University of Bologna.

ABOVE: The scene in the Front Quad during a fundraising Bazaar and Fete held at UCL in July 1909. Three days of fairs, dances, concerts, exhibitions and dramatic performances took place (College Archives, Photographs).

OPPOSITE: This cartoon of 1825 by Robert Cruikshank depicts Henry Brougham MP (later Lord Brougham amd Vaux) hawking shares in the projected University around Lincoln's Inn. Their sale sought to raise money for the new London University (now UCL) (College Archives, Artworks).

1911 also saw the arrival of the Folklore Society library deposit, now regarded as one of the world's principal folk collections. Two years later the first modern professorial collection was bequeathed to the Library – that of Sir William Ramsay, who discovered the rare gases of argon, helium, krypton, neon and xenon. It contains the original notebooks recording his laboratory experiments (p.168). This was followed by the papers of W P Ker, English Professor 1889–1922, and those of Sir Ambrose Fleming, inventor of the thermionic valve that marked the birth of modern electronics. His notebooks record the first-ever transmission of wireless signals (p.169). Other new arrivals include the Johnston-Lavis Collection of volcanology (p.35), and the First World War Collection of contemporary memorabilia, which the alumnus Leonard Magnus bequeathed in 1925 (p.176).

Professor Hale Bellot's centenary history of UCL (published 1929) led to the acquisition of printed and other historical material which forms the College Collection. This now consists of a large, and unique accumulation of photographs and ephemera that document the story of UCL (p.164). The Library has always been a repository for UCL's own archives, the most important group of which comprises over 5,000 items of correspondence between 1825 and 1840, shedding important light on early developments and the struggles that took place on a day-to-day level.

During the same period two more fine rare book collections were presented: Sir Herbert Thompson's Castiglione Collection and the library of Sir John Rotton, who served on the College Committee from 1869 to 1906. Later added to from the

The POLITICAL, TOY-MAN.

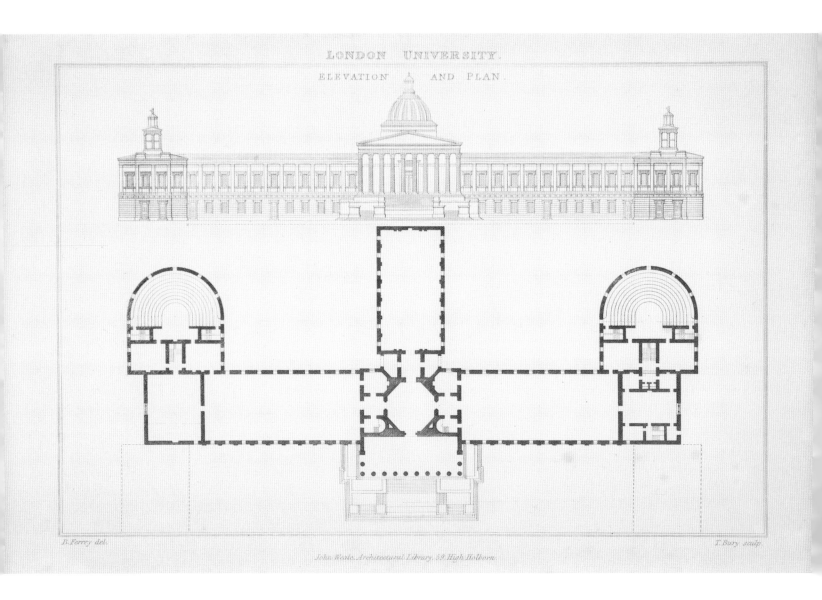

B.Ferrey del.

T.Bury sculp.

John Weale, Architectural Library, 59 High Holborn.

ABOVE: Elevation and Plan of University College London (then University of London) as designed by William Wilkins, 1826. Significantly, there was to be no chapel. Instead the main entrance was intended to give on to the three principal rooms for the University: the Museum of Natural History (left), the Library (right), and the Great Hall directly ahead (College Archives, Plans).

LEFT: The Library room given over to the Mocatta Collection, early 20th century (College Archives, Photographs).

collection of Huxley St John Brooks, the first of these now constitutes one of the most complete collections (102 separate editions) of Baldessare Castiglione's *Il libro del cortegiano* known to exist, containing five Aldine editions printed between 1518 and 1547 (p.94). The splendid Rotton Collection comprises over 30,000 finely bound volumes. Specialising in the 18th century, they cover the literatures and histories of England, France and Italy, in addition to classics, economics, law and fine art.

Three other special book collections also entered the Library at this time. These were Sir Herman Gollancz's own extremely rare tracts on the Jews in England, some dating from the 17th century, and the historical collection of Lansdowne and Halifax Tracts, which originally came from the London Institution and amount to nearly 6,000 items. Acquisitions of special collections in the 1930s and 1940s continued to build up a broad range of subjects (Anglo-Jewish, German History, palaeontology, London History, Latin American history), as well as those of learned societies (mathematics, malacology [the study of molluscs] and natural history).

1940s to 1960s

During the Second World War UCL suffered more damage than any other British university. In September 1940 and April 1941 two incendiary bombs caused extensive damage to buildings on the Gower Street site; the Main Library, located under the Wilkins dome, was almost completely gutted. Manuscripts and rare books had been evacuated to Aberystwyth, joining the treasures of many other libraries and galleries in the solid rock cellars beneath the National Library of Wales; they were returned in 1948–9. The less rare collections that remained in the capital saw heavy losses, with some 100,000 books and pamphlets destroyed.

Many supporters and friends rallied round with gifts or bequests. Lady Fleming donated 500 volumes from her husband's library in 1941 and Professor Dawes Hicks bequeathed his library of 4,000 volumes of philosophical works, together with archival material. In the same year a significant collection of Hebraica and Judaica collections was given by the Guildhall Library, while in 1943 the books of R W Chambers (the UCL Librarian before the Second World War) were presented by his sister. They contained valuable material on Sir Thomas More.

The year 1953 heralded the second highly proactive era of extensive activity of acquisitions for UCL Library Services' Special Collections, beginning with the purchase of what is probably its greatest manuscripts and rare books collection, that of Charles K Ogden. Inventor of the ground-breaking *Basic English*, to promote which he founded the Orthological Institute in 1927, Ogden (1889–1957) was considered an eccentric polymath by many. Purchased with generous assistance from the Nuffield Foundation, to 'serve as a basis for studies in the field of human communication', the collection contains around 5,000 volumes; it includes 21 incunabula and over

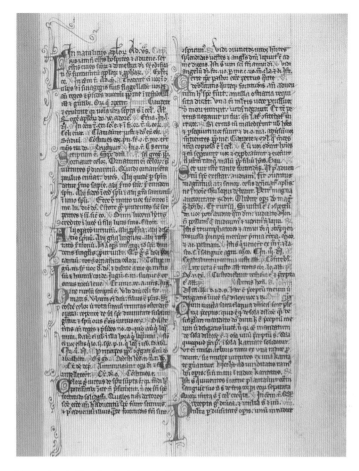

13th-century *Lectionarium* displaying a text fragment from the Common of the Saints in the breviary, showing January, February and March (MS LAT 6, fol. 6r).

100 individual and small manuscript collections, dating from the 14th to 20th centuries. The largest, that of Henry, 1st Lord Brougham, amounts to over 90,000 items, with numerous letters from several important contemporary figures. They include Charles Dickens, Queen Caroline, Prince Albert and Benjamin Disraeli, to name just a few, making it one of the most extraordinary sources for the Victorian age in the UK.

Ogden was a prolific book collector, and the collection contains some of the finest early printed books and manuscript collections at UCL, frequently being 're-discovered' by researchers (p.96). The most notable names represented in the Ogden Library (first editions, association copies and/or manuscripts, letters, diaries, related source material) include Francis Bacon, John Milton, John Dee, Samuel Coleridge, Robert Boyle, Ben Jonson, William Shakespeare, Percy Shelley, Lord Byron, Emile Zola, Dante Rossetti, John Bright, Joseph Conrad, André Gide and Arnold Bennett.

The themes of 19th-century radical, political and educational reform continued to be central to the collecting

Hand-coloured lithographic plate of the
Lettered Aracari bird (*Pteroglossus Inscriptus*),
from John Gould, *A monograph of the
Ramphastidae: or family of toucans*, 1834
(S R E Folio 920 G6.1/1–3).

Plate from Charles Lemaire (ed), *L'Illustration
horticole*, vol. 14, 1867, of the *Lilium
Haematochroum*, a former name of the
Lilum bulbiferum, of the Lily family
(R 910 ILL).

policy of Special Collections in the early 1960s. The papers of
the parliamentary solicitor and political reformer Joseph Parkes
were purchased in 1960 from his great-granddaughter, the
Countess of Iddesleigh, and in 1965 the papers of a group of
late 18th-century and 19th-century nonconformists, including
such well-known figures as the poet Samuel Rogers and the
philanthropist Samuel Sharpe, were presented by Egon Pearson,
a descendant through his mother, Maria Sharpe. More is
said of the Pearson family below. One of the most surprising
19th-century collections to be added in the late 1960s were
the papers of George Bellas Greenough, the first President of
the Geological Society of London. A prolific artist and writer,
his travels took him across Europe. Between them the Ogden,

Parkes, Sharpe and Greenough manuscript collections contain
fascinating travel journals, personal diaries and sketchbooks.
They also feature the letters of contemporary celebrities such
as James Burton, Samuel Coleridge, William Gladstone, John
Ruskin, Lord Tennyson, Walter Scott and William Wordsworth.

Professorial collections in subject specialities were also
expanding, with the acquisition of papers of physiologists,
chemists, geologists and physicists, and further learned society
deposits. The most important new strong areas to be proactively
established during the 1960s, however, were the Little
Magazines Collection, the Poetry Store Collection, the George
Orwell Archive and the Latin American Business Archives. The
Little Magazines was set up in 1964 as a Library initiative with

the original aim of collecting all current UK little magazines (small press and independent publications); this was soon broadened to encompass North American, Commonwealth and a smaller number of significant European titles. A section of Alternative Press (or Underground Press) publications was added in the mid-1960s, and the collection also features various community newsletters, underground comics such as *Oz*, *Frendz* and *International Times*, arts bulletins and radical papers. The Poetry Store was started shortly after the Little Magazines, in recognition of the affinity and interrelationship between the two. Now totalling over 7,000 titles, it contains small press publications, mostly of poetry but also including fiction and creative work in other media. Both the Little Magazines and Poetry Store holdings are at their strongest from the mid-1960s onwards, but there has also been a good deal of retrospective acquisition of earlier publications. Among these important early titles, in original form or facsimile reprint, are *Blast*, *The Germ* and *The Yellow Book*.

Sonia Orwell, George Orwell's widow, chose UCL Library Services to house the precious manuscripts and notebooks of the author of *Nineteen Eighty-Four* and *Animal Farm*. Attracted by its growing reputation as a world-class repository of modern literary papers and collections, she presented the works on permanent loan in 1960, on behalf of the George Orwell Archive Trust. Today the Archive is still the most comprehensive body of source material for Orwell studies anywhere (p.182).

The extensive collection of archives relating to South America incorporates the records of over 20 firms. On permanent loan from British companies with trading and commercial interests throughout South America in the 19th and 20th centuries, their acquisition established the largest primary resource for Latin American economic and social history outside the Americas. Threatened with their wholesale destruction by liquidators, many of the archives were rescued and deposited with UCL via the good offices of Professor Christopher Platt, a leading historian in the field.

The largest three of these collections are the archives of the fur and tea merchants Frederick Huth and Company (which traded all over the world and has records dating back to 1812), the Bank of London and South America (which looked after British banking interests and has over 1,000 volumes, from 1862) and the Peruvian Corporation (a company with major dealings in land, produce, property, construction and the management of railways, roads, canals and telegraphs). The Corporation was also involved in constructing and managing docks and harbours, ships, mines and beds of nitrates, and acting as agents of the Peruvian Government. Its archive, which spans over a century, encompasses more than 20,000 records, including much rare photographic and other illustrative material.

1970s

The policy of expansiveness continued through the 1970s and 1980s. These decades saw the highest proportion of added

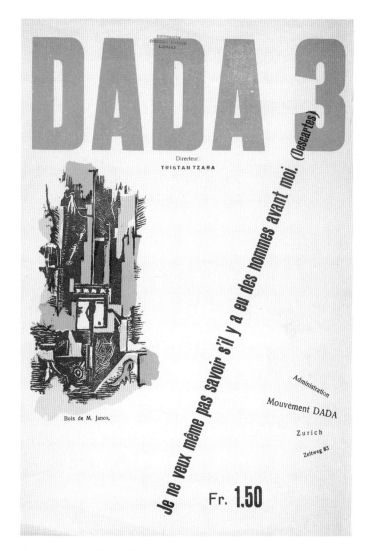

The front cover of *Dada: Recueil littéraire et artistique*, no.3, Zurich, December 1918. The periodical was edited by Tristan Tzara, a seminal figure for the Paris Dadaist group, an avant-garde movement of the early 20th century (Little Magazines DAD).

manuscripts and archive collections in the Library's history, with the possible exception of the 1990s. Some were bequeathed or presented, others purchased or transferred from departments.

Top of the list are three important groups of papers relating to the foundation and early history of the science of genetics. Francis Galton, Charles Darwin's half-cousin, had a lifelong interest in the study of inherited human characteristics. He endowed the first UCL Chair in Eugenics in 1911, bequeathing his voluminous research papers and correspondence at the same time, though they did not come to the Library until the early 1970s (p.156). Galton's successor and biographer, and first UCL Professor of Applied Mathematics, was Karl Pearson, and his papers were accessioned in 1973 (p.158). Last of this group were the papers of Lionel Penrose, Galton Professor of Genetics from 1945 to 1965, which cover his research work into the hereditary aspect of mental illness. They were also acquired in 1973.

Galton's data-collecting activities, including his pioneering work on composite photography and fingerprints, are comprehensively documented. Karl Pearson's interests beyond those of science included involvement in the establishment of the Men and Women's Club, with his wife Maria Sharpe, and provide fascinating insight into the social mores of the time. The papers of their son, Egon Sharpe Pearson, a member of staff in UCL's Department of Statistics since 1921, made Professor in 1935, also later came to the Library, containing extensive historical family material as well as important research papers. In other areas of science, medical collections such as the papers of pioneering neurosurgeon Victor Horsley (p.166), anatomist George Dancer Thane, and neurologist Francis Walshe were added to the manuscript collections.

In the arts and humanities, significant literary and artistic collections acquired include the papers of the writer and painter Richard Rees, whose correspondents included many well-known literary and public figures of the 20th century (among them George Orwell, whose literary estate he managed), and the letters and journals of William Townsend, Slade Professor of Fine Art at UCL 1968–73. They also featured the papers and drawings of Alex Helm, the English folk drama authority, the literary and political correspondence of poet and physician Alex Comfort and the illustrated printed books of Laurence Housman (p.172). The James Joyce Centre, which now holds a number of rare editions (p.178) and a significant archival collection, was set up in 1973 with the help of the Trustees of the Joyce Estate.

The other major acquisitions of the 1970s, which expanded the 19th-century British history theme, were the archives of Routledge and Kegan Paul, dating from 1853. The records of these ground-breaking publishers of books for the general public, including authors' contracts and publication records, had been stored in a riverside basement that frequently flooded. The vast personal correspondence and papers of Moses Gaster, Chief Rabbi of the Sephardic (Spanish and Portuguese) Jewish community in England between 1857 and 1918, were given in 1974; they amount to over 200,000 items. Family diaries and papers of the writers T Humphrey and Mary Ward, and of the historians George and Harriet Grote, also came to the Library during this period.

1980s

In addition to the acquisition of the Egon Pearson papers already mentioned, the year 1980 was significant for the deposit of another major collection. The papers of Hugh Gaitskell, Chancellor of the Exchequer 1950–1 and Leader of the Labour Party 1955–63, fill over 260 boxes and include a large quantity of correspondence. They are an extremely important resource for British and world political history during the first half of the 20th century, touching on many significant events such as the Suez Crisis of 1956.

Early on in the decade an important, previously unknown archive relating to James Joyce's daughter, Lucia, was bequeathed by her executor, Jane Lidderdale, while Lawrence Gowing, Professor of Fine Art at the Slade School, presented his wife Julia Strachey's papers during the same period. The latter contain interesting correspondence of the noted Strachey family, among them Julia's uncle, the critic and biographer Lytton Strachey, and the artist Dora Carrington. Another surprising collection, discovered in the Department of Electrical and Electronic Engineering and handed over to the Library in the 1980s, was the collection of autograph letters by Odo Russell (1829–84), whose family had strong connections with the Bloomsbury locality. The letters contain a handwritten note by the legendary composer Beethoven (p.142) and a manuscript letter of Goethe amongst material which is otherwise predominantly the correspondence of botanists.

The field of 20th-century biological sciences was further strengthened at this time when two of the most important and largest collections were donated: the papers of the geneticist J B S Haldane, and those of zoologist J Z Young. Haldane was a controversial figure whose lively personality and extreme left-wing views pepper the collection of his personal and scientific papers, providing an entertaining window on the political struggles of the time. J Z Young's pioneering work on the workings of the human brain is still highly influential today. Robert Carswell's famous drawings of pathological conditions were transferred to Special Collections towards the end of this decade from the Medical School (p.144). So too were the voluminous archives and records of UCL Hospital and Medical School, dating from their beginnings into the mid-20th century and featuring casebooks of well-known surgeons from the early days of modern surgery and medical practices, such as John Elliotson and Robert Liston (p.154).

1990s to the Present

Scientists' papers of former UCL professors who were chief specialists in their chosen field have continued to dominate the scene over the last two decades. Three of the greatest late 20th-century figures stand out. Kathleen Lonsdale, crystallographer, attained a number of highly significant scientific firsts. One of the first two women elected a Fellow of the Royal Society, she also became the first female tenured professor at UCL, first female president of the International Union of Crystallography and first female president of the British Association for the Advancement of Science (p.170). James Lighthill, also a Fellow of the Royal Society, was an applied mathematician and former Provost of UCL who pioneered work in the field of aeroacoustics. Bernard Katz, who fled to Britain from Nazi Germany in 1935, is noted for his work on nerve biochemistry. He was awarded the Nobel Prize for Physiology in 1970.

New additions in the humanities, less voluminous in size, have been no less notable in terms of importance. In this period they have come from the linguist and university politician Randolph Quirk (b. 1920), the distinguished Renaissance art historian John Hale, and the philosopher Richard Wollheim. Archival material previously housed in separate departments at UCL was transferred to Special Collections for safe keeping in 1997, the most notable and sizeable collections being the archives of the Slade School of Fine Art and of the Institute of Archaeology. Such large and important archive collections contain a wealth of historical research material.

It is heartening to know that smaller collections which strengthen both the 19th-century material and the wide range of outstanding academic achievements sprung from UCL's community in the 20th century continue to be bequeathed, offered and accepted as gifts from relatives, estates or biographers. Five such acquisitions from 1990 to 1999 worth noting here are the papers of the phoneticist Daniel Jones, who produced the first description of the pronunciation of the English language; the letters of the social reformer Francis Place (1771–1864); two notebooks of the writer Vita Sackville-West; correspondence between George Orwell and David Astor; and the books, papers and family archive of the Jewish studies scholar Alexander Altmann. More recently the Library has received the papers and books of Peter Davison, editor of the *Complete Works of George Orwell*, the papers of the archaeologist Mortimer Wheeler, who first brought archaeology to the general public through television, papers relating to the philosopher A J Ayer and the papers of the social anthropologist Mary Douglas.

The spirit and tradition of bequeathing papers and collections to the Library for use by present and future researchers remains as vibrant today as over the last two centuries. The challenge now facing those who care for and manage collections is to find the best way to do so in the digital age.

A selection of Treasures from Special Collections. The beautiful Dutch red morrocco binding of the Portuguese *Calendar* of 1667 and the tortoiseshell cover of the Spanish *Order of Daily Prayers* from 1717 are visible on the centre shelf.

Illuminated Bible of the 13th or 14th century, Italy

Biblia Latina

Latin. Parchment manuscript written in Italy, late 13th or early 14th century. 626 leaves. 350 × 235 mm.

Provenance: given by William Steere, 1859.

MS LAT 9

ABOVE: Decorative edges of pages from a *Biblia Latina* of the 13th/14th century. They are painted with a floral design in red and blue, while the outer edge features an ornate brass clasp.

RIGHT: *Biblia Latina*, opened at the beginning of the four New Testament Gospels. The ornate capital 'E' for Evangelists is just visible, inside left.

OPPOSITE: *Biblia Latina*, detail of miniature from the Book of Baruch (Old Testament), from the 'Explicit' or Introduction. Baruch was the prophet Jeremiah's scribe and is often depicted as such, as here (fol. 374 v).

This handsome manuscript volume containing books of the Bible in Latin is remarkable for two main reasons. Firstly, it is an outstanding example of well-preserved medieval painted edge decoration. It is highly unusual for coloured ornate decoration to be so clearly defined in an item of this age. Secondly, the story of what happened to the original binding is a fascinating tale in itself, and the reason why the book is exceptional and unique to UCL. The volume is now re-bound in half-red goatskin, with oak boards and a large ornate brass clasp. A delicate floral design is stamped on the border.

The story of this Bible's early history is laid out in a manuscript letter tipped into the fly leaf, dated October 1859. According to the letter, the book belonged to an unnamed Spanish lawyer who was obliged to leave Spain owing to his political opinions and resided in England as a refugee for some years. Before it reached England's shores, however, the original substantial bindings were 'violently torn away', to make it a lighter load for transporting 'on the backs of Mules' across Spain, and 'still worse the Manuscripts (*sic*) fell into very bad hands'. Whether the original owner re-bound it or not is unknown, but we know the half-red goatskin and oak boards replacement was bound by W H Smith, probably in 1904.

The manuscript is written throughout by the same hand in a very neat, well-executed Gothic minuscule of the 13th (or perhaps 14th) century. It is in brownish ink, with text laid over two columns with 47 lines per column. Set within 69 larger initials are beautifully executed miniatures on a blue background, overlaid with silver, red and blue flourishes. Images from the Gospels dominate the pages and delight the eye – though a number of them are missing, having been cut out, according to the manuscript letter, 'as was believed, to give away to Women and Children, and other leaves taken, to be used, as and for thread papers'. These losses are the only defects in an otherwise magnificent example of medieval craftsmanship.

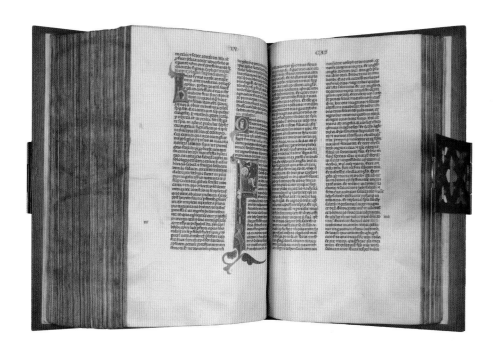

plura habens uobis scribere:
nolui p cartam 7 atramentum
8 spero enim me futurum apud
uos: et os ad os loqui. ut gau
dium urin sit plenum. Salu
tant te filii sororis tue electe.
Gra tecum amen. Explic epla
iohis ſa. Incipit argm in terciam.

Gaium pietatis causa ex
tollit. atqz ut in uia pie
tate maneat exhortat.
Diotrepem impietatis 7 supe
be causa obiurgat. demetrio
autem bonum testimonium
pibet cum frib3 uniuerſis. Ex
plicit argm tm. Incip epla ter.

Senior gaio ca
rissimo quem
ego diligo in
ueritate. Ka
rissime de oi
b3 orationes
facio. p spere
te ingredier
ualere. sicut
p spere agit anima tua. Gauiſ
sum ualde uenientib3 fribus
et testimonium pbilentibus
ueritati tue: sicut tu in ueritate
ambulas. maiorem horum ne
mo habeo gram. quam ut audi
am filios meos in ueritate am
bulare. karissime fideli facis
quicquid operas in fres. et hoc
in pegrinos qui testimonium
reddiderunt caritati tue. in co
spectu ecclie. quos benefacis
deducens digne deo. p nomie
enim eius profecti sunt. nichil
accipientes a gentib3. Nos igit
debemus suscipe huiusmodi
ut cooperatores simus ueritati.
Scripsissem forsitan ecclie. si
is qui amat primatum gerere
in eis diotrepes. non recipit nos.
ppter hoc si uenero commoneam

eius opa. que facit uerbis mali
gnis garriens in nos. Et qui
ei ista sufficiant. nz ipe suscip
fres: 7 eos qui suscipiunt phi
bet: 7 de ecca eicit. karissime no
li imitari malum: s qd bonum
est. Qui bene facit ex deo est. qui
male facit non uidit deum. De
metrio testimonium reddit
ab omnib3: et ab ipa ueritate
7 nos ei testimonium phibe
mus: 7 nosti qm testimonium
nrm uerum e. Multa habui t
scribere: s nolui p atramentu
et calamum scribere tibi. Spo
autem protinus te uidere. 7 os
ad os loquemur. pax tibi. Sa
lutant te amici. Salutant te
amici. Saluta tu amicos no
iatim. Explicit epla tcia. Incip
argm tum in epla iude.

Iudas apls frater iacobi.
scribit de corruptorib3 uie ue
ritatis ita informat. ut il
licitum ee disserat. de sub iugo
semel erutis p futuris denuo
opam suam officiis nouiter f
uilib3.

Iudas ihu xpi ſuus
frater autem iacobi. hijs
qui in deo patre di
lectis. 7 ihu xpo con
seruatis. et uocatis.
qia uobis px cari
tas adimpleatur.
ksſim omnem solli
citudinem faciens
scribendi uobis de
comuni ura salute
necce habui scribe
uobis: deprecans f
certari. semel trditi
scis fidei. Subitro
ierunt enim quidam
homines qui olim scp
ti sunt in hoc iudici

אל יי אלהי אבותינו וישמע
יי את קולנו וירא את ענינו
ואת עמלנו ואת לחצנו

Jewish service book of the 13th or 14th century, Spain

Castilian Haggadah

Hebrew. Parchment manuscript written probably in Castile, late 13th or early 14th century. 58 leaves. 242 × 188 mm.

Provenance: given as part of the library of F D Mocatta, 1906.

MS MOCATTA 1

OPPOSITE: Verses Deuteronomy 26:7 from the Mocatta Haggadah (fol. 29v). The candelabrum-shaped micrographic bands on the outer margin are typical of Catalan Hebrew biblical manuscripts from 14th century.

RIGHT: Detail of the Mocatta Haggadah, fol. 33v. The wording translated as 'and with awe' is decorated in gold leaf.

OVERLEAF, LEFT: An entire page from the Mocatta Haggadah (fol. 40r) depicting the *Dayenu* (a song of thanksgiving), decorated in gold leaf.

OVERLEAF, RIGHT: A *piyut* (liturgical poem), with candelabrum-shaped micrographic bands and ornate script, deorated with gold leaf, on light red background (fol. 55v).

Originating in Spain, this Haggadah is an exquisitely decorated manuscript volume in ink, gouache, silver and gold leaf on parchment. In Jewish homes it is central to the rituals enacted to commemorate the Israelite redemption from Egypt in biblical times. A compilation of biblical passages, prayers, hymns and rabbinic literature, the Haggadah was probably assembled sometime during the Second Temple period in Palestine (between 538 BCE and 70 CE) and was meant to be read during the Passover Seder, a ritual feast.

Illuminations represent biblical scenes as well as scenes from rabbinic legends. Many illuminated Haggadot, most of which were produced in Europe in the Middle Ages, depict the preparations for the holiday and the celebration of the Seder itself, giving later generations glimpses into the domestic landscape of Jewish communities spread across the globe. The first printed version of the Haggadah was published in Guadalajara in 1482, just ten years before the expulsion of the Jews from Spain. The first Haggadah to be printed with illustrations was produced in Prague in 1526. It was the first in a long line of printed illustrated Haggadot, a tradition that continues to this day.

The family of Frederic Mocatta (d. 1905) can trace its origins back to the 15th century, and one can imagine the Mocatta Haggadah being carefully passed down the generations. The work dates back to a crossover point for Jewish folk art in the stylistic trends of Hebrew book illumination in Spain. Opinions vary as to the date of the Mocatta work's creation, as the decoration encompasses various types of Hebrew manuscript illustration prevalent at the turn of the 13th/14th centuries. This was probably due to the use of several models, each of different origin.

The lack of uniformity in the design suggests that it was executed in various phases over a period of time. The numerous grotesque figures, contained within the panels or extending from the corners, point to a model of French origin, while the micrographic ornaments filled with colour that run along the script in the outer margins occur in biblical manuscripts of Aragon and southwestern France or Languedoc. The micrography is possibly the work of Jacob, the scribe of the Rylands Haggadah, the Catalan Mahzor and the Nahum Bible, who was working in Barcelona in the second quarter of the 14th century. On some pages these micrographic bands form a candelabrum, a motif mainly used in 14th-century Catalan Bibles. Catalan influence is also discernible in the manuscript's only illustration, the full-page representation of the *matzah*, or unleavened bread (fol. 43r). The ornamental disc, with gold fillet interlaces and painted colour fillings, became typical of the 14th-century Haggadot of Catalonia.

העניר־ט בתוכו

כחרבה ולא שק

צריעו בתוכו

שקע צריעו בתוכו

ולאספק צרכנו

כמדנר ארכע שנ

ספק צרכנו כמדנ

ארבעים שנה ולא

חא כלנו את תמ

מצרים מושיע
בתינו הציל
חורות נערו
אריות ואין מציל
עיר חל קראת ורא

מצרים ספי לא
כאהם שחירת
חורות ערין נגה
לכו ער לם שחית
עיר חל קראתי וראה

A beautiful *Lectionarium*, or reader, with fragments of two texts

13th-century Lectionary

Latin. Parchment manuscript, probably written in England in the 13th century. 27 leaves. 136 × 86 mm.

Provenance: probably among the fragments purchased in Bonn in 1921.

MS LAT 6

This tiny, delicate manuscript comprises fragments of two different texts: a *Breviarium*, or breviary (fols. 1–18), written for Franciscan use and including hagiographical texts, and a *Missale*, or missal (fols. 19–27). A member of the clergy or a devout lay person would have been the proud owner of this very personal and pleasurable *Lectionarium*, or reader, from which he or she could read scripture extracts on appointed saints' days, holy days and festivals.

The Latin text is written in ink by three different hands. All is in minute, neat Gothic minuscule on very fine vellum, rubricated throughout with gold, red and blue initials. On folio 19 there is a skilfully executed, though slightly damaged, miniature of the Crucifixion, painted on a blue background. Other interesting features of this work include the graded calendar in the breviary, written entirely in black, with the word 'pape' and the entry of St Thomas of Canterbury on 29 December erased, and the variations regarding standard Franciscan saints' days – for example, All Souls (2 Nov), Clare (12 Aug) and Bernard (20 Aug) are all missing. Following the Reformation it was common practice to remove references to the Pope and to specific saints, as a reaction against the Church of Rome. Three English saints have, however, been added in the 14th century: Wulstan, Chad and William (19 Jan, 2 Mar and 8 June). Folios 17–18 contain the Office of St Anthony, also added in the 14th century.

The first initial of the second fragment, the Office of the Mass, which starts on folio 19, is an historiated *T* of *Te igitur*, in a frame. It is followed on folios 20–27 by the text of the *Sanctorale*, devotional saints' days 21 March to 21 December, the common of the saints, a dedication of church and altar, and votives. For most feasts, including that of St Francis (the one modern saint), only the collect, secret and postcommunion are provided, finishing with the Office for the Sick on folio 27. The common of the saints, the collect, secret and postcommunion are part of the services of the Roman Church.

OPPOSITE First initial of of the second fragment in a 13th-century *Lectionarium* beginning the Office of the Mass, the '*Te igitur*'. A historiated capital '*T*' is configured as a crucifix on a blue background (fol. 19r, slightly damaged).

OVERLEAF, LEFT: 13th-century *Lectionarium*, a text fragment from the common of the saints in the breviary, showing January, February and March (fol. 6r).

OVERLEAF, RIGHT: First leaf of the *Lectionarium*, beginning the common of the saints, with exaggerated blue and red flourishes on the initials (fol. 1r).

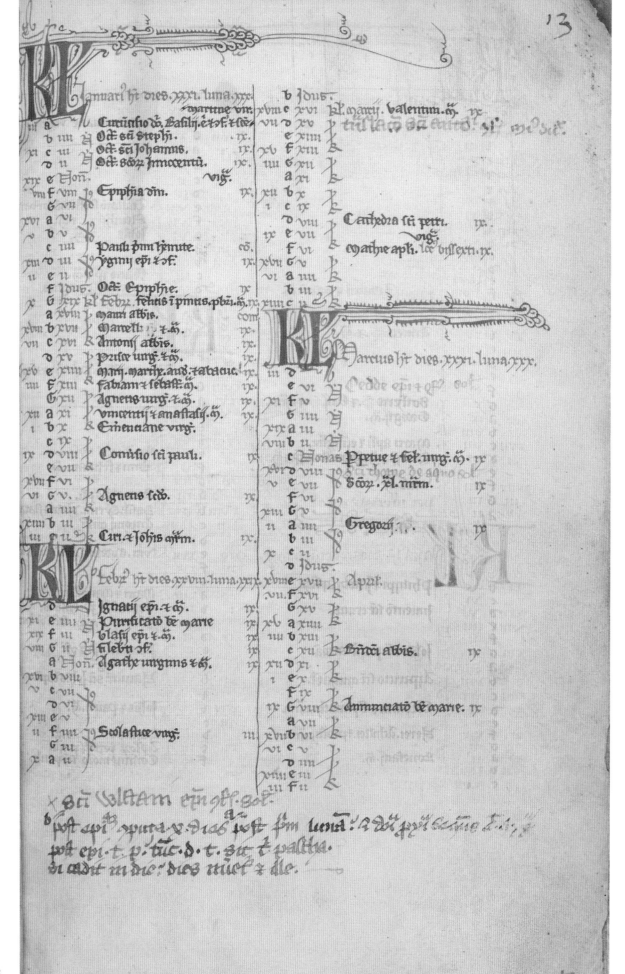

Januari ht dies .xxxi. luna .xxx. b Idus.

Martine vir. xviii c xvi Kł marcij valentini. m̃. ix

a iiii Circūcisio dñi. Basilij .c̃. t̃. iscd̃ vii d xv y trit̃ laco de eunt̃ Kł me d̃c̃.
b iii Oct̃. sci Stephi. ix. e xiiii
c ii Oct̃. sci Johannis. xvi f xiii
d Oct̃. sctoꝝ Innocentū. ix. iiii g xii
xii e Non. viij a xi
viii f viii Epiphia dñi. ix. xii b x
g vii ix c ix
xvi a vi d viii Cathedra sci petri. ix.
b v vii f vii
c iiii Pauli pmi heite. cō. ix f vii Agathie apłi. ic̃ bissexti. ix.
xiii d iii Ygini epi t̃ c̃. ix. xviii g vi
ii e ii vi a v
f Idus. Oct̃. Epiphie. ix. b iiii
x g xix kł febr. felicis in pincis. pbr̃. c̃. ix. xiiii c iii
a xviii y mauri abłis. cō
xviii b xvii y Marcelli t̃ c̃. ix.
vii c xvi k Antonij abłis. ix. Marcius ht dies .xxxi. luna .xxx.
d xv y Prisce uirg. t̃ c̃. ix. iii d Cedde epi t̃ c̃. ix
xv e xiiii mariū martiū aud̃ t̃ abacuc. ix. e vi y
iiii f xiii k fabiani t̃ sebłi. c̃. ix. xi f v y
g xii y Agnetis uirg. t̃ c̃. ix. vi g iiii y
xii a xi y vincentij t̃ anastasij. c̃. ix. xix a iii
i b x k Emerentiane uirg. viii b ii y
c ix y c Nonas Ppetue t̃ fel. uirg. c̃. ix
ix d viii y Conuersio sci pauli. ix. xvi d vii Thome de aquo cō
e vii k v e vii Sctoꝝ .xl. mrm. ix
xviii f vi vi k xiii g v
vi g v y Agnetis scdo. ix. ii a iii Gregorij. ix
a iiii k b iii
xiiii b iii x c ii
iii c ii k Ciri t̃ Johis epm̃. ix. d Idus.
xviii e xvii y Aprut̃
Febr ht dies .xxviii. luna .xxx. vii f xvi
d Ignatij epi t̃ c̃. ix. g xv
xi e iii y Purificatio be marie xvi a xiiii
xix f ii y Blasij epi t̃ c̃. ix. iiii b xiii
viii g ii y Tilebri c̃. ix. c xii Brici abłis. ix
a Non. Agathe uirginis t̃ c̃. ix. xii d xi
xvi b viii i e x
v c vii f ix
d vi ix g viii Annunciatio be marie. ix
xiii e v a vii
ii f iiii y Scolastice uirg. iii xviii b vi
g iii vi c v
x a ii d iiii
xiiii e iii
iii f ii

x sc̃ wiłłm epi gł sol.
b post epi epua x dies post sm leuit̃ t̃ dñi prī iciue t̃ t̃
post epi t̃ p tuc d t̃ sit t̃ palm̃.
bi cadit in die dies miet t̃ dłe.

In natalicijs aplox Ad.vs. Cap.
gz iam tn estis hospites z aduene. set
estis ciues scox z domestici dñ si edifica
ti si sunt suntu eplox z pphax. Exst.
ce. In cēm t. Ad.ch. Tradent ei uos i d
ncilijs tī sinagogis suis flagellabi uos et
añ reges tpsices ducemi ipi me i testimoniū
illi z gntibz. Orz q̃ ppetit. Sauuete
z exultate qz noia ura sepia st i coel. At.
Legē aplox do. w. Adore. Etña. Jn.c.
S. In cēm t. exi so. e. z i si. oz. t. ü. coz.
Celi enar. Clamauint iusti z do ex eos.
Benedica. Cōstitues eos. pn. st. o. t. me. est
nois tui do. Crydaunt. Jn.o. t. Csermo
scriptum e. Spe dñi. Tot. t. sci gref. ip.
ornauit celos. Ornatum ei celox. st
uirtutes p dicantū. Q̃urdz ornamēta
paulus enuiat. uices. Alij quoz p spm
daturz sermo sapie. alij sermo scie. p eundem
spm. Alij fides i eod spu z alij gra sanitatū
i uno spu. Ecce e mitto uos sic oues i
me. lu. diē do. Estote gz prudentes siē ser
pentes z si. sie co. Dum lucem htis
credite i lucē ut filij lucis sitis. Estote.
Alij opato uirtutū. alij pphia. alij disce
tio spuū. Alij gña linguax. Alij inter
tatō knionū. Hã opñs un atqz id scie dum
dens singlis. put uult. Qz g s sua pdi
cantū. tot s ornamēta celox. Tollite iu
gū. m. sr uos. d. do. z discite a me qz mitis
sū z humil corde. Jugū. e. m. siuaue z et
onus meū leue. Et inue.re. a. uris. Jug
nne rursū scriptū e. Vbo dñi celi fir
mati s. Vbum ei dñi. filius e pris. Sz
coscē celo. ut tota simul trinitas ostenda
opita. repente de sci spc diuinitate subun
gitur. z spu ous e ois uirtus cox. Du ste
tius añ reges z psides no. co. quo au q̃ lo
mini. Dabz ei uob i illa hoza q̃ loximini. nõ
ei uos estis q̃ lo. sz spc p.u. q̃ loqi i ub. Dabi.
Jn.ü.S. Principes ppli congregati sci do
abraham. Os go. Dedisti hoc n.ū.t. do.
Cz e de dez. Anunciauint opa dī z sacta e
antellexēt. Cz.dz.o. Cōstitues e.
Celox g uirtus de spu suipta e. qz midi sz
pptestant. Jur n psunent. n eos sci spc
fortitudo solidast. Quales nsz dertozes
scē ecce añ h aduentū spc fiūt scimus.
z p aduentu illius q̃te fortitudis sci sint.

ospicium. Vidi iuuētos inox hntes
splendidas uestes z angls dñ loquit e ad
me dicens. Jsti s uiri sci sci amuti di. Vidi
angelū di. fo. uo. p. me. t. uo. m. cla. z di. Jsti
certe ipe pastor ecce petrus q̃tte
debilitatis q̃utez fortitudis añ aduen
tium li spc fiūt. ancilla ostiaria requi
sita dicat. una ei mstris uece ptissi nz
do moui timuit. uerta negauit. Et tñ pe
trus negauit in tra. qn lat ostedat in
tute. Bi eritis cū maledixerint ub hōs
z psequuti uos fūrint z di. o. mã. apusiū uez
inticientes ipi me. Sauuete z exl. q̃ mces
ura copiosa e i coel. Cū uos odirint hoies
tū sepauuto uos. z exprobrauint z eiecint
n urm tanq̃ malū ip filiū hōis. Gau
ter uir iste tante fortitudis. qz p aduen
tū spc extitat. audiam. sit euentus
magistatuū atz senioz. eosis dentiam aplis
ne i noie ihu loqui debeant. Petrus magna
auctoritate rz dit. Ordine opz do mag
q̃ hoibz. Et rursū. Si iustu e i cōspctu
dei uos poti audire q̃m dm. iudicate. Jsõn
ei possim q̃ audiuim z uidim n loqui.
Jsti s triumphatores z amici dñ q̃ stephen
tes uista pntcipi merint pmia etña. ch co.
z at. palmam. Jstis q̃ ueneēt ex m̄ t. Na
sto. c. i sanguie agni. ch co. Cn. ü. S.
Exaltabimur cornua iusti att. Cōstitebi.
Lux orta e iusto att rectis coz. le. att.
Do.n.ez. Custodiebant testimonia e z p̃cepta
e att. Sumis hoñ. S. John
S. iñ t̄z. d.i.v.s. Hoc e p̃ceptū meum ut
diligatis iuice sic dilexi uos z Bc.
Dum iuicta sacra eloquia dñicis sint ple
na p̃ceptis. quid eq̃ de sola dilcce qu de
singlari mandato do dicit. h e p̃ceptū me
um ut diligatis iuice. n qz cē mandatum
de sola dilcce e. z ois uniti p̃ceptū s. Quia
quicqud pripi. i sola karitate solidatur.
Vt ei multi arbores rami ex una radice p
deunt. sic multe uirtutes ex una karita
te gñantur. Hec li ad uinditatis rami
bo opis. siū man̄z i radice karitatis.
Jsti s uiuuentes i carne plantati nr eosm
sanguie suo nz s de tris cozpis cox sepatata
Oziox iusta s i coel coeqta. Jn cēm. t. Orz
rtcepta g dñica. z inuita s z iusti. uiu.
Inuita p duisitatē opis. unu i radue

4

A rare late medieval chemise binding

Passio Christi ('Passion of Christ')

German. Paper manuscript written in Bavarian dialect, late 15th century. 166 leaves. 500 × 105 mm.

Bound in original alum-tawed sheepskin cover, stained pink, over oak boards. Secondary chemise covering, also alum-tawed and stained pink, cut with head and tail flap to create the chemise. Contemporary single brass clasp.

Provenance: presented by Sir Edgar Speyer, 1911.

MS GERM 20

An account of Christ's Passion, in two hands, this uses a Gothic cursive script, with red ornamented initial letters throughout. This is a fine example of a late medieval 'chemise' binding that has survived the destruction of libraries and books during the Reformation of the Roman Catholic Church which swept across Europe in the early 16th century.

As a result of this political and religious turmoil most chemise bindings, which quickly become part of the symbolism of the old Catholic Church, were either deliberately damaged or had their chemise coverings removed so the books could be re-bound. The chemise style of binding, only applied to the most precious and venerated texts, was also used as a visual display of personal piety. The bindings played a significant role in the iconography of late medieval painting, sculpture and manuscript illumination. Although the tail flap on this example has been shortened (no doubt to allow the book to be stored upright on the shelf alongside others), it would once have been long enough to be carried by the hand or to slip under the belt in readiness for use. The contemporary single clasp is fashioned with charming little 'duck heads' – the only decoration on the binding.   FREDERICK BEARMAN

FAR LEFT AND LEFT: The *Passio Christi*, with late 15th-century chemise binding, showing cover and brass clasp. The clasp is fashioned with a charming 'duck head'.

OPPOSITE: The *Passio Christi*, late 15th century, clearly written in a deep black, well-preserved ink in a cursive script, in the Bavarian dialect. The initials throughout are ornamented with red vertical strokes (fols. 97r–98v).

...lin was kume re notdurft
zu kauffen auf die osterlich
en zeit Nun het got gepo
ten das all iuden zu ostern
pei dem tempel solten sein
Dar umb so was in d' zeit
groß volk in d' stat die sa
hen den herrn so andelich
en furen mit gepunden
henden auf dem ruck ho
kom dem den herrn das
lang tuch vnd die fuß
das der her dan fiel on
alle stewr vn̄ den vnflat
mit seine benedite ant
lutz so gar geswall vn
den wunden die er dar
ein gefallen het vnd das

plut vmisthet sich den
mit dem vnflat das sein
frolichen antlutz so gar
vngestalt wart vn so
merclichen on ze sehen das
es in himel vn erden
erparmt mocht haben
Das groß leiden vnd
vnschuld an vnserm
lieben herrn sach pilatus
was vn erparmte sie vnd
ant zu pilato das er mit
hosu mehts zu schaffen het
mit der gestalt prachten
die iuden den herrn ihesu
fur pilato petrus darma
sterus der cardinal prucht
also von erlichen gespot

5

Early edition of Rabanus Maurus's commentaries

Rabanus Maurus, *De Sermonum proprietate, sive Opus de universo.* Strassburg: Adolf Rusch, before 20 July 1467.

Latin. 167 leaves. 415 × 280 mm.

Provenance: bequeathed as part of the Graves Library, 1870.

INCUNABULA FOLIO 1a

This early edition of the *De Sermonum proprietate* of Rabanus Maurus is the oldest printed book owned by UCL. It is itself a fine example of a very important stage in the history of early printing. Roman script, eventually the standard throughout Europe, was not universally accepted at first (very few books were in this form of script before 1480), representing as it did the move away from the ornate 'medieval' styles to embrace the new 'humanist' form. Leaders of this movement, emanating from Italy, saw it as giving a more classical appearance to printed text. Adolf Rusch, based in Strasbourg, was one of the first printers to possess a typeface in roman script type, earning him the title 'the R-printer'. He used it for the first edition of Rabanus Maurus's *De rerum naturis* (*On the Nature of Things* – an early form of encyclopedia) before 1467.

Rabanus Maurus Magnentius (*c.* 780–856), also known as Hrabanus of Rhabanus, was a Frankish Benedictine monk, the Archbishop of Mainz and a theologian. His *De rerum naturis,* also known as *De universo,* is an encyclopedic compilation which he assembled between 842 and 846. It is chiefly a rearrangement, in 22 books and 325 chapters, of Isidore's *Etymologies,* with several omissions and additions. Maurus's arrangement, beginning with God and the angels, long prevailed in methodical encyclopedias. UCL is fortunate to own another work by Rabanus, a 13th-century manuscript of his commentary on St Matthew's Gospel, from Pontigny, purchased in 1919 (MS. LAT.7).

The outstanding collection of books and manuscripts from the library of John Thomas Graves (d. 1870) has already been mentioned (p.13), but it is worth saying more about this remarkable man. Graves's interests covered not only law, but also classics and mathematics. He published many articles in Smith's *Dictionary of classical antiquities,* as well as in the *Proceedings of the Royal Society, the Philosophical Magazine* and the *Transactions of the Royal Irish Academy.* A lifelong book lover, his amassed collection is principally devoted to early mathematics, but also embraces the history of physics, applied mathematics in all its branches, chemistry and the biological sciences. The Graves incunabula collection, numbering 75 altogether, accounts for nearly half of all UCL's collection, including this splendid volume.

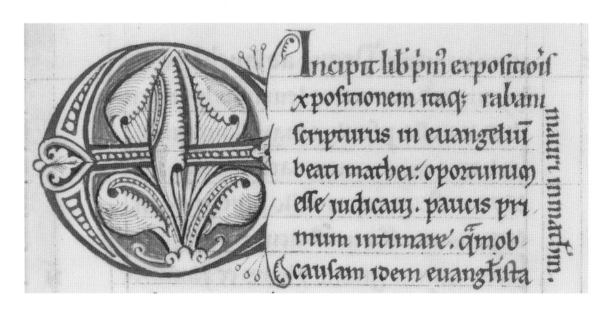

LEFT: Detail from Rabanus, commentary on St Matthew's Gospel, 13th-century manuscript (MS LAT 7). The historiated initial 'E', for 'Expositionem', appears at the beginning of the work, and the words '*mauri in matheum*' (commentary of Maurus upon Matthew) are written vertically in the margin (fol. 3r).

OPPOSITE: A page from the chapter entitled 'De Civibus', at the end of Book XVI in Rabanus Maurus's commentaries, printed early 1467. Contemporary handwritten annotations can just be seen in the centre space (unnumbered page).

clamauit & dominus exaudiuit eum . Pau=
peres sancti qui humiles spiritu sunt . vt in
euangelio. Beati pauperes spiritu & in psal=
terio. Non spreuit neq; despexit preces pau=
perum. Aliter pauperes diuites seculi hui9
virtutibus vacui vt est illud in apocalipsi Di
cis quia diues sum & ditatus . & nescis quia
tu es pauper & mendicus. Inops populus gē
tium humilis. vt in psalterio. Suscitans a ter
ra inopem. & alibi. Eripiens inopem de ma/
nu fortioris. hoc est de potestate dyaboli .
Mancipium est quicquid manu capi aut sub=
di potest . vt homo. equus ouis. Hec enim ani
malia statim vt nata sunt. mancipium esse pu
tantur. Nam & ea que in bestiarum numero
sunt. tunc videntur mancipium esse . quando
capi siue domari ceperint. Ingenui dicti quia
in genere habent libertatem nō in facto sicut
liberti. vnde & eos greci eugenos vocant q̱d
sint boni generis . Libertus autem vocatus
quasi liberatus . erat enim prius iugo serui=
tutis addictus libertorum filii apud anti/
quos libertini appellabantur . quasi de liber=
tis nati. Nunc vero libertinus aut a liberto
factus aut possessus . Liberti enim spirita/i
ter illi dicuntur. qui cristiana libertate bene
vtuntur . Vnde apostolus ait . Qui enim in
domino vocatus est seruus libertus est domi
ni. Similiter qui liber vocatus est seruus est
cristi. Hic enim omnino seruus est qui impru
denter agit . sicut & veteribus placuit . qui
omnes sapientes liberos appellauerūt. impru
dentes autem omnes seruos. Vnde salomon
Seruo inquit sapienti liberi seruient. Hic er
go qui credit ac si seruus sit ad tempus quia
rem facit prudenter vt credat in cristam li=
bertus sit domini. Si ergo peccata seruos fa
ciunt sicut cham filius noe peccati & impru=
dentie causa factus est seruus. Cum accepe/
rit remissionem peccatorum libertus effici=
tur. Similiter inquit qui liber vocatus est ser
uus est cristi. profectus est ex libero seruum
fieri cristi. liber enim a deo quod maximum
crimen est ideo amissa amara & contraria li=
bertate seruilem cōditionem sortitus est que
prodesset. sicut dicit dominus. Tollite iugū
meum super vos. quia suaue est. & onus me=
um leue est. Manumissus dicitur quasi ma/
nu emissus Apud veteres enim quotiens ma
nu mittebant alapa percussos circumagebāt
vnde & manumissi dicti eoq; manu mitteré
tur. Ciues romani postea dicti sub consuli=
bus per testamenta in vrbe romana sunt ef=
fecti . dicti autem ciues romani quia testa=
mento liberi effecti in numero romarorum
ciuium rediguntur. His primum aditus erat

in vrbe roma commorari . Ceteris autem li=
bertis prohibebatur ne vel in vrbe roma vel
infra septimum ab vrbe miliarium comma=
nerent. licet legamus paulum apostolum ne
cessitate compulsum propter sedicionem ex=
ortam ciuem romanum se appellasse. multo
gloriosius est quod se cum ceteris fidelibus
ciuem celestis hierusalem nuncupauit. vnde
ad ephesios scribens ait. Ergo iam non estis
hospites & aduene sed estis ciues sanctorum
& domestici dei superedificati super funda=
mentum apostolorum & prophetarum. hoc
est super nouum & vetus testamentum collo
cati. que enim apostoli predicauerunt. ppĥe
te futura dixerunt. hoc est non solum nos sed
& celestes potestates pariter fieri habitacu=
lum dei in spiritusancto. Heredis nomen im
posuit census eris. consuluit enim tributum
actoris in hoc enim vocabulo prima successio
est hereditatis & generis vt sunt filii vel ne
potes. Proheres qui loco heredis fungitur .
quasi pro herede. Est enim aut institut9 aut
substitutus . Heredes autem mistice sancti
dei possunt intelligi. & qui celestis patrie pos
sessores futuri sunt Vnde apostolus ad roma
nos scribens ait . Ipse spiritus testimonium
reddet spiritui nostro quod sumus filii dei.
Si autem filii & heredes . Heredes quidem
dei coheredes autē ixp̄i. Vt ergo promptos
ad obediendum deo patri faceret hac spe ex
hortatur. dicens. dei nos futuros heredes.
coheredes autē ixp̄i. vt quia magna spes pre
mii est tantomagis in dei rebus propensiores
essemus postponentes curam mundanorum
quid sit autem coheredem esse filii dei ab apo
stolo iohanne docemur. inter cetera enim ait
Scimus quoniam cum apparuerit similes ei
erimus.

Explicit liber sedecimus.

Genealogical roll chronicle of the kings of England, from a Yorkist

Chronicon genealogicum regum anglorum

Latin. Parchment manuscript roll, written in England, early 1460s. Coloured roundels surmounted by gold crowns, coloured initials, rubrics. 8 membranes, pasted together, measuring 5955 × 308 mm unrolled.

Provenance: bequeathed by Gertrude Moseley, 1918.

MS ANGL 3

RIGHT: Section of *Chronicon genealogicum regum anglorum* (genealogical roll chronicle of the kings of England), written in the early 1460s. The largest crowned roundel at the bottom features Edward IV, the line tracing back from Richard Duke of York in the centre of the image, and thence from Richard Earl of Cambridge and Anna (on the right and left of the image respectively).

OVERLEAF, LEFT: A section of the *Chronicon genealogicum regum anglorum* tracing, from the top, Richard I, John, Henry III, Edward I and Edward II. The monarchs are signified by crowned roundels down the centre of the image.

OVERLEAF, RIGHT: A section of the *Chronicon genealogicum regum anglorum*, showing the line of descent of Edward III, Richard II and Henry IV.

'*Ricardus Dux Eboracensis desponsavit filiam … domini Westmorland*' ('Richard Duke of York married the daughter … of the lord of Westmoreland').

Ms. Angl. 3 belongs to a genre of genealogical chronicles well established in the later Middle Ages. This roll is potentially a most valuable source for 15th-century attitudes to Britain's past, tracing the lineage of England's Plantaganet rulers right back to Adam himself. It is also a visually attractive object.

The illustration shown appears at the end of the roll. Prominent in it is the second and largest roundel, to the left, which features a crown top and the text: '*Edwardus dei gratia verus heres et rex istius Britannie, Francie et Hispanie*' ('Edward, by the grace of God, true heir and king of this Britain [presumably as opposed to Brittany], of France and Spain').

The lines leading to the illustration show Edward IV's claim to the throne. Retracing them, we arrive first at the name of Richard Duke of York, in a circle saying that he married the daughter of the lord [in fact the Duke] of Westmoreland. Following the diagonal line on the right upwards, we get to a roundel saying that '*Ricardus Comes Cantibrigie desponsavit Annam*' ('Richard Earl of Cambridge married Anna'). Again from Richard Duke of York, a double red and blue line leads up to a corresponding roundel on the left-hand side which says the same in reverse: '*Anna nupta domino Ricardo comiti Cantibrigie*' ('Anna married to Richard Earl of Cambridge').

Following these two lines up from Anna's circle on the left, we are led back through Roger Mortimer and other intermediaries to King Edward III. From Edward III, a single green line leads down to Edmund Langley Duke of York. We are then taken by a red line down to the roundels already mentioned to Richard Earl of Cambridge, and so on down through Richard Duke of York to Edward IV.

We may infer that the compiler of the genealogical history was on the Yorkist side in the Wars of the Roses – and that he finished his work before Edward IV's death in 1483, since Edward is the last king recorded in the roll. He probably wrote it over a period of time, since at the beginning he says he will take it up to Henry VI, then the reigning monarch.

The chronicler-genealogist was patriotic. He admires Henry V, calling him '*precipuus inter omnes reges cristianos tam in temporali policia quam in armis militaribus*' ('pre-eminent among all Christian kings both in statesmanship and in feats of arms') and stressing his conquests in France.

Rolls such as this were used to prove one's noble ancestry and to support claims to titles, arms and other accoutrements of nobility. A table of the kings of England to Edward IV, this one traces their descent from Adam and Eve, including legendary figures such as Brutus, the first king of Britain, and King Arthur. The genealogy is preceded by a brief preface, beginning '*Considerans cronicorum prolixitatem*' and ending with '*ad Henricum sextum originaliter finem perduxi*' which summarises the content of the document. We know the date of the last entry, which appears in the text adjacent to the roundel depicting Edward IV as king ('*anno domini mccccliii*', or 1453). As Edward's marriage is not given, this roll was presumably completed before 1465, when he married Elizabeth Woodville.   DAVID D'AVRAY

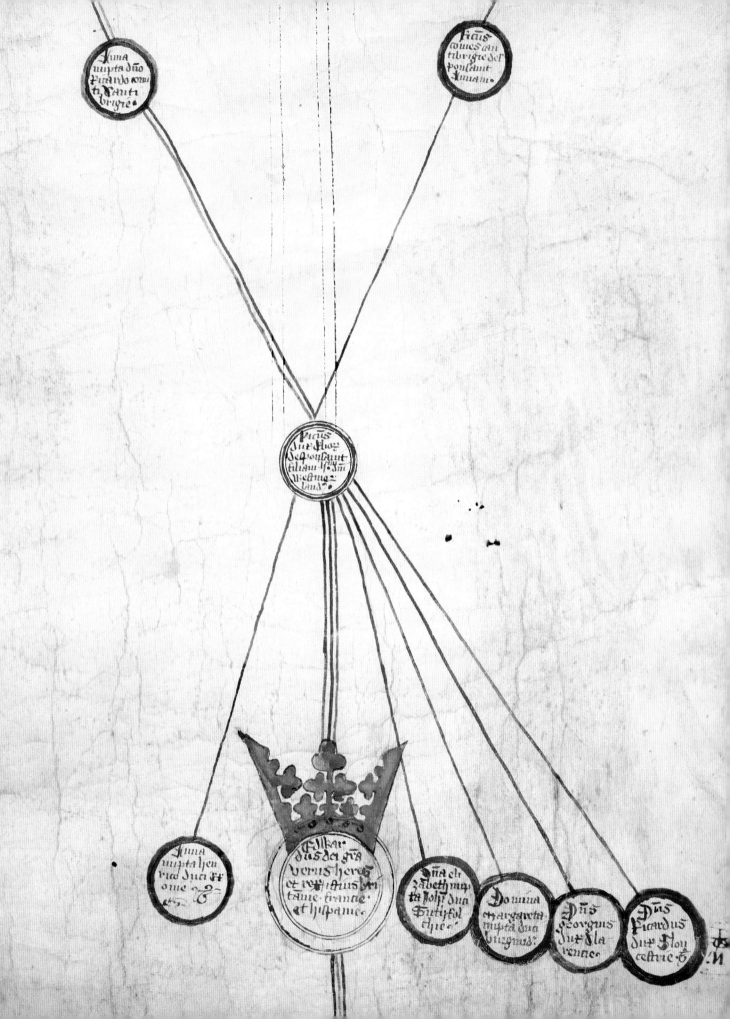

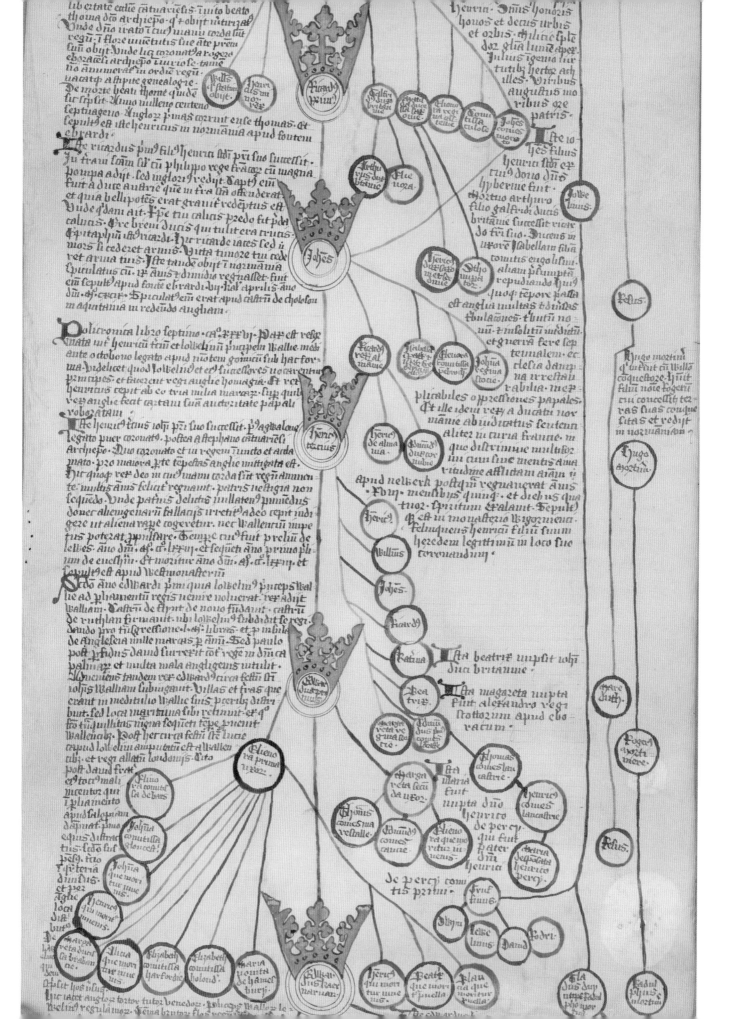

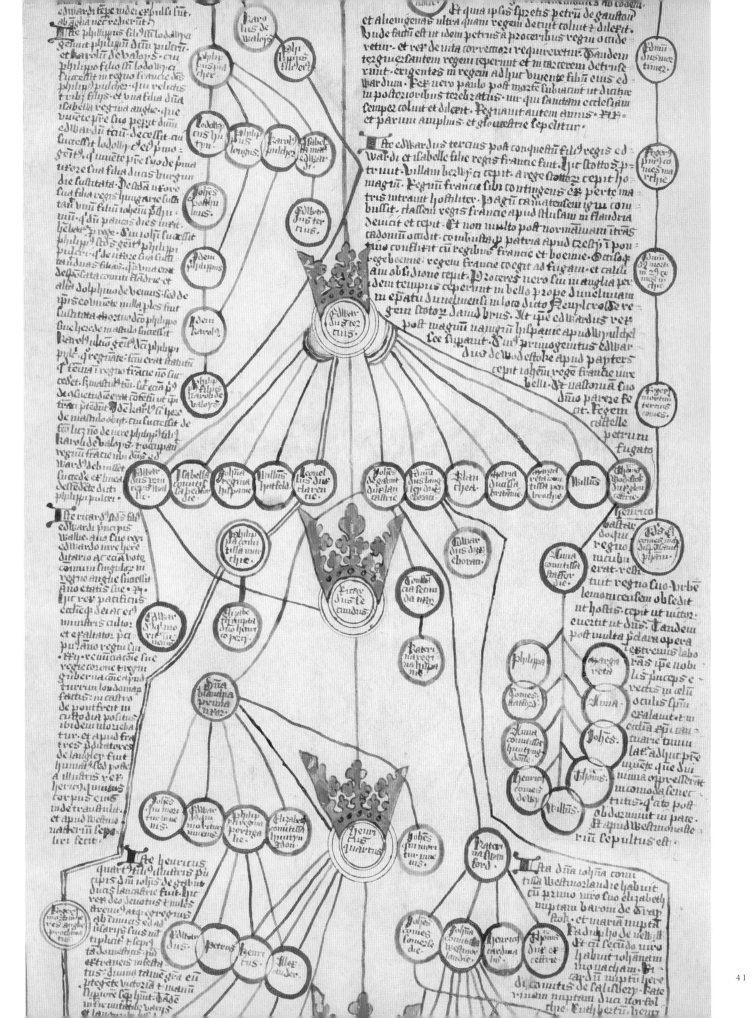

41

Book of Hours from the late 15th century, adapted for the Victorian market

Officium Beatae Mariae Virginis

Latin. Parchment manuscript written in Italy, *c.* 1470–80, with 19th-century English additions. 124 leaves, originally 106 leaves. 140 × 100 mm.

Provenance: given by Professor L S Penrose, 1949.

MS LAT 25

This exquisite illuminated devotional text, beginning with the *Officium Beatae Mariae Virginis*, would have been a privately treasured possession when it was first created. The fore-edges of the leaves are embellished with gilt. Written in a humanistic script, with beautifully decorated initials in blue and red, the text would have been in daily use by its owner. Eighteen of the initials have illuminated miniatures, in red, blue and gold on patterned coloured backgrounds. The scribe is known to be a Venetian, Marcus de Cribellariis or Marcus de Vincenze. The extraordinary feature of this tiny Book of Hours, however, is the fact that eight of the full-page colour illustrations, including a Crucifixion, plus decorated borders and a calendar, were added in 19th-century England.

Originally dating from probably the 1470s, this small manuscript book is a curious example of the taste for owning medieval manuscripts in the Victorian age. This trend was amply serviced by Caleb Wing (fl. 1826–60), well known as a professional facsimilist, and his work has often subsequently been regarded as genuine. The additions are thought to have been made while the work was in the possession of John Bykett Jarman, a collector and dealer with premises off Bond Street in the 1840s. After his death the manuscript was bought in the Jarman sale of 1864 by the bookseller Lilly, who sold it to William Bragge of Sheffield. It was bought by Quaritch at the Bragge sale in 1876, but returned, probably due to the fake additions.

In 1881 the book was sold at Sotheby's to Alexander, Baron Peckover of Wisbech, the grandfather of the donor, Lionel Penrose. The Peckover bookplate is attached to the second end page. It was also exhibited at the National Exhibition of Works of Art in Leeds in 1868. At some point in the late 19th or early 20th century the work was bound with emerald green velvet cloth and fastened with brass clasps. It was then re-housed in a nondescript slipcase made of wooden boards and cloth-covered, but the finished product no doubt appealed to a gentleman of the age.

RIGHT: A 15th-century Book of Hours with a 19th-century cover of green velvet, with brass clasps.

OPPOSITE: Illuminated leaf, folio 1 of the Book of Hours, the 'Incipit', or beginning, of the Office of the Blessed Virgin Mary – a convincing addition from the 19th century (fol. 1 r).

INCIPIT OFFICIŪ
BEATÆ MARIĘ VIR
GINIS SECŪDVM
CONSVETVDINE RO
MANĘ CVRIĘ. ad mat.
VERSVS:
OMINE
LABIA
MEA A
PERIES
ET OS M
EVMAN

43

RIGHT AND OPPOSITE: A double-page spread showing two faked illuminated leaves from the 15th-century Book of Hours (fols. 50v–51r).

Amen. AD NONAM.
DEVS INAD
IVTORIVM
MEVM INTÉ
DE DOMINE
AD ADIVVAN

dum me festina Gloria pa
tri et filio et spiritui sancto.
Sicut erat in principio nūc
et semper & in secula seculox
Amen. Alleluia. Hymnus.
MEmento salutis auctor

8

Witch-hunting handbook with a Ben Jonson connection

Jakob Sprenger and Heinrich Kramer, Institoris, *Malleus Maleficarum*. Nuremberg: Anton Koberger, 1494.

Latin. With manuscript marginalia. 146 leaves. 230 × 170 mm. Original quarter pigskin-covered boards, remains of clasp; title written on top edge.

Provenance: purchased as part of the Ogden Library, 1953.

INCUNABULA 2o

Also known as *Hexenhammer*, or *The Hammer of Witches*, this work has been called 'the most important and most sinister work on demonology ever written'. A handbook for witchfinders, it was first printed in 1486 and went through 13 editions before 1520. The work owed its authority to several factors, not least the scholastic reputation of its authors, both Dominicans: Jakob Sprenger (1436–95), Dean of Cologne University, and Prior Heinrich Kramer (*c.* 1430–1505). It relied heavily on Innocent VIII's Papal Bull of 1484, which declared disbelief in witchcraft to be heresy.

The Library also holds a 1615 edition of the same work, *Mallei Maleficarum*, (Vols 2–4, SR OGDEN A 291). This book has an additional significance because one of its former owners was the poet and playwright Ben Jonson (1572–1637). The Ben Jonson collection accumulated by C K Ogden includes no less than five books from Jonson's library, printed between 1537 and 1615. The tell-tale inscriptions ('*tanquam explorator*' at the head and '*sum Ben Jonsonij*' at the foot) also appear on the title pages of Vitruvius's *De Architectura* (1586) and Despautere's *Commentarii grammaticii* (1537), which also have underlinings and annotations, while Jonson's copy of Otto van Veen's *Amorum emblemata* (1608) has a verse added in his handwriting. Jonson found the tag '*tanquam explorator*' in an epistle of Seneca, who in turn had found it in the writings of the Greek philosopher Epicurus. Seneca writes '*non tanquam transfigura, sed tanquam explorator*' (translated roughly to mean that when visiting an enemy's camp he entered not as a deserter, but as a scout – in other words, in the spirit of exploration rather than confrontation). Also included in this group is Jonson's annotated copy of Greneway's 1598 translation of Tacitus. Many of Jonson's books survive and are readily identifiable by the characteristic signature and marginal annotations.

The printer for the 1494 edition, Anton Koberger, godfather of Albrecht Dürer (p.100), was the greatest publisher in Europe at this time, producing outstanding illustrated books for which he employed the wood engraver Michael Wolgemut. Koberger commissioned 2,000 cuts for the production of the famous Hartmann Schedel's *Liber Cronicarum*, known in English as the *Nuremberg Chronicle*, of which UCL owns a copy (Incunabula Folio 2n). A landmark in the history of early printing, this work integrated text and painted woodcuts in unprecedented numbers and variations of formats.

TOP: Two pages from Part 1 of
C K Ogden's copy of the *Malleus
Maleficarum*, 1494, with marginalia.
It features an extract from Question
Five, which asks about the source of
the increase of '*Works of Witchcraft*'
(unnumbered pages).

LEFT AND ABOVE: Front cover of the
Malleus Maleficarum (left) and detail,
showing handwritten title added by an
unknown previous owner.

9

Part of Book V of
Confessio Amantis
(*'The Lover's Confession'*)

John Gower, *Confessio Amantis*

English and Latin. Parchment manuscript fragment written in England, early 15th century. Two leaves. Illuminated initials. 399 × 275 mm.

Provenance: formerly Phillipps 22914, given by Dr W Seton and Dr R W Chambers, 1911.

MS FRAG ANGL 1

This charming manuscript fragment, the earliest in the Library written in English, belonged to the baronet, antiquary and bibliophile Sir Thomas Phillipps (1792–1872). His collection included *c.* 60,000 manuscripts of various kinds – among them some relating to the administration of Swiss towns, manuscripts which UCL also holds. Many manuscripts were sold after Sir Thomas's death, some to the German government, and were dispersed to several libraries.

In this verse piece, part of Book V, summaries in Latin are inserted in the same script, a neat Gothic minuscule. The parchment is thick and well-preserved, and the mauve-decorated gold leaf of the initials, alternated with blue and ornamented with red flourishes, is as vivid today as when the text was completed. The black ink is also very well preserved – the slight discolouration, and the presence of a few stains on the vellum, only add to its charm and speak volumes about the work's heavy use. The two leaves are bound in a modern binding, incorrectly, it would seem, according to a study by G C Macaulay in 1900, with omissions and in the wrong order. Nevertheless it is a prized item of the UCL collection, recorded in *A Companion to Gower*, edited by Siân Echard and published in 2004.

John Gower was born a squire around 1330. A close friend of Geoffrey Chaucer, he wrote poetry in the tradition of courtly love and moral allegory, very popular in its time. Gower's major works were *Speculum Meditantis*, a French poem on vice and virtue, *Vox Clamantis*, a Latin elegaic poem, and *Confessio Amantis*, in English. The first version of the *Confessio* was composed about 1383 at the request of Richard II, to whom it was dedicated. For the second version, however, which appeared around 1393, the dedication and Gower's allegiance were transferred to Henry of Lancaster (afterwards Henry IV). He died in 1408, and the *Confessio Amantis* was first published by Caxton in 1483, one of Caxton's earliest printed works.

RIGHT: Detail from early 15th-century manuscript of Gower's *Confessio Amantis*, showing the illuminated initial 'T' from lines 5.1453 and 5.1454: 'The king of Bragmans Dindimus Wrot unto Alesandre thus' (fol. 4v). In popular medieval romances, Dindimus was the king of the Brahmans, who lived by the River Ganges. Alexander [the Great] and Dindimus disagreed on their different manners and customs.

OPPOSITE: Lines 5.871 to 5.966 of the *Confessio Amantis* fragment. The verse at the end of the second column evokes the Roman god Vulcan, 'the god of fyr' (fol. 1r).

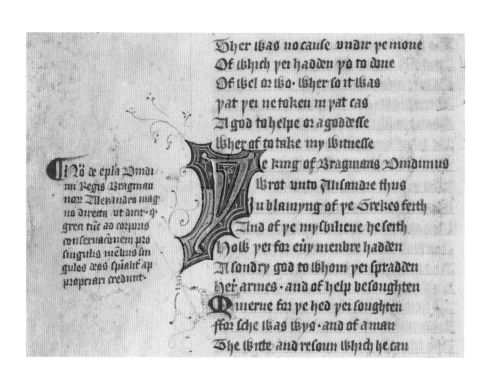

Which Iuno hadde vn to his wyf
And zit alecchour al his lyf
He was and in avonterye
He wroughte many a tricherye
And for he was so foule of vices
Thei clepid him god of delices
Of whom if y wolt more write
Ouide þe poete haþ write
But zit her sterres boþe two
Saturne and Jupiter also
þei haue al þough þei be to blame
Attitled to her owne name

Mars · deus belli ·

Mars was anoþ in þat laiþe
þe which in Mace was forth drawe
Of whom þe clerk vegeans
wroot in his book and tolde þus
Howe he in to Itaile cam
And suche fortune þe he nam
þat he amaiden haþ oppressid
which in hir ordre was pfessid
Als sche which was þe prioresse
In Vestes temple the goddesse
So was he wel þe more to blame
Dame ylia · this lady name
men clepe and ek sche was also
þe kinges daughter þat was þo
which aimitor be name highte
So þat aзem þe lawes righte
amars þilke time vppon hire þat
Remus and Romulus begat
which aftir whan þei come in age
Of knighthode and of vasselage
ytaile al hol þei ouercome
And foundeden þe grete Rome
In armes and of such emprise
They weren þat in þilke wise
Here fadr amars for þe rivaile
The god was cleped of bataile
They were his children boþe two
þurgh hem he took is name so
Ther was non oþe cause why
And zit asterre vppon the sky
He haþ vnto his name applied
In which þat he is signified

Apollo · deus Sapiencie ·

Anoþ god þei hadden eke
To whom for counseil they beseke
þe which was broþ to venus
Apollo men him clepe thus

He was an hunte vppon þe helles
Ther was wiþ him no vertu elles
wher of þat eny lukes karpe
But only þat he couþe harpe
which whan he walked ouer londe
fful ofte time he toke on honde
To gete him wiþ his sustenance
ffor lack of oþe purueiance
And oþ wile of his falshede
He feyned him to conne arede
Of þing which aftir schulde falle
wher off among his sleightes alle
He haþ þe leiþed folk deceyued
So þat þe bette he was receyued
Lo now þorugh what creacion
He hath deificacion
And cleped is þe god oflicht
To suche as be the foles zit

Mercurius deus Marchator et ffurtorum ·

Anoþ god to whom þei soghte
mercurie hihte and him ne roghte
what þing he stal ne whom he slough
Of sorcerie he couþe ynough
þat whan he wolde him self transforme
fful ofte tyme he tok þe forme
Of woman · and his owne lefte
So dide he wel þe more þefte
A gret spekere in alle þinges
He was also · and of lesinges
An auctour · þat men wiste nom
A noþ suche as he was on
And zit þei maden of þis þeef
Al god which was vnto hem leef
And cleped him in þo beleeues
The god of marchantes & of þeeues
But zit asterre vppon þe heuene
He haþ of þe planetes seuene

Vulcanus deus ignis ·

But vulcanus of whom I spak
He hadde a courbe vppon þe bak
And þeto he was hepehalt
Of whom you vndirstonde schalt
He was a schrewe in al his зouþe
And he nam oþe vertu couþe
Of craft to helpe him selue wiþ
But only þat he was a smith
wiþ Jupit which in his forge
Diuerse þinges made hym forge
So bot I nought for what desire
They clepen him þe god of fire

The crafte to lyue well and to dye well ·

A guide to the good Christian life

Andrew Chertsey, *The crafte to lyve well and to dye well*. London: Wynkyn de Worde, 1505.

English. 150 leaves. Woodcuts. 260 × 185 mm.

Provenance: unknown.

S R B Quarto 1505 C3

OPPOSITE: Title page of Chertsey's *The crafte to lyve well and to dye well*, 1505. It also bears the title of the chapter, 'The arte or crafte to lyve well', and features a charming, full-page woodcut (fol. 1r).

BELOW: Front cover of the early 16th-century work by Chertsey. It has a re-worded title tooled in gilt and a fine modern binding by Douglas Cockerell.

BELOW, RIGHT: A woodcut illustrating the commonly held medieval belief of the dire consequences of a non-Christian life, with buildings and trees collapsing (detail, fol. CIXr).

Guides to the good Christian life, and especially the good Christian death, were extremely popular in the late Middle Ages. This very handsome copy of a typical handbook of the age, which starts with *Here foloweth a right devoute medytacyon of the soule the which thynketh on his departynge from the body for to have socours,* is lavishly illustrated with fine woodcuts. It is also the earliest English printed book in the Library. An English translation by Andrew Chertsey of *L'art de bien vivre et de bien mourir,* this edition is a fairly close reprint of the Paris edition of 1503 ascribed to Antoine Vérard, a French publisher active between 1485 and 1512. It bears the printer's device of England's better known printer, William Caxton (d. 1491), which can be explained by the fact that de Worde worked with Caxton and became his successor, inheriting his premises, types, woodcuts and printer's device.

By the first decade of the 16th century the chief printers in England were from the continent. Wynken de Worde, who printed over 700 works, mostly schoolbooks, up to his death in 1535, came from Worth in Alsace; he had probably come from Bruges with Caxton, who had established his first press in the city in 1473. The 'W C' printer's device, as well as Caxton's famous 'Sun in splendour' motif, plus a greyhound and centaur, are all present in this work. De Worde also introduced italic type into England and pioneered the printing of music from moveable type. He rarely printed a book without illustration, and the use of woodcuts lent an accessible and memorable format for the increasing numbers of devout and literate layfolk, among others, who wanted devotional material made available in English.

UCL's copy has a modern, dyed red-brown goatskin binding with five raised bands on the spine and blind tooled and gilt ornaments. It is signed 'DC 1904' on the rear endpaper, indicating the craftmanship of Douglas Cockerell (1870–1945), a British master bookbinder.

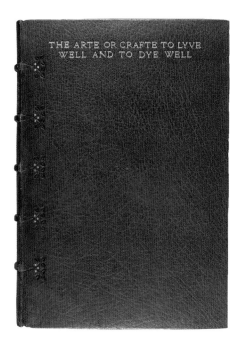

Ur god Imperatour & creatour of heuen and of þ erthe / in the begynnynge of the tyme & of all creatures / created all thynges of nought without ony matere lyenge before. And all these sayd thynges create conteyned in foure thynges / the whiche ben euen That is to saye of one tyme & of one aege / in the whiche shyneth þ ryght souerayne puyssaunce of the creature / The sayd foure thynges ben the Imperyal nature angelyque / þ ma

tere of the foure elementes and the tyme. And that is none other thynge but the werke of the redempcyon the whiche hath ben made euermore before. After foloweth the werke of the dystyncion / in þ whiche shyneth the souerayne wysdome of the creature / of that the whiche was made in the thre fyrst dayes. For the fyrst daye god made the lyght. That is to vnderstonde a clere cloude gyuynge lyght vnto the partyes superyours of the worlde / of a lytell clerte or clerenes suche as men hath accustumed

A ii

52

OPPOSITE: Folio 2 of the first chapter of *The arte or crafte to lyve well* – an excellent example of type and woodcuts on the same page, from the early period of printing technology.

ABOVE: Detail from the end page of *The crafte to lyve well and to dye well*. It features the printer's device of Wynkyn de Worde, the printer of this work who inherited Caxton's 'Sun in Spendour' motif.

Miles Coverdale and the genesis of the Bible in English

Miles Coverdale, *Biblia: the Byble: that is the holy Scripture of the Olde and New Testament / faythfully and truly translated out of Douche and Latyn in to Englyshe*. Marburg: Eucharius Cervicornus and Johannes Soter, 1535.

English. [8], xc, cxx, lii, cii, lxxxi [ie lxxxiii], [1], cxiii, [1] leaves, [1] folded leaf of plates, woodcuts, 1 map; 320 mm.

Fine modern binding, signed and dated by Douglas Cockerell 1901, of reddish-brown goat, gold tooled, with frames and ornaments and title in gold on front cover. Five raised bands on spine and two plaited leather clasps.

Provenance: unknown, former owner Thomas Holme, 1680.

S R B 1535 B4

OPPOSITE AND LEFT: Front cover and spine of the 1535 first edition of the Coverdale Bible. This fine example of gold-tooled ornamented and framed goatskin leather binding by Douglas Cockerell possesses a full gilt spine with five raised bands and leather claps, produced in 1901.

Miles Coverdale's *Bible* is one of the most important works ever published in the English language. It was produced in the context of a movement towards reform in the England of the 1530s.

The Vulgate, the Latin text of the Bible (*editio vulgata*) most widely used in the West, is largely the work of St Jerome (*c.* 342–420). Following Jerome's translation of the text, Erasmus issued his own edition of the Greek *New Testament* in 1516. The *Novum Instrumentum Omne* of Erasmus is a version of the *New Testament* containing a newly collated Greek text and an updated Latin text of the Vulgate. The work exercised a tremendous influence on the contemporary study of philology, although based on insufficient manuscript sources. Erasmus made himself the focus of attention for systematic biblical scholarship, his *New Testament* exerting a special influence upon the early English Lutherans. Thomas Bilney, who was martyred for his beliefs in 1531, certainly read the work, attracted in the first place by Erasmus's Latin translation rather than theological truth.

Following his refusal to recant at the Diet of Worms in 1521, Martin Luther spent some months in seclusion at the Wartburg, the summer residence of the Elector of Saxony set high in the Thuringian hills. It was here that he completed, in two and a half months, a German translation of the *New Testament*. Luther had two requirements of any such translation: that it be founded on original texts and that it use a form of German that all native speakers could understand. The *September Testament* was finished shortly before 21 September 1522 and 3,000 copies were printed. The text is remarkable for its vitality, bringing the *New Testament* to life in idiomatic German.

William Tyndale was responsible for producing the first printed English translation of the *New Testament*. Like Erasmus, Tyndale translated directly from the original Hebrew and Greek. Production of the work began at Cologne in 1525, but, following attacks by the authorities, printing activities were moved up river to Worms. Six thousand copies of the *New Testament* from Worms were printed, to be sold for two shillings each. When the text first arrived in England, it was attacked by William Warham, archbishop of Canterbury, Cuthbert Tunstall, bishop of London, and Thomas More.

Miles Coverdale was responsible for the first full translation of the Bible into English, a work published in 1535 and printed on the continent of Europe, probably at Cologne or Marburg. Coverdale did not translate directly from Hebrew or Greek, but used a number of sources. It is most heavily based on Leo Jud's and Ulrich Zwingli's Swiss-German version of 1524/29 and the Latin of Pagninus of 1528. He also used Luther's German text, the Vulgate and the work of Tyndale. Following Tyndale, for example, the word 'church' was translated into English as 'congregation', removing any possible allusion to the hierarchy of the late medieval Roman Church. Professor David Daniell, Emeritus Professor of English at UCL, has suggested that Coverdale's Bible was probably printed in Antwerp by Martin de Keyser, with sponsorship from Jacob Van Meteren, an Antwerp merchant trading with England.

In England, Thomas Matthew's Bible arrived from the Low Countries in August 1537, a year after Tyndale had been executed as a heretic outside Brussels. Only the first five books of the Old Testament, the Pentateuch, had appeared in print. John Rogers rescued Tyndale's translations of

Joshua-II Chronicles and he also used Coverdale's translation of the second half of the Old Testament. The New Testament was from Tyndale's revision of 1534. Using all these texts, Rogers produced a complete translation of the Bible, issued under the pseudonym of Thomas Matthew and printed at Antwerp.

On 4 August 1537 archbishop Thomas Cranmer sent Thomas Cromwell a copy of this Bible. Both Cromwell and Cranmer were keen to see the English Bible available in every parish in England. It was not possible to reprint Coverdale's Bible as, not being from the original languages, this was seen as insufficient. Cromwell therefore authorised a revision of the Matthew Bible to be undertaken in Paris, with Coverdale being responsible for the revision. Cromwell's original 1536 Injunctions to the English Church contained no stipulation concerning the use of the English Bible. They could not have done, as Coverdale's 1535 Bible was not officially licensed. The appearance of the Matthew Bible changed that, with later copies of the 1536 Injunctions indeed stipulating the provision of an English Bible.

In his 1538 set of Injunctions, Cromwell certainly required that a Bible of the largest volume in English be set up in every parish church by Christmas 1538. However, work in Paris on the revision of the Matthew Bible did not proceed apace. The French authorities turned hostile (egged on by English adversaries) and all the bound copies printed in France were burned. Fresh printing then began in London and, supplemented by copies from France, the Great Bible was ready by April 1539, although no copy was available before November. Thomas Cranmer wrote an important *Preface* to the April 1540 edition commending the reading of Scripture in the common tongue.

UCL's copy of Coverdale's Bible of 1535 is not perfect. It lacks the title page and preliminary matter before the list of the books of the Apocrypha and New Testament. Also missing is all text after folio lxxviii of the New Testament (II Cor. ch. III) except for a fragment of the last page, bearing on the recto a part of the Book of Revelation and on the verso part of the Colophon, with date MDXXXV. The volume has been severely cropped, but there is an Inscription on the verso of folio XC [1st count] which reads 'Thomas Holme his own Booke Anno Domini 1680' and gives a clue to previous ownership. Many annotations and drawings throughout, including recipes, sketches, notes on family history etc, also make this copy unique.

The exact edition is uncertain because the volume is so damaged. However, it is recorded in the Short Title Catalogue (2nd ed), 2063.3?, STC (2nd ed), 2063? and Darlow & Moule (rev. 1968), 18. The place of publication could be Antwerp or Southwark, with the work printed by Martin de Keyser and J Nicolson. Other clues of note are the Creation Date, which is M.D.XXXV. [1535 (4 October)], given in the colophon, and the Dedication present in this copy: 'Dedicated to King Henry VIII, and preceded by "A prologe: Myles Couerdale vnto the Christian reader"'.   PAUL AYRIS

BELOW: Detail (left) and page (right) from the Book of the Machabees, Chapter XIII, showing the inscription of Rowland Wright, 1649, a possible former owner.

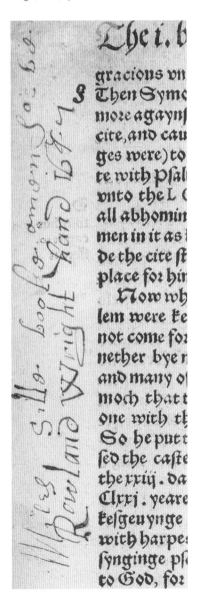

12

The art of practising Judaism in the 16th century

Italian *Mahzor*

Hebrew. Parchment manuscript, written in Italy, early 16th century. 392 leaves. 172 × 134 × 70 mm.

Provenance: bequeathed as part of the library of F D Mocatta, 1906.

MS MOCATTA 2

The Mocatta *Mahzor* is the second most highly-prized Jewish item, after the Haggadah (p.26), in UCL Library Services. It is a richly illuminated festival prayer book for the whole year according to the Italian rite, including some additional prayers and ceremonies. The *Mahzor* is beautifully executed in fine Hebrew script, with the superscriptions and initial words painted in gold. Possibly dating from around 1400, but generally recorded as early 16th century, the manuscript is in immaculate condition. The title page is particularly exquisite, featuring gold and a variety of other colours such as red, blue, black and green. It shows the coat of arms of a Kohen (priest) at the bottom of the page, depicting the blessing given by the priest (or *Kohen*) in certain Jewish prayer rituals.

Apart from its intrinsic artistic merit, this *Mahzor* has a unique history. Censorship of Jewish books was undertaken on a large scale in Italy, with individuals appointed by the Inquisition from the 13th century, and the tell-tale signatures of four censors appear on the last two leaves. The earliest is that of Jacob Geraldino, dated 1555; the others are Caesar Bellicosus (undated), Camillo Jaghel, 1619, and Antonio Franc Enrique, 1688.

BELOW: Highly stylised intricate pattern detail from the Italian *Mahzor*, early 16th century, with gold-painted initials (fols. 69v–70r).

RIGHT: Title page of the *Mahzor*. Exquisitely executed with a variety of colours, it features the coat of arms of a priest or *Kohen* (centre, top).

13

Islamic art in the 15th century

Fragment of the Holy Qur'an

Arabic. Illuminated parchment manuscript fragment, written probably in Syria or Egypt, probably 16th century. 8 leaves, in modern board covers. 380 × 270 mm.

Provenance: bequeathed as part of the library of F D Mocatta, 1906.

MS MOCATTA 20

Mocatta was an accomplished scholar in his own right and this exquisitely crafted fragment, one of the many religious texts accumulated by him, is a valued part of UCL's small Mocatta manuscipts collection. This short fragment is written in the Muhaqqaq script, one of the six main types of calligraphic script in Arabic. The Arabic word *muhaqqaq* means 'consummate' or 'clear', and originally was used to denote any accomplished piece of calligraphy.

Often used to copy *masahif* (singular *mushaf*), meaning loose sheets of Qur'an texts, this majestic type of script was considered one of the most beautiful, as well as one of the most difficult to execute well. The script saw its greatest use in the Mameluk era (1250–1516/1517).

The fragment contains part of the 19th section of the Qur'an and may date from the late Mameluk period in the 14th and 15th centuries; the style is typical for the time and place. Small roundels mark the end of the verse, and larger ones occur at the end of every fifth verse, the largest at every tenth verse. The fragment covers *Sūra* [chapter] xxv, verse 23 to the beginning of verse 63, with the text beginning on folio 1 verso; it has a decorative first opening, and the bottom border states that it is part 19 of 30. The name Abu Sa'id can just be recognised from a partially erased note on folio 1 recto – possibly the name of the patron who commissioned the work, or the person to whom it was originally donated.

It is very rare for complete 30 verse sets to have survived from this period. These eight leaves bear the signs of heavy usage and of being moved from place to place, but the gold illuminations are as fresh as ever.

RIGHT: Second page of the text of verse 23 of Sura [chapter] xxv of the 16th-century manuscript fragment of the Holy Qur'an (fol. 2r).

OPPOSITE: Penultimate page of the Qur'an fragment, illustrating the highly accomplished Muhaqqaq script commonly in use in the Mameluk period (1250–1517) (fol. 6r).

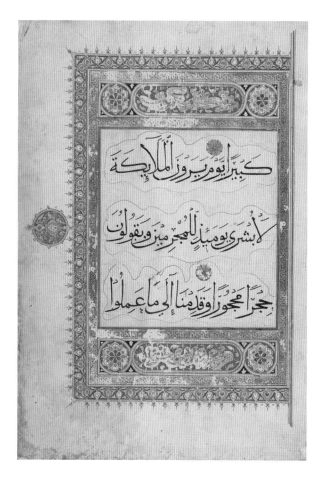

إِنْ هُمْ إِلَّا كَالْأَنْعَامِ بَلْ هُمْ أَضَلُّ سَبِيلًا

أَلَمْ تَرَ إِلَى رَبِّكَ كَيْفَ مَدَّ الظِّلَّ وَلَوْ شَاءَ لَجَعَلَهُ

سَاكِنًا ثُمَّ جَعَلْنَا الشَّمْسَ عَلَيْهِ دَلِيلًا

ثُمَّ قَبَضْنَاهُ إِلَيْنَا قَبْضًا يَسِيرًا وَهُوَ الَّذِي

جَعَلَ لَكُمُ اللَّيْلَ لِبَاسًا وَالنَّوْمَ سُبَاتًا

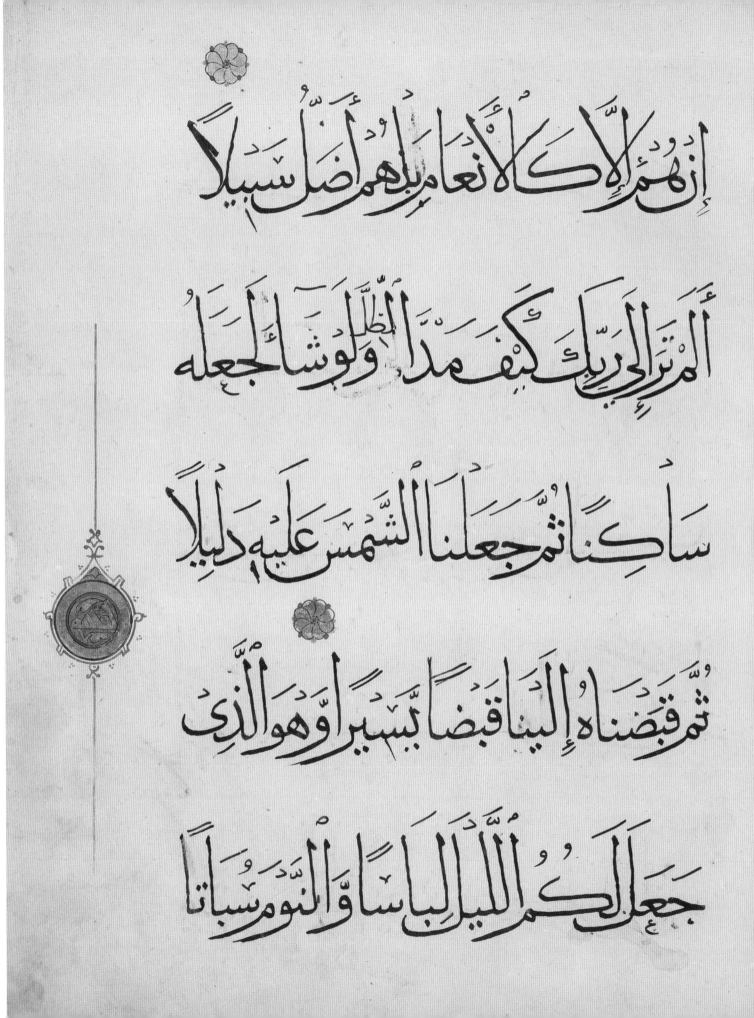

14

A very rare medieval astronomical text

Johannes De Sacrobosco, *Tractatus de Sphera* and other tracts

Latin. Parchment manuscript volume written in Italy, early 14th century. 33 leaves. 217 × 162 mm.

Provenance: bequeathed as part of the Graves Library, 1870.

MS LAT 15

The *Tractatus de Sphera*, composed around 1233, one of the greatest scientific textbooks of the 13th century, formed the fundamental work on astronomy in the medieval period. Based on Ptolemaic principles, it discusses the terrestrial globe, the rising and setting of stars, and the orbs and movements of the planets. Manuscripts of the mathematician and astronomer Johannes de Sacrobosco (also known as John of Hollywood) circulated throughout the Middle Ages, but very little is known about the author; he is thought to have been born in Yorkshire, settling in Paris around 1220. Sacrobosco's other great text is the *Algorismus* or *Tractatus de Arte Numerandi*, a textbook on arithmetic. It uses Arabic numerals in the text, which contributed significantly to their adoption by the modern world in place of roman numerals. According to the census undertaken by

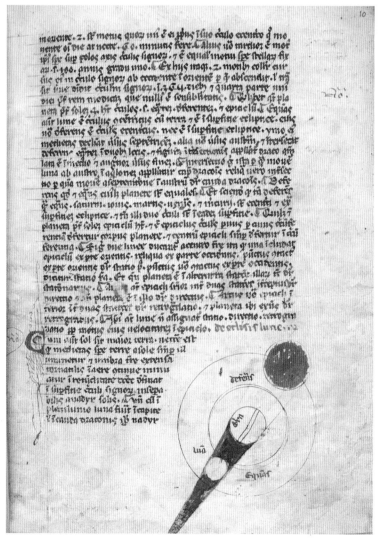
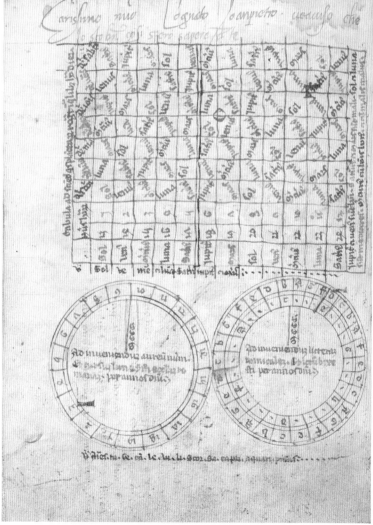

Seymour De Ricci (1881–1942), only three 14th-century copies of these two texts have been recorded.

The UCL manuscript is a palimpsest, the erased text still visible on some of the leaves. The upper texts, which consist of the *Tractatus de Sphera* (fols. 2r–10v), the *Tractatus algorismi* (fols. 11r–16r), *De lapidibus* (fol. 16r), *De Geometria* (fol. 16v) and others, are written continuously, in various minuscule hands of the 14th century, in inks of various tints, and rubricated. Headings and paragraph marks are in red, with diagrams accompanying the text in red, or red and black. Other interesting features are a list of the titles in Latin on the first folio, with an entry in another hand dated 1383. Below this also appear the date 1340 and the identity of a possible former owner, A S Dawes, dated March 1782, at the base.

LEFT TO RIGHT: From the early 14th-century Latin manuscript of Sacrobosco's *Tractatus de Sphera*, showing the earth at the centre of the universe (fol. 10r); astronomical texts, with lunar and solar tables (fols. 18r and 18v); title page (verso).

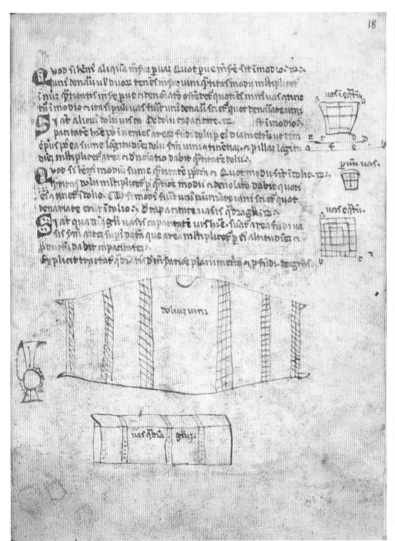

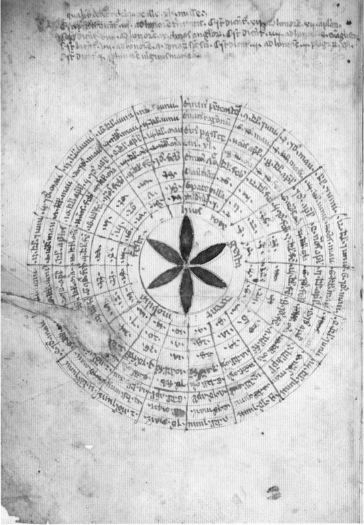

15

First printed edition of Euclid's *Elements*

Euclid of Megara, *Elementa geometriae*

Latin. Translated by Adelard of Bath, edited with a commentary by Giovanni Campano Novarese. Venice: Erhard Ratdolt [1st edition]. 25 May 1482. 137 ff; woodcuts, diagrams. 230 × 190 mm.

Provenance: bequeathed as part of the Graves Library, 1870.

INCUNABULA QUARTO 5q

The first printing of one of the most important texts from the Middle Ages, and one of the very earliest mathematical works to be printed, posed a challenge to the new technology, requiring ingenuity, skill and innovation to replicate the all-important diagrams. Erhard Ratdolt (1447?–1527/8), who printed works in Augsburg, his birthplace, and in Venice succeeded spectacularly, and this first edition is the result – a true masterpiece of early printing technique.

The first printing to use colours and and a title page, this 1482 edition of Euclid's *Elementa* is technically brilliant in integrating the diagrams with the text. The inclusion of woodcuts and other design flourishes, such as the use of red in the headings and paragraph marks, as well as underlinings, all combine to make this intrinsically technical work both a joy and an immensely practical tool to own.

This work forms part of the Graves Library (p.13), in which the works of the ancient Greek mathematician Euclid form a separately identified group – an important collection of over 400 volumes. Among them are 83 of the editions of works by Euclid printed before 1640, including this *editio princeps*, published by Erhard Ratdolt at Venice in 1482, and many other first editions of translations. The most notable are the first translations of Euclid into any modern language: Italian (1543), German (1562), French (1564), English (John Day's edition, with John Dee's preface of 1570) and Arabic (1594). Graves complemented these very early, priceless editions with later translations into Turkish, Chinese, Persian, Hebrew, Finnish and other languages, added to by the Library well into the 20th century.

Adelard of Bath (*c*. 1080–1152) was a 12th-century English natural philosopher. He made the first full translation of Euclid's *Elements* from an Arabic translation into Latin.

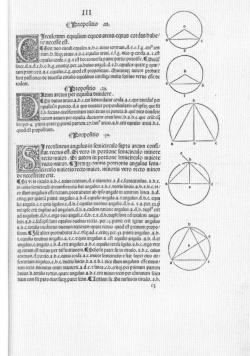

FAR LEFT: Section from Book 1 of the first printing of Euclid's *Elements* in 1482, showing propositions relating to triangles. The heading at the bottom of the page, Proposition 5, is misplaced (fol. 2v).

LEFT: Propositions 28–30 from the 'Theory of Circles' in Euclid's work (unnumbered page). Printing technology had advanced by this stage to enable images to be integrated with the printed text, instead of being added afterwards.

OPPOSITE: Lavishly ornamented opening page of the Ratdolt edition of Euclid's *Elements*, 1482. The 'P' for 'Punctus' (point), in a decorated framed background, launches the great work.

Preclariffimus liber elementozum Euclidis perfpi/ caciffimi:in artem Geometrie incipit quáfoeliciffime:

PUnctus eft cuius ps nó eft. ¶Linea eft lógitudo fine latitudine cui⁹ quidé ex/ tremitates fr duo púcta. ¶Linea recta é ab vno púcto ad aliú bzeuiffima exté/ fio i extremitates fuas vtrúqz eoz reci piens. ¶Supficies é q lógitudiné z lati tudiné tm bz:cui⁹termi quidé fút linee. ¶Supficies plana é ab vna linea ad a/ lia extéfio i extremitates fuas recipiés ¶Angulus planus é duarú lincarú al/ ternus ptactus:quaz expáfio é fup fup/ ficié applicatioqz nó directa. ¶Quádo aút angulum ptinét due linee recte rectiline⁹ angulus noiaf. ¶Mñ recta linea fup rectá fteterit duoqz anguli ytrobiqz fuerit eqles:eoz yterqz rect⁹erit ¶Lineaqz linee fupftás ei cui fupftat ppendicularis vocaf. ¶An gulus vo qui recto maioz é obtufus dicif. ¶Angul⁹ vo minoz re cto acut⁹appellaf. ¶Termin⁹ é qd vniuícuiuiqz fnis é. ¶Figura é q tmino vl termis ptinef. ¶Circul⁹ é figura plana vna qdem li/ nea pteta: q circúferentia noiaf:in cui⁹medio púct⁹é: a quo⁹oés linee recte ad circúferétiá exeútes fibiinicez fút equales. Et bic quidé púct⁹cétrú circuli dz. ¶Diameter circuli é linea recta que fup ei⁹centz tráfiens extremitatefqz fuas circúferétie applicans circulú i duo media diuidit. ¶Semicirculus é figura plana dia/ metro circuli z medietate circúferentie ptéta. ¶Poztio circu/ li é figura plana recta linea z parte circúferétie ptéta: femicircu/ lo quidé aut maioz aut minoz. ¶Rectilinee figure fút q rectis li/ neis cótinenf quarú quedá trilatere q trib⁹rectis lineis: quedá quadrilatere q qtuoz rectis lineis. qdá mltilatere que pluribus qz quatuoz rectis lineis continenf. ¶Figurarú trilaterarú:alia eft triangulus bñs tria latera equalia. Alia triangulus duo bñs eqlia latera. Alia triangulus triú inequalium laterú. Paz iterú alia eft ozthogoniú:vnú .f. rectum angulum babens.Alia é am bligonium aliquem obtufum angulum babens.Alia eft ozigoni um:in qua tres anguli funt acuti. ¶Figurarú antê quadrilateraz Alia eft qdratum quod eft equilaterú atqz rectangulú. Alia eft tetragon⁹long⁹:q eft figura rectangula : fed equilatera non eft. Alia eft belmuaym: que eft equilatera : fed rectangula non eft.

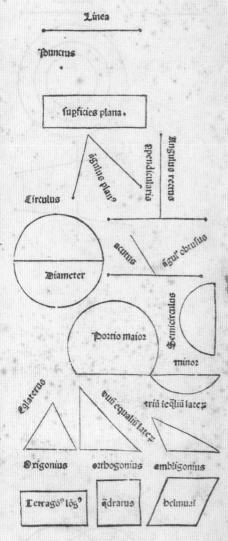

65

16

An early printed herbal

Anonymous, *Herbarius latinus: Herbarius seu de virtutibus herbarum*. Passau: Johann Petri, 1485.

Latin. 174 leaves. Coloured woodcuts. 215 × 145 mm.

Provenance: deposited with the Library of the Hertfordshire Natural History Society and Field Club, 1935.

INCUNABULA 2S

This work, such a valuable and popular pharmacopoeia that it went through a number of editions, is known under many titles, for example *Herbarius in Latino, Aggregator in simplicibus, Herbarius Moguntinus* and *Herbarius Patavinus*. It was first published as a small quarto in 1484 by Peter Scoeffer in Mainz. Other early editions and translations appeared in Bavaria, the Netherlands, Italy and France, still using the same plants that were native to Germany. Among the most familiar are garlic, basil, camomile, ivy, gentian, lily, marjoram and mandrake. Rarer plants are also featured, such as artemisia or mugwort, a plant used in the past to treat female problems and illnesses.

The purpose of the work was entirely practical. It served as a domestic manual, in case of accidents or illnesses and other misfortunes – another traditional use of mugwort was to keep demons away from the home. The illustrations are stylised, simple and full of charm, with names printed clearly in capital letters, so that the plants could be easily identified by, and accessible to, a barely literate public. In UCL's copy the woodcuts are crudely coloured by hand, and the title page and first 'chapter' are missing, but it is a charming work nevertheless. All the initials are rubricated and it contains a manuscript index at the back, along with some manuscript notes.

Like many medieval herbals, the work is anonymous, consisting of a compilation from the works of a number of medieval writers and some classical and Arab authors. Most of the authorities quoted wrote before 1300 and no featured author is later than the mid-14th century, which suggests that there was a previous manuscript edition.

RIGHT: Delicately coloured images and description of the plant *Artemisia*, also known as wormwood, sagebrush or mugwort. Its healing properties are traditionally associated with women's conditions (no.xii).

OPPOSITE: The Mandrake plant, *Mandragora* in Latin, features as no. cxiiii. The older Arab authority on plants, Avicenna, is referenced in the second line.

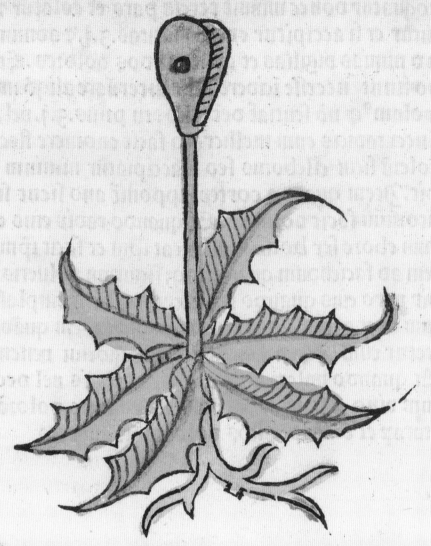

Mandragora   Dilwurtz

Mandragora est frigida et humida in tercio gradu
scōm Auicennam. sed scōm Pandectā est frigida in
tercio et est in ea cum hoc caliditas pauca· sed in po
mis mandragore est humiditas et ꝓpter hanc causaz
inducūt subet. io est somnum ꝓfundum sed cortex ei⁹
radicis est frigidus multum et cum hoc desiccat . Et
qñ ex ista radice exhibet̃ alicui inpotu vel ĩ cibo cum
pãe icidit sumẽs eã ĩ subet.i. sonũ. z ido vtũt cirogici

17

A very rare book of lunar tables

Bernat de Granollachs, *Lunarium ab anno 1490 ad annum 1550. Summario de la luna*

Venice: Guilelmus Anima Mia, Tridenensis, *c.* 1489–90. Latin. 31 leaves, un-numbered; woodcut; 180 × 140 mm.

Provenance: bequeathed as part of the Graves Library, 1870.

INCUNABULA 5 sss

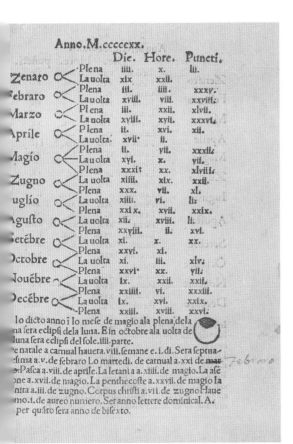

The *Lunarium*, or *Lunari* as it was known, of the Barcelona-born Bernat de Granollachs (*c.* 1400–87) was a bestselling work of astronomical literature in the first decades of early printing. It was first published most probably in 1485, in Catalan as well as in Latin. The Catalan edition is considered to be the *editio princeps*, of which only one copy survives, in the Biblioteca de Catalunya in Barcelona. UCL's copy of De Granollachs' work is the Library's second rarest book after its Milton first edition (p.130) – it is one of only three recorded copies in the world, the other two being in Italy.

This well-preserved book sets out the phases of the moon, giving all the details of the month, day, hours and minutes for the new and full moons from 1485 to 1550 on a yearly basis. Each page covers one year, beginning in January, and supplies information on the dates of Easter, Corpus Christi and other moveable feasts in the Christian liturgical calendar. The *Lunari,* as it was known, also specifies the golden number and the dominical letter of that year, as well the time and magnitude of 70 eclipses visible at the latitude of Barcelona (31 solar eclipses and 39 lunar ones).

Readers were probably not only astronomers, but also those looking for an easy and accurate way to determine the dates of Christian liturgical feasts, or those simply curious about astonomical phenomena. The *Lunari* was a useful and celebrated book for those with no special interest or training in astronomy, but was also an important work for those who had some knowledge. The solar eclipse of 16 March 1485 is recorded, for instance, as is the lunar eclipse of 25 August of the same year. UCL's copy has a number of manuscript corrections and scored-out inscriptions, which speaks of its previous owners, and contains the full-page woodcut at the front, which is absolutely charming. The fine vellum binding from the 19th century, probably added by Graves, adds to its appeal, with its gilt ruling, ornaments and edges.

Some details of De Granollachs' life are known. His uncle became the first chancellor at the University of Barcelona in 1481, and Bernat first studied medicine there. After gaining his master's degree at Montpellier in 1440, De Granollachs joined the faculty of the University of Barcelona and became active in public affairs. He spent some time in jail on alleged bribery charges, but by 1471 was re-elected to the municipal council. Although the date of his death is not accurately known, it is usually taken as 1487, thus making the *Lunari* a work of De Granollachs' middle age.

The *Lunari* is not a long work, which made its transmission across Europe all the wider. It went into 60 editions within 40 years, mostly in Italy, but also in Spain and France. Sacrobosco's *Tractatus de Sphera*, of which UCL holds an early 14th-century manuscript copy (p.62), was one of the other major incunabula works of astronomy of the time. The Library also possesses no fewer than eight incunabula of treatises of Sacrobosco.

OPPOSITE: This charming, full-page woodcut forms the title page of De Granollachs' *Lunarium*, printed *c.* 1489–90.

LEFT: The phases of the moon given in detail for the year 1520, from the *Lunarium* (unnumbered page).

re:qrū dentes sese ꝯiūgerent sic.

Et ista cōiunctio offis cum offe

facta fuit sic in capite ꝓpter iuuamēta que sciuisti. nulluz enim aliud os cum offe sic coniungif. ℂ Sub offe lau de est vnum os ualde durum in medio ꝑforatū:q̔ om nia offa capitis sustinet:quod uocatur basillare : ⁊ conti nuatur inferius cum pzima spondili colli. ℂ Figura vo ꝯiunctionis illoꝛ. v. offiuz capitis est sic.

ℂ A latere vo pzedictorum dextro ⁊ si nistro offium nerualiuz:que sunt ƀm lō gum capitis in summo duo sunt offa in qualibet parte. vnum cum quadam adiacentia firma nō per inferratio nem serralem illis nerualibus supponunf:que uocanf offa mēdofa. Sed quoniā ƀec offa in vna sui parte sunt multum dura:ubi sunt aures ꝑforata:⁊ ibi dicunf petro fa:ab aliquibus dicunf effe q̔tuoꝛ offa duo ab vna parte.

ℂ Lum aūt ƀec offa capitis ad innicem coniunganf in uenis ꝙ offa capitis fex sunt ƀm ueritatem:ponendo os coronale ufq̔ ad supcilia vnum:⁊ offa mēdofa duo:vnū scilicet coronale:duo nerualia:vnum alauda:duo mēdo fa:⁊ septimum est os basillare:q̔ non est de offibus ca pitis:sed offa capitis sustinens:⁊ sit cōiū ctio offiū ut dictū est tribᵒ ueris cōmiffu ris sic:⁊ duabus cōmiffuris mēdofis sic.

Et cum est perfecta tota per ƀunc moduz capitis compofitio stant sic.

ℂ Jsta eni est forma capitis naturalis:ut sit rotūdum ut ꝯtineat:⁊ minus lefionibus supponaf: ⁊ sit oblonguz ƀabens ante ⁊ retro eminētiaz ut locū inueniat neruo rū exitus a porta/videlicet ⁊ a puppi. Est etiā impoffibile ut uoluit optimus Hyp poc.⁊ eius interpzes Gal. Tres alie com pofitiones capitis inuenire. ℂ Una fi eminētia non fiat in anteriori:fed fiat in anteriori planum:per ƀoc perde ret cōmiffura coronalis. ℂ Secūda fi eminentia poste rioꝛ amittaf:⁊ fit posterius planum:⁊ abꝑdaf cōmiffu

The standard medieval manual of surgery

Guy de Chauliac, *Cyrurgia* [with other medical tracts]. Venice: Simon de Luere, 23 December 1499.

Latin. 269, [1] leaves; small woodcuts. 270 × 190 mm.

Provenance: given by Sir John Tweedy, 1924.

INCUNABULA QUARTO 5rrr

The *Chirurgia Magna,* or *Cyrurgia,* was the most important and influential medieval manual of surgery, illustrated with woodcuts of surgical instruments. Its author, Guy de Chauliac (*c.* 1300–68), was the most famous surgeon of the Middle Ages. He had studied medicine at the universities of Toulouse, Montpellier and Bologna, becoming a Magister in 1325, and rose to the position of personal physician to the Avignon Popes Clement VII (1342–52), Innocent VI (1352–62) and Urban V (1362–70).

De Chauliac's chief work was the *Inventorium sive collectorium in parte chirurgicale medicine*, usually referred to simply as *Chirurgia* or *Chirurgia Magna*, completed in 1363. The text went through numerous editions and was translated into Provençal, French, English, Dutch, Italian and Hebrew. Regarded as the standard surgical text of its age, it was frequently found in manuscript form before its first printed publication in 1478, and continued to be used until at least the 17th century.

The prologue is a fascinating essay on the general facts that de Chauliac thought every surgeon should know about the liberal arts, diet, surgical instruments and the manner of conducting an operation. It also gives a brief history of medicine and surgery. He urged surgeons to study anatomy, though his own knowledge of this subject seems to have been sketchy. De Chauliac was a teacher rather than a scientist, and probably represents an accurate picture of the medical knowledge of his time.

This fascinating work also contains nine medical texts by eminent medieval writers, including Roger of Palermo, Chancellor of the University of Montpellier (*Practica*, folios 147r–170v), his pupil Roland of Parma (*Libellus de Cyrurgia*, folios 135r–146v) and Lanfranc of Milan (*Parva Cyrurgia*, folios 171r–175v), who formed a college of surgeons in Paris in the 13th century. A previous owner of UCL's copy is Marcus Beck, a distinguished surgeon who held various posts at University College Hospital from 1863 until his death in 1893.

OPPOSITE: Detail from Guy de Chauliac's *Cyrurgia*, 1499. The work integrated text and woodcuts on the same page to aid the book's user in treating head wounds – an unusual feature for the time (fol.183v).

LEFT: A section on surgical instruments used for treating head wounds, with woodcut images, from Guy de Chauliac's *Cyrurgia*, 1499 (fol. 184v).

BELOW: Detail from the title page of the 1499 *Cyrurgia*, listing the other writers whose works also appear.

First translation of Vitruvius's *De Architectura* in Italian

Cesare Cesariano (ed), *Di Lucio Vitruvio Pollione De Architectura Libri Dieci traducti del Latino in Vulgare affigurati: Commentati et con mirando ordine Insignitii.* Como: Gottardus da Ponte, 1521.

Italian. [8], 183, [1] leaves; woodcuts. 550 × 600 mm.

Provenance: bequeathed as part of the Graves Library, 1870.

S R Folio 1521 V4

Cesariano's Vitruvius is a showy book. Its claim to fame lies in being the first translation into a modern vernacular language of the only surviving text from antiquity on architecture. For Latin versions of Vitruvius's *De Architectura* had started to appear in print soon after the development of printing, the first in 1486. The most authoritative of these, collating the various manuscript versions of Vitruvius, was Fra Giocondo's, published in Venice in 1511 (UCL has a copy of the pocket-size octavo edition, published in 1513).

Cesare Cesariano (1475–1543) was an architect and engineer from Milan. He formed part of the humanist circle (including Leonardo da Vinci) that was assembled in the city by its prince, Ludovico Sforza. Cesariano's was not the first attempt to translate Vitruvius into Italian, but the difficulties were such that no one else had completed the task. Obscure points in the text, or confusing terms that Vitruvius had used, had no contemporary equivalents, while the illustrations to which he referred to had been lost in the manuscript copies, if they had ever existed at all. Cesariano's solution was to write an extensive commentary – and he became so carried away that the commentary is more than five times as long as the text. Pretentious and often erroneous – Cesariano was convinced, for example, that Milan's Gothic cathedral was the perfect demonstration of Vitruvius's principles, apparently unaware of the anachronism – the commentary nonetheless successfully cast architecture as a branch of humanistic learning.

He also drew illustrations to explain what Vitruvius was referring to. These in fact are the book's most original feature: Fra Giocondo's edition also had woodcut illustrations, but they were crude and clumsy. Cesariano's, by contrast, are beautiful, composite images that combined all kinds of information about antique architecture within individual plates. Nothing like this had been seen before. While there is certainly much licence in the illustrations, they present classical architecture as an intellectually coherent system, and make it seem rich, sensuous and desirable.

Cesariano had almost completed the translation and commentary by 1513. To publish the book, he went into partnership with two noblemen and two scholars who were to edit the text. He procrastinated, however, and by 1521 had still not finished the last two sections. His partners grew so exasperated that they took matters into their own hands: a publisher in Como printed the book with the partners' own version for the last two sections, and illustrated them with stock images. Yet the final product is a remarkable tribute to the printer's craft in the way it integrates text, commentary and images, wrapping the commentary elegantly around the text.

Cesariano's Vitruvius was not the most influential architecture book of the 16th century – that must be Sebastiano Serlio's *Tutte l'opere d'architettura et prospetiva*, or possibly Andrea Palladio's *Quattro libri dell'architettura* – but it was certainly the most spectacular. The result was less a work of scholarship and more a visual device to position architecture as a liberal art, distant from the building trades – an intellectual pursuit for educated men. Cesariano's translation stands at the beginning of a long tradition of architectural publishing with similar purposes.   ADRIAN FORTY

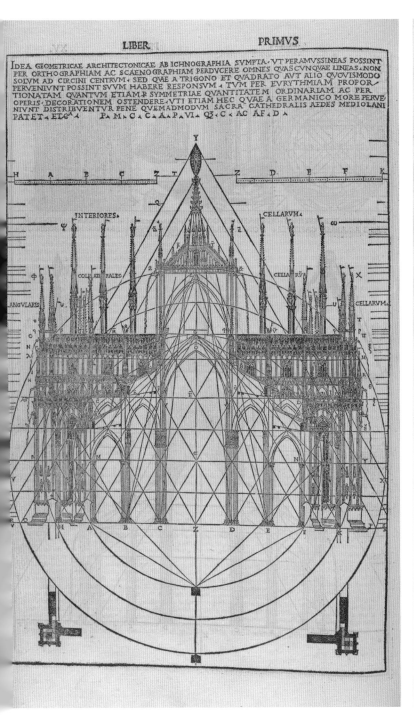

OPPOSITE: A magnificent detail from *Di Lucio Vitruvio Pollione De Architectura*, translated by Cesare Cesariano and published in 1521 (Book 1, unnumbered page).

ABOVE: Cesariano's anachronistic rendering of the elevation of Milan Cathedral, from his Italian translation of Vitruvius's *De Architectura*, 1521 (Book 1, unnumbered page).

ABOVE: Cesariano's rich, detailed illustrations of classical architectural features were highly original drawings for the period (Book 1, unnumbered page).

20

Medical treatises from the East

Haly Abbas [Ali ibn-al-'Abbas al Majusi].
Liber totius medicine necessaria continens quam sapientissimus Haly filius abbas discipulus AbimeberMmoysi filii Seiar edidit ['*The Complete Medical Art*']... Lugduni: Typis Jacobiniyt, 1523.

Latin. [4] 319 leaves; woodcuts, 200 × 190 mm.

Provenance: given by Sir John Tweedy, 1924.

S R C 1523 M15

In the 16th century, Persian and Arab authorities in medicine were referred to largely at the same time as the classical medical texts of Hippocrates and Galen. The latter based their theories on the idea of the human body's four humours and the importance of prognostication, which remained dominant until William Harvey's discoveries in the early 17th century (p.102).

Very little is known about Haly Abbas (d. late 10th century), the Persian author of the original text of this work, but the *Kämil al-Sinä'ah al Tibbiyyah* ('*The Complete Medical Art*') was an important medical book. It was known as the *al-Maliki*, or *Liber Regius*, in the Latin translation here produced for European consumption at the beginning of the printing age. The work remained the leading treatise of medicine for a hundred years, until displaced in the following century by Avicenna's *Canon*, which covered the whole range of medicine and consolidated the notion of the balance between internal and external factors in medical diagnosis and treatment.

The *Liber Regius* consists of 20 treatises on the theory and practice of medicine, giving ten on each. Haly Abbas was in favour of a sensible diet, bathing, exercise and plenty of sleep, advice that has a very modern ring to it. UCL has two copies of this work, the one featured having originally been given to the Medical School Library by Sir John Tweedy and bearing his bookplate. The other (SRC 1523 M1) is a slightly less perfect copy; previously owned by Frederic North, 5th Earl of Guilford, it was sold as part of his library sometime between 1828 and 1835. The front fly leaf bears the signature of James Copland, M D.

FAR LEFT: *The Complete Book of the Medical Art*, here the Latin translation published in 1523, was divided into two large 'books', Theory and Practice. Each was made up of 10 chapters. This detail, from the tenth book of Practice, features recipes for medicine using various herbs and plants (fol. 304v).

LEFT: From the Theory section of *The Complete Book of the Medical Art*, the 'Incipit', or beginning, of the Prologue. Highlighted in red, top left, it contains a reference to Haly Abbas, bottom right (fol. 5r).

OPPOSITE: The elegantly designed, if slightly flawed, title page of '*The Complete Book of the Medical Art*', as this Latin translation, printed in 1523, of an earlier work by Haly Abbas was known.

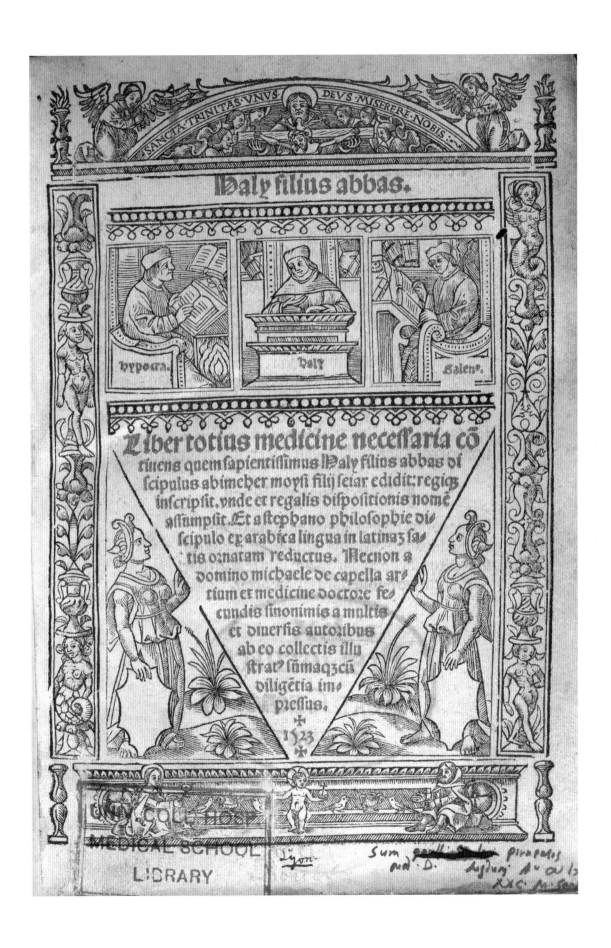

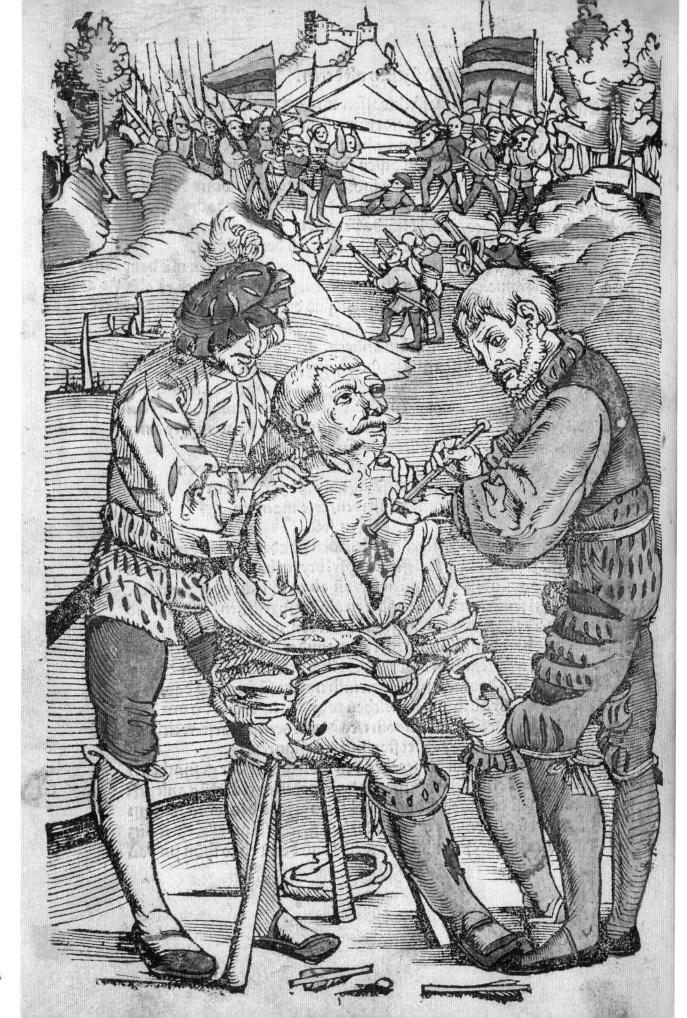

Battlefield surgery techniques: a 16th-century self-help manual

Hans von Gersdorff, *Feldtbuch der Wundartzney. Neulich getrucht und gebessert* ('Fieldbook of Wound Dressing'). Strassburg: Hans Schotten, 1530.

German. [5] 105 folios, 2 folded tables; woodcuts, some coloured. 215 × 160 mm.

Provenance: bequeathed by Sir John Tweedy, 1924.

S R C 1530 G2

OPPOSITE: This detailed battle scene features a full-page coloured woodcut from the *Feldtbuch der Wurdartzney* of Hans von Gersdorff, 1530, showing how to treat an arrow wound (unnumbered page).

BELOW: Employing a tourniquet, detail from von Gersdorff, *Feldtbuch*, 1530 (unnumbered page).

For centuries the main advances in practical medicine were the achievements of the despised, 'unlearned' army doctors and surgeons. Gersdorff (*c.* 1455–1529) was a practising surgeon who performed over 500 amputations, and this book describes his own experiences, based on his original work in the field. It proved to be so popular a manual that it went through about a dozen editions between the date of first publication (1517) and the early 17th century.

The *Feldtbuch* was widely quoted, referred to and plagiarised as a handbook of military surgery. It was illustrated throughout with woodcuts by Johannes Wechtlin, some hand-tinted and including two large folded plates. The title page of this edition and the second edition of 1526 depicts a battlefield scene. Printed in red and black, the imposition of the red ink may appear rather crude, but it adds to its patina, not to mention the mysterious, dark red stains on several of the pages (perhaps not so mysterious, given the circumstances in which the work was used...). These are probably the best surgical illustrations of the period, and include the first printed depiction of an amputation.

In this collection of instructions in the care and treatment of the wounded, Gersdorff describes the extraction of arrows and bullets in detail, accompanied by illustrations of the probes and of the forceps employed. He also describes the processes of his amputation in great detail: employing a tourniquet to control the bleeding, treating bleeding vessels

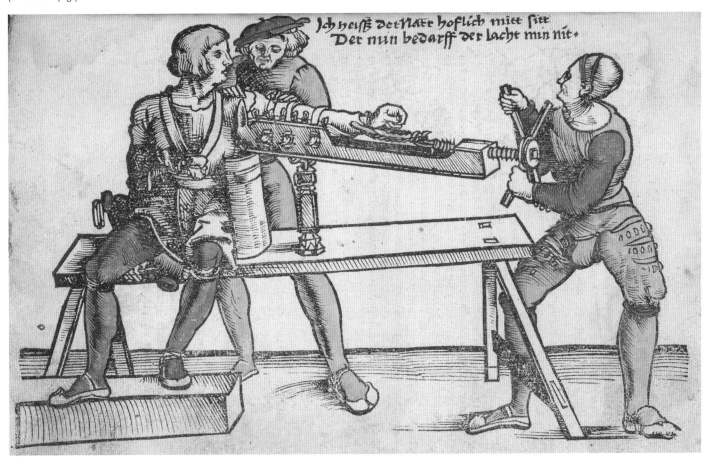

with compression or cauterisation, and covering the stump with a beef or pig bladder. He also mentions a soporific drink for dulling the pain before the operation, and gives its formula. Gersdorff makes no great display of learning and quotes relatively few medical authorities, although he does mention Galen, Albucasis, Avicenna, Haly Abbas (p.74) Roger, Lanfranchi, Mondeville and Guy de Chauliac (p.70).

RIGHT: The Wounded Man', a full-page, hand-coloured woodcut illustration from von Gersdorff's *Feldtbuch*, displays a variety of possible wounds.

OPPOSITE: A full-page, hand-coloured woodcut illustration from von Gersdorff's *Feldtbuch*, showing the detailed treatment of a skull injury with contemporary instruments (unnumbered page).

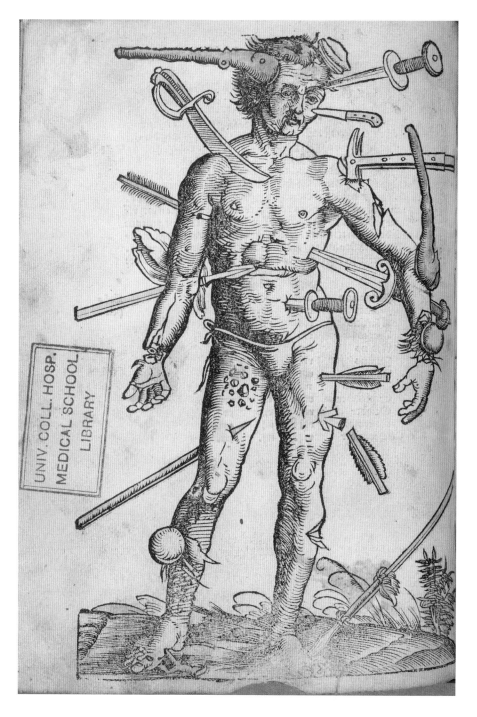

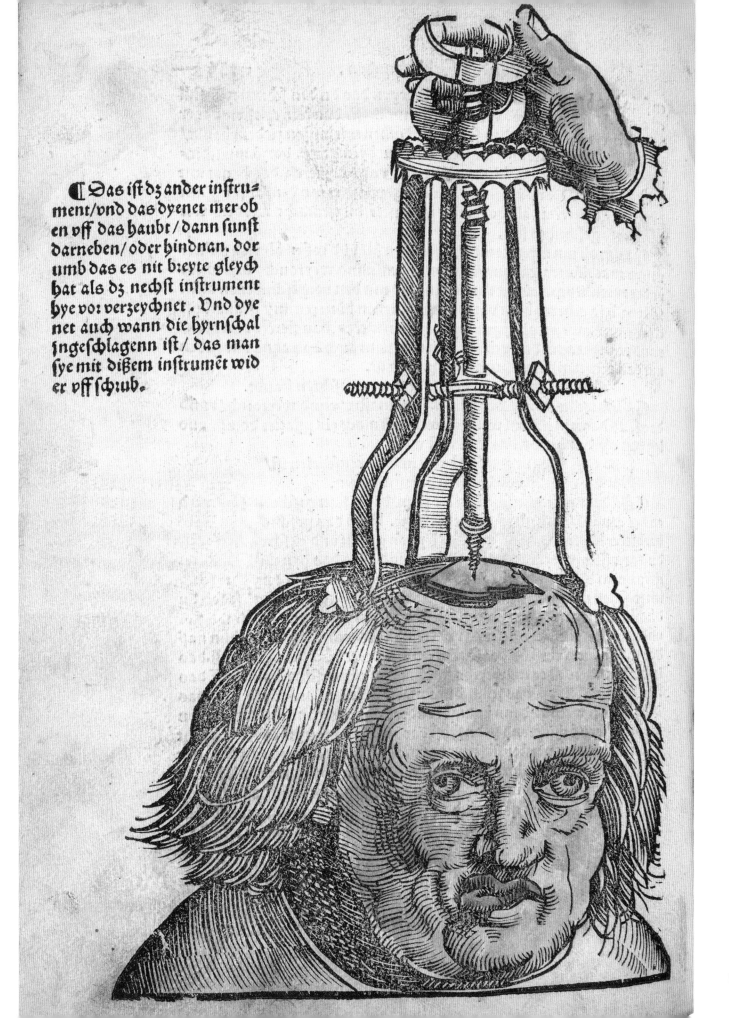

Das ift dz ander inftru=
ment/vnd das dyenet mer ob
en vff das haubt/dann funft
darneben/oder hindnan. dor
umb das es nit breyte gleych
hat als dz nechft inftrument
hye voz verzeychnet. Vnd dye
net auch wann die hyrnfchal
jngefchlagenn ift/das man
fye mit dißem inftrumēt wid
er vff fchiub.

Copernicus – the first publication on a heliocentric universe

Nicolaus Copernicus, *De revolutionibus orbium coelestium, Libri VI: Habes in hoc opere iam recens nato, & aedito, studiose lector, Motus stellarum, tam fixarum, quam erraticarum, cum ex veteribus, tum etiam ex recentibus observationibus restitutos: & novis insuper ac admirabilibus hypothesibus ornatos. Habes etiam Tabulas expeditisimas, ex quibus eosdem ad quodvis tempus quam facillime calculare poteris. Igitur eme, lege, fruere.* Nuremberg: Apud Joh. Petreium, 1543.

Latin. [6] 196 leaves; woodcut initials, tables and diagrams. 270 × 190 mm.

Provenance: bequeathed as part of the Graves Library, 1870.

S R C 1543 C6

This first edition of the most famous scientific work of the 16th century is undoubtedly another of UCL Library Services' most treasured possessions. In the 15th century Europeans were beginning to explore the earth's surface, and sea-going navigation relied solely on accurate observation of the heavens. Accuracy for both latitude and longitude was also crucial to successful commerce, but before the invention of the spring-clock the position of the stars was the only tool available. Ptolemy's theory of the geocentric universe, expressed in his *Almagest*, ruled. Then in 1543 came the publication of a book that turned this theory on its head and rocked the religious establishment: Nicolaus Copernicus's *De revolutionibus orbium coelestium* (*On the revolutions of the celestial spheres*).

The Polish astronomer Copernicus (1473–1543) asserted that the earth and planets revolved around the sun; the earth was no longer at the centre of the universe, but merely an orbiting body. His observations were neither entirely original nor especially accurate, but he did inspire debate and laid the path that others, such as Brahe, Kepler and Galileo, would follow. Copernicus's famous text circulated in manuscript for many years before its first publication in 1543. It was immediately condemned by the Catholic Church, forcing the author to recant some of his views.

Many of the threads of Copernicus's theories can actually be traced back to the classical age. In the Egyptian city of Alexandria classical astronomy flourished, with the curators of the city's fabulous library using geometry to measure the size of the earth and its distance from the sun and moon. These ancient astronomers were surprisingly accurate. Eratosthenes's measurement of the circumference of the earth was only about 50 miles out, while Hipparchus's determination of the distance from the earth to the moon was out by no more than 5 per cent. The culmination of the Alexandrian system was Ptolemy's *Almagest*; first published about AD 150, it ruled supreme for more than a thousand years. In Ptolemy's universe the earth was at the centre with the sun, moon, stars and planets its acolytes, moving around the earth in perfect circles. The scheme had great religious appeal and was officially approved by the Church.

We tend to think nowadays that *De revolutionibus orbium coelestium* caused a huge furore on publication, but in truth it did not. The medieval view of the universe was, literally, earth-centred, with all the heavenly bodies believed to rotate around the earth in a neat, circular fashion. The

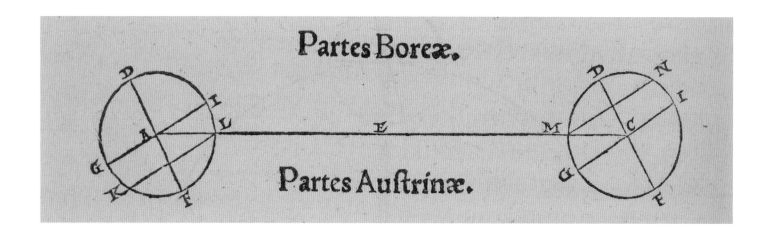

NICOLAI COPERNICI
SIGNORVM STELLARVMQVE DE-
SCRIPTIO CANONICA, ET PRIMO
quæ sunt Septentrionalis plagæ.

Formæ stellarum	Lōgitu dinis partes.	Lati= tudinis partes	magnitudo
VRSAE MINORIS SIVE CYNOSVRAE.			
In extremo caudæ.	53 1/2	66 0	3
Sequens in cauda.	55 1/2	70 0	4
In eductione caudæ.	69	74 0	4
In latere q̄dráguli p̄cedēte australior	83 0	75 1/3	4
Eiusdem lateris Borea.	87 0	77 1/2 1/3	4
Earū quæ in latere sequēte australior	100 1/2	72 1/2 1/6	2
Eiusdem lateris Borea.	109 1/2	74 1/2 1/3	2

Stellæ 7.quarum secudæ magnitudinis 2.tertiæ 1.quartæ 4.

Et q̄ circa Cynosurā informis in latere sequēte ad rectā linea maxie aust.	103 1/3	71 1/6	4

VRSÆ MAIORIS QVAM ELICEN VOCANT.

Quæ in rostro.	78 1/2 1/6	39 1/2 1/3	4
In binis oculis præcedens.	79	43 0	5
Sequens hanc.	79 1/2 1/6	43 0	5
In fronte duarum præcedens.	79	47 1/2 1/6	5
Sequens in fronte.	81 0	47 0	5
Quæ in dextra auricula præcedente.	81 1/2	50 1/2	5
Duarum in collo antecedens.	85 1/2 1/3	43 1/2 1/3	4
Sequens.	92 1/2 1/3	44 1/2 1/3	4
In pectore duarum Borea.	94	44 0	4
Australior.	93 1/3	42 0	4
In genu sinistro anteriori.	89 0	35 0	3
Duarū in pede sinistro priori borea.	89 1/2	29 0	3
Quæ magis ad Austrum.	88 1/2 1/6	28 1/2	3
In genu dextro priori.	89 0	36 0	4
Quæ sub ipso genu.	101	33 1/2	4
Quæ in humero.	104 0	49 0	2
Quæ in ilibus.	105 1/2	44 1/2	2
Quæ in eductione caudæ.	116 1/2	51 0	3
In sinistro crure posteriore.	117 1/3	46 1/2	2
Duarū p̄cedēs in pede sinistro poster.	106 0	29 1/2 1/3	3
Sequens hanc.	107 1/2	28 1/4	3

Quæ

BOREAE PLAGAE.

Formæ stellarum. VRSAE MAIORIS &c.	Lōgit. partes.	Latit. partes	magnitu.
Quæ in sinistra cauitate.	115 0	35 1/4 1/6	4
Duarū q̄ in pede dextro posteriore	123 1/2 1/6	25 1/2 1/3	3
Quæ magis ad Austrū. (Borea)	123 1/2 1/6	25 0	3
Prima triū in cauda post eductionē.	125 1/2	53 1/2 1/3	2
Media earum.	131	55 1/2 1/6	2
Vltima & in extrema cauda.	143	54 0	2

Stellæ 27.quarū secundæ magnitud. 6.tertiæ 8.quartæ 8.qntæ.5.

QVAE CIRCA ELICEN INFORMES.

Quæ à cauda in Austrum.	141 1/2 1/6	39 1/2 1/4	3
Antecedens hanc obscurior.	133	41 1/2	5
Inter ursæ pedes priores, & caput Le	98 1/2 1/3	17 1/2 1/6	4
Quæ magis ab hac in borea. (onis.)	96 1/2 1/6	19 1/2 1/6	4
Vltima trium obscurarum.	99	20 0	obscura
Antecedens hanc.	95 1/2	22 1/2 1/4	obscura
Quæ magis antecedit.	94	23 1/2	obscura
Quæ intra priores pedes & geminos.	100 1/3	22 1/2	obscura

Informiū 8.quarū magnitud.tertiæ 1.quartæ 2.quintæ 1.obscuræ 4

DRACONIS.

Quæ in lingua.	200 0	76 1/2 1/3	4
In ore.	215 1/2 1/6	78 1/2 1/3	4 maior
Supra oculum.	216 1/2	75 1/2 1/6	3
In gena.	229 1/2 1/3	75 1/2	4
Supra caput.	233 1/2 1/6	75 1/2 1/3	3
In prima colli inflexione Borea.	258 1/2 1/3	82 1/2 1/3	4
Australis ipsarum.	295 1/2 1/3	78 1/2 1/6	4
Media earundem.	262	80 1/2 1/3	4
Quæ seq̄ has ab ortu i cōuersiōe se	282 1/2 1/3	81 0	4
Austrina lateris p̄cedētis q̄drilateri.	331 1/3	81 1/2 1/6	4
Borea eiusdem lateris.	343 1/3	83 0	4
Borea lateris sequentis.	1 0	78 1/2 1/3	4
Australis eiusdem lateris.	346 1/6	77 1/2 1/3	4
In inflexiōe tertia australis trianguli	4 0	80 1/2 1/3	4
Reliquarum trianguli præcedens.	15 0	81 1/2 1/6	5
Quæ sequitur.	19 1/2	80 1/2 1/4	5
In triangulo antecedente trium.	66 1/2	84 1/2	4
Reliquarū eiusdē trianguli australis.	43 1/2 1/1	83 1/3	4

m iij — Quæ

OPPOSITE: A diagram of the earth's axis points with reference to the northern and southern hemispheres, from Copernicus's *De Revolutionibus*, 1543 (detail, fol.11v).

ABOVE: This extract from Book II of Copernicus's *De Revolutionibus, 1543*, provides detailed calculations of the astronomy of fixed stars (fols. 46v–47r).

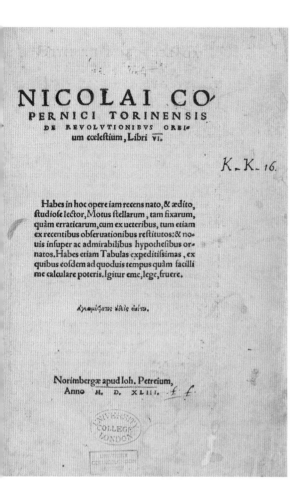

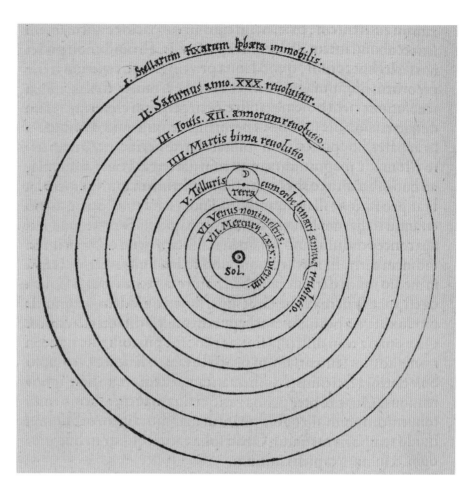

theory was not without its critics, however. As noted, Copernicus's ideas were not actually that new and his work had circulated in manuscript for some years prior to publication. In the printed book a preface appears, unsigned but known to be the work of Andreas Osiander, a German Lutheran theologian (1498–1552), who oversaw the publication of the work. In it he presents the Copernican planetary model purely as a hypothesis for discussion, without Copernicus's knowledge at the time, and many readers assumed he too held this view. Following publication the theories were commented on by scholars, notably the leading Jesuit astronomer Christoph Clavius, who opposed the heliocentric view but recognised there were problems with the orthodox model. There was even a second edition of the work published in 1566.

uel è conuerſo. H igitur in lineam A B reclinabitur:alioqui accide

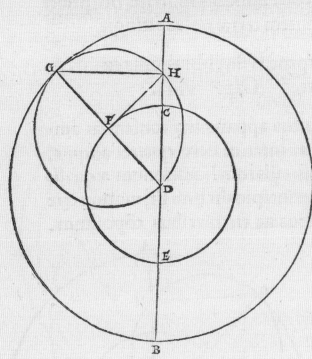

ret partem eſſe, maiorē ſuo
toto, quod facile puto intel
ligi. Receſsit autem à prio=
ri loco ſecundum longitudi
nem A H retractam per infra
ctam lineam D F H, æqualem
ipſi A D, eo interuallo quo di
metiens D F G excedit ſnbten
ſam D H. Et hoc modo per=
ducetur H ad D centrum, q̃d
erit in contingente D H G cir
culo, A B rectam lineam, dũ
uidelicet G D ad rectos angu
los ipſi A B ſteterit, ac deinde
in B alterum limitem perue=
niet, à quo rurſus ſimili rati

one reuertetur. Patet igitur è duobus motibus circularibus, &
hoc modo ſibi inuicem occurrentibus in rectam lineam motũ
componi, & ex æqualibus reciprocũ & inæqualem, quod erat
demonſtrandum. E quibus etiam ſequitur, quod G H recta linea
ſemper erit ad angulos rectos ipſi A B: rectum enim angulum in
ſemicirculo D H G linea compræhendent. Et idcirco G H ſemiſsis
erit ſubtendentis duplam A G circumferentiam, & D H altera ſe=
miſsis ſubtendentis duplum eius, quod ſupereſt ex A G quadran
tis circuli, eo quòd A G B circulus duplus exiſtat ipſi H G D ſecun=
dum diametrum.

Inæqualitatis anticipantium æquinoctiorum & obli= quitatis demonſtratio.   Cap. v.

A M ob cauſam uocare poſſumus motum hunc circu
li in latitudinem, hoc eſt in diametrum, cuius tamen
periodum & æqualitatem in circumcurrente: at di
menſionem in ſubtenſis lineis accipimus, ipſum pro
pterea inæqualem apparère, & uelociorem circa centrum, ac tar
diorem

A physician's handbook for the Elizabethan age

Pier Andrea Mattioli, *Commentarii, in libros sex Pedacii Dioscorides Anazarbei, de medica materia*. Venice: in officina Erasmiana, apud Vincentium Valgrisium, 1554.

Latin. [48], 707 pages; coloured woodcuts. 330 × 220 mm. Fine binding of pale leather, with gilt decoration and gilded pages.

Provenance: given by Anthony Todd Thomson, Professor of Materia Medica, before 1836.

S R C Quarto 1554 M1

One of the most famous works of the 16th century, this edition of the translation with commentaries of the largest pharmaceutical guide of antiquity, the *De materia medica* of Pedanus Dioscorides, is largely regarded as the masterpiece of Pier Mattioli (1500–77), first published in 1544. The text of *De materia medica* was hugely popular and influential from its first printing in Latin in 1478. By 1544 approximately 35 editions of Dioscorides' translations and commentaries had been produced, with Mattioli's being the most popular. Intended for daily use by physicans, herbalists and others, the work provided Greek and Latin synonyms and equivalents in other languages for all entries. The woodcuts in this volume are exceptionally fine.

Pedanus Dioscorides of Anazarbus lived in the middle of the 1st century AD. Little is known of his life, and he has only this one work definitely attributed to him. In five books *De materia medica* deals with over 600 plants, 35 animal products and 90 minerals, and it determined the style of later pharmacopoeias in the East and West. For each item Dioscorides gives the original name (often deriving from Persian, Egyptian, Armenian or African languages) and its Greek synonym. There then follows a description of the substance's origin and its medicinal uses. Dioscorides is largely responsible for determining modern plant nomenclature, both scientific and popular.

Mattioli was a surgeon with an abiding interest in medicinal botany, borne out by the many additional descriptions of plants not known to Dioscorides. This hugely influential work constitutes a lasting achievement of medical and botanical scholarship in its own right.

Detail from Mattioli's *Commentarii*, 1554, depicting a typical farm scene of milking and butter-making (fol. 205r).

ELEPHAS.

utuntur. Os gerunt pectori proximum, ut quod cum fuillo ineat fimilitudinem : è cuius fuperna parte dentes duo prominent præcipuæ magnitudinis (quales plurimi uenales confpiciuntur Venetijs in publico foro uulgò Merceria dicto, ac in alijs Italiæ emporijs) qui proni cufpide deorfum uergunt. Pedibus nituntur rotundis, difci inftar, latitudine duûm, triumúe palmorum, quos callofa materia obducit : ungulis quinque circùm, rotundis, mediocrium concharum

Error quorû dam. magnitudine. Crura ijs magna, ac fortia, neque (ut quidam imperiti exiftimant) uno tantùm offe conftant unduifa, fed genua flectunt, utpote & cætera quadrupeda. Quamobrem Elephanti (ut refert Aloifius Cadamuftus, qui claffe in Aethiopiam, & ad Calicut nauigauit) ut eos, qui deferri uolunt, fufcipiant, genua fubmittunt, fefeque erigunt deinde. Elephantis cauda bubali, trium palmorum circiter longitudine, rarißimis fetis referta. Quocirca haud facile fe tueri poffent à mufcarum iniuria, nifi aliam illis induftriam natura tribuiffet, qua ab ijs fe uindicent : quandoquidem ferientibus mufcis, cutim, quam cancellatam obtinent, contrahunt. Quo fit, ut arctatis in rugas repente cancellis, mufcas comprehenfas enecent. Hominibus non nifi laceßiti nocent. Veruntamen irritati homines promufcide comprehenfos, adeò in fublime iaciunt, ut priufquàm in terram decidant, fuffocentur, & pereant. Ad hæc nullus hominum tantæ pernicitatis inuenitur, quem mox Elephas non comprehendat, etiam non currens, fed gradatim incedens. Id efficit uafta animalis moles : quandoquidem fui greffus longitudine, humanam omnem pernicitatem euincat. Victitant arborum tam frondibus, quàm fructibus : neq; ulla tam ingens eft arbos, quam ij promufcide non profternant, frangant, ac dilacerêt. Adolefcunt ad fexdecim palmorum altitudinem. quapropter qui eos confcendere non affuecere, non fecus faftidio afficiuntur, ac illi, qui nauibus non affueti maria fulcant. Effrenes præterea adeò natura Elephanti funt, ut nullis habenis cohiberi poßint. quo fit, ut liberi incedere dimittantur : uerùm cum maximè gubernantibus fuarum regionum hominibus pareant, & eorum fermonem intelligant, idcirco uerbis facilè reguntur. Adeò confpectum ignem expauefcunt, ut eo territi à fuga reuocari non queant. Qua re ab ijs non cogniti, qui eius Elephanti curam gerebant Romæ, in cuius dorfo oppidulum conftruxerant, eo die, quo Iulianus Medices Pontificis Max. frater uxorem è Gallia duxit, in magno fanè difcrimine uerfati funt : nam ubi bellica tormenta ignem eructantia confpexiffet, magnumq;, ac terrificum fonum fenfiffet, tantæ fe fugæ dedit, ut nunquam cohiberi uoluerit, donec unà cum conclufis in oppidulo hominibus in Tyberim fefe commiferit. Elephanti non coëunt, neq; gignunt, nifi an-

Plinij lapfus. num uigefimum agant, ut autor eft Ariftoteles lib. V I. cap. XXVII. de hift. animalium. Qua in re Plinij error manifeftus deprehenditur : quippe qui marem quinquenné, fœminam decennem generare memoriæ prodiderit. Elephanti nulla nouere adulteria : nam unius tantùm fœminæ coitu utuntur, eamq; cùm uterum gerentem uiderint, non amplius tangunt. Quantum uerò temporis unaquæq; fœmina utero gerat, haud quaquam fciri poteft : quòd Elephanti pudore nunquam nifi in abdito coëant. Idcirco alij eis annum & fex menfes ftatuerunt, alij biennium, alij deniq; triennium. Pariunt fœminæ cum dolore, quemadmodum & mulieres. Pullum editum ore lambunt, qui ftatim cum natus eft, cernit, & ambulat. Viuere Elephantos (ut inquit Ariftoteles) tradunt quidam annos ducentos : fed florere ætate circa fexagefimum, uel feptuagefimum narrant. Iidem hyemis, ac frigoris impatientes funt. Gaudent amnibus maximè, circaq; fluuios uagantur, quos intrant libenter bubalorum more. Cæterùm Elephanti ingenio, & intellectu hominibus proximi funt : fiquidem patrios fermones intelligunt, fummam præftant obedientiam, prudentiam feruant, & religionem præ fe ferunt : folem nanq; ac lunam uenerantur. Cuius rei autores funt Mauritani, in quorum regionibus Elephanti innumeri confpiciuntur : qui gregatim noua nitefcente luna ad amnes defcendunt, ibiq; lauantur : mox purificati genibus flexis falutant fidus, & in fyluas reuertuntur. Sunt, qui tradant tanta intellectus fagacitate Elephantos pollere, ut maria tranfituri ad alienas regiones, non antea naues confcendere uoluerint, quàm ij, qui eos ducebant, iuramentum de reditu promiferint. In fyluas ituri gregatim ferè femper ingrediuntur, quorum agmen ducit, natu maximus : cogit uerò ætate illi proximus. Produnt Elephantos à uenatoribus circumuentos, cùm fciant prædam folùm in dentibus fuis ab illis expeti, dentibus uehementer impingentes arboribus eos fibi euellere, prædáq; fe redimere. Quod facilè

Μύρων σύνθεσις.   VNGVENTORVM COMPOSITIO.   CAP. XLI.

De ratione vnguentorum consequenter tractandum existimauimus : quandoquidem ea in nonnullis corporum uitijs, aut medicamentis mista, aut corpori perfusa, aut naribus obiecta, plurimùm prosunt. in quorum probationibus consulere nares oportet, an ea oleant, ex quibus temperantur. Optimum huiuscemodi iudicium. quod tamen in quibusdam planè obseruari non potest, propter ea, quæ admiscentur, odore cæteris præualentia : ut in amaracino, & crocino, telino, & plerisque alijs, quæ crebra circa hæc meditatione experiri conueniet.

Ῥόδινον.   ROSACEVM.   CAP. XLII.

ROSACEVM sic fit. Iunci odorati quinque libras & bessem tundito, & subactas aqua in uiginti olei libris, & quincunce subinde mouedo, coquito : dumque percolaueris, in olei libras uiginti, & quincuncem, adijcito rosas non madefactas numero mille, & manibus melle peruncis identidem moueto, interdiu premens, sinito nocte tota macerari, postea exprimito : & ubi recrementum ierit, mutato uase, in craterem melleillitu recondito . Cæterùm rosas, quæ antea pressæ fuerunt, in labellum demittito, & assutis octo libris & quadrante spissati olei, iterum premito, eritque secundarium oleum . Quòd si tertias usque, quartasue perfusiones insundens exprimere voles, secundarium fiet, tertiarium, & quartarium vnguentum . Sed quoties ita fecerit, uasa melle oblini debent . Si verò secundam infusionem instituere libet, in expressum oleum, numero pari recentes rosas, nullo humore imbutas inijcito : manibus melle præmadefactis agitans premito : & iterum tertiò, aut quartò simili modo exprimens facito, totiesque recentes rosas detractis vnguibus immittito : fiet enim ita oleum multò validius . nam septies oleum rosarum infusionem admittit, nec amplius . Prælum melle perungatur, oleum à succo diligenter secerni oportet : nam si minimum quid relinquatur, vnguentum corrumpet.

Alij autem detractis vnguibus, rosas tantùm oleo macerant in sole hoc modo . Rosæ, quæ selibram pondere æquant, in sextario olei diebus octo madescunt, & usque tertiam perfusionem quadraginta diebus insolantur, & sic oleum reconditur . Alij calamo, aut aspalatho prius olei spissamenta saciunt. Alij coloris causa anchusam admiscent, & salem, quò minus oleat . Vim astringendi, & refrigerandi obtinet : fomentis, & cataplasmatibus utile . Potum soluit aluum : stomachi ardorem restinguit : vlcera caua replet, & mulcet, quæ cacoëthe uocantur : vlceribus in capite manantibus, atque seruidis eruptionibus illinitur : caput dolens eo perfunditur : dentes inter initia doloris collui prodest : ad genarum durities illitum efficax est. ad lacessita interanea, & concitatas vuluas utilissimè subijcitur.

Hoc sub olei nomine comprehendit Dioscorides oleum omne, quod per se tantùm, nulla alterius olei admixtione, aut ex arborum fructibus, aut herbarum diuersorum generum seminibus, aut stirpium resinis elicitur . Sed vnguenti appellatione intelligit oleum omne genus, cui & odoramenta, & alia simplicia medicamenta admiscentur, ut in præsentia de Rosaceo agens, & deinde in sequentibus manifestè ostendit . Quo sit, ut apud Dioscoridem oleum uocetur, quod simpliciter expressum sit : vnguentum verò oleum quodlibet, cuius componendi ratio pluribus constet medicamentis . Quapropter Galenus lib. vi. simp.med.de oleo agens, sic inquit . Ex dictis cognoscere iam liceat, & de alijs olei generibus, quæ æquiuocè ipsis dicuntur, puta rosaceo, melino, liliaceo, & quæcunq; ab alijs floribus, fructibus, germinibus, folijs in oleo maceratis conficiuntur. Horum quodq; ubi unà cum aromatibus præparatur, unguentum efficitur . Cæterùm oleum rosaceum, quod hoc tempore officinæ completum appellant, à Dioscoridis rosaceo longè dissidet, quod etiam eo præstantius existimandum est, siquidem ob artificium, quod in ipsa parandi ratione diligentiores adhibent myropolæ . Quòd eorum tamen perpauci (ita ut ingenium est multorum à labore procliue ad ignauiam) illud secundùm Mesuem temperant ; tametsi plures ab eo optimi rosacei conficiendi modum sint consecuti.

Fit etiamnum rosaceum rosis non affatim defidescentibus in omphacinum demissis, modò calentis balnei uiribus (ut in quibusdam alijs superius adnotauimus) modò insolatu perquàm longo . Sunt & qui, ut magis uiribus præstet, oleum prius ex aqua rosacea luunt, deinde plusculo temporis spatio ter, aut quater rosas insundunt, quæ haud penitus satiscant, demum expressione peracta immaturarum rosarum succum adijciunt, ac inde diu insolant. Postremò oleum à

succo

strangulationibus obnoxias mirum in modum iuuat, adeò ut eas à strangulatu liberet, & sanet . Equidem noui multere, quotidie serè per annos hoc morbo uexatam, quæ tandem à quodam uulgari herbario edocta, ut uinum album biberet, in quo uitis albæ radicis uncia efferbuisset dormitum itura semel in hebdomada, cùm hac medicina per annum usa fuisset, optimè ex illo morbo conualuit . Vitis albæ meminit Galenus libro vi. simplicium medicamentorum, de eius uiribus ita scribens. Vitis albæ, quam & Bryoniam, & Psilothrum uocant, prima quidem germina ab omnibus pro more in uere eduntur, utpote edulium stomacho, eo quod adstringat, gratum . Habent etiam subamaram, & modice acrem adstrictionem : quare & urinam moderatè cient . At radix & abstergentem, & deficcantem, & tenuium partium, ac moderatè calidam uim obtinet : quamobrem & lienes induratos liquat, tum epota, tum soris cum sicubus imposita : & psoram, & lepram sanat . Porrò fructus eius racemi specie præferens, ijs qui coria tingunt, utilis est.

Ἄμπελος μέλαινα.   VITIS NIGRA.   CAP. CLXXVII.

NIGRA uitis, quam aliqui nigram bryoniam uocant, folia fert hederæ, smilaceis proxima, sed maiora : caules etiam cognatos : capreolis suis arbores, quasi adminicula, comprehendit : fructus racematim cohærent, qui inter principia uirent, & post maturitatem nigrescunt : radix foris nigra, intus buxeo colore nitet . Viticulæ, quæ primo germinum partu erumpunt, in olera recipiuntur . menses pellunt, urinas cient, lienem absumunt : uertiginosis, comitialibus, neruorum resolutione tentatis prosunt . Radix eadem, quæ uitis alba præstat, sed inefficacius . Folia cum uino exulceratis iumentorum ceruicibus commodissimè illinuntur : luxatis itidem imponuntur.

VITIS nigra Hetruscis uulgò appellatur Tamaro, corrupto à tamno uocabulo . Sunt enim qui hanc tamnum, siue tamnum etiam uocent, unde Latinis eius uua Taminia dicta est . Huius uiticulæ, quæ uere primùm è terra erumpunt, quòd asparagis similes sint, eorum more decoctæ, hac etiam tempestate manduntur, quamuis non eam, quam asparagi, cũ palato ineant gratiam . Frequentissimæ hæc in Hetruria prouenit, quin & in Goritiensi comitatu, ubi Martio & Aprili mensibus, eius cauliculi in fasciculos digesti in foro ueniunt ad ciborum usum. Huic tamen, quæ in Italia nascitur, illud tantùm obijci posse putauerim, quòd in uuarum colore ab illa dissidere inueniatur, quam Dioscorides repræsentauit, quòd huic uuæ post maturitatem nigrescant, nostræ verò perpetuo rubentes spectentur : cætera enim, meo quidem iudicio, inter se maximè conueniunt . Sed illud nihil me mouet, neque facit, ut mutare debeam sententiam, & credere hanc aliam esse à Vite nigra, quòd

sæpe uiderim solanum hortense quibusdam in locis uuas ferre modò nigras, modò rubentes, modò quàdā dam natura plerumq; cum florum, & fructuum colore ludere soleat, ut in uuis, ecrasis, moris, sicubus, prunis, malis, & alijs compluribus perspicuo cernitur . Idcirco nil mirum esse debet, si in Italia Vitis nigra rubentes uuas proferat, albi uerò nigras, ut in Græcia, Asia, alijsq; calidioribus regionibus, quòd huiusmodi discrimina sæpenumero cœli, ac soli diuersitate contingant . Hac igitur ratione fretus, quæ, ni fallor, illam obiectionem diluit, non dubitauerim asserere, hanc plantam, cuius etiam hic effigiem pictam damus, esse ueram ac genuinam Vitem nigram, quoniam cæteræ omnes prorsus notæ illi adstipulari deprehenduntur . Cæterùm credidit Leonardus Fuchsius, medicus nostræ ætatis celebris, eam stirpem esse legitimam Vitem nigram, quam nostris in Hetruria uulgò Vitalba dicitur, quamq; alteram esse Dioscoridis clematidem superius huius libri initio abunde ostëdimus . Verùm hæc eius opinio nobis, pace sua, planè reprobanda uidetur . Siquidem nostra Vitalba non habet radicem foris nigram, sed modò rubens colore : non fert fructus hedere à maiora, sed potius minora, & per ambitum laciniata : nec semen edit in racemi modum, sed simul compactim, nulla cum uuis similitudine. Adde, quòd eadem sua facultate exulcerat . Vitis verò nigra exulceratis boum ceruicibus medetur, & luxatis ob adstringentem uim, quam habet, utilissimè imponitur . Vitis nigræ uires paucis peristrinxit Galenus lib. vi. simplicium medicamentorum, sic inquiens . Vitis nigra : uocatur ubi hæc proprie bryonia, uti albæ ad omnia similis, nisi quòd imbecillior . hactenus Galenus de uite nigra. Huius autem succo (ut est auctor Mesues) nihil ualentius ad struinas sanandas, si cum uini, & mellis æquali portione is hauriatur. Præstat ad idem radix quoq; si tusa, & melle except à illinatur . Sed quoniam Vites tam alba, quàm nigra, de quibus hactenus dictum est, multi in mentem eam herbam redegerunt, quæ aliquibus uulgò uocatur Viticella, alijs Balsamina, alijs Mordica, alijs Caranza, cùm ueteribus nihil de ea posteritatis memoriæ proditum sit, sitq; dotibus quàm plurimis non obscuris

OPPOSITE: Description and image of the elephant in the *De Materia Medica*, 1543 (p.192).

ABOVE: Entries from the plant section in Mattioli's *De Materia Medica*, with delightful illustrations of *Rosacea*, the rose, and *Vitris Nigra*, the vine (pp. 554–5).

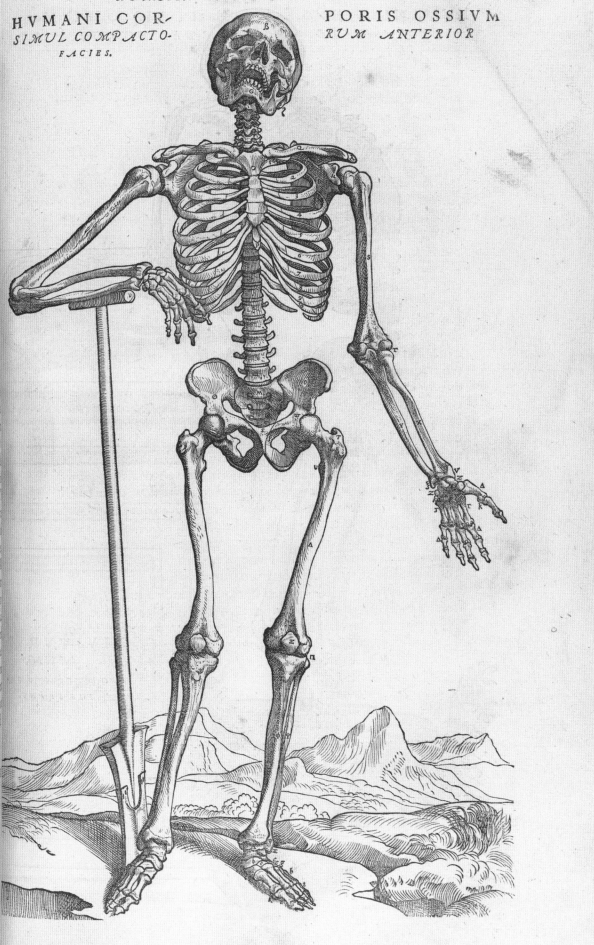

Second expanded edition of Vesalius's *De Fabrica*, the first book of scientific anatomy

Andreas Vesalius, *De humani corporis fabrica libri septem*. Basileae: Ioannem Oporinum, 1555.

Latin. [12] 824 [48] pages. Woodcuts throughout. 440 mm.

Provenance: unknown; housed in the office of the Dean of the Medical School for many years.

S R C Folio 1555 V28

First published in 1543, Vesalius's work was the greatest medical book of the 16th century. It heralded the beginning of true scientific anatomy: Vesalius did his own dissections and the illustrations come from his direct observations. This second, much expanded and improved edition dates from 1555. UCL has three copies of this edition.

Vesalius (1514–64) enjoyed imperial patronage and a steady supply of bodies for dissection. In this, his *magnum opus*, he spared no effort or expense, hiring the best draughtsmen, engravers and printer. Both drawings and woodcuts were executed in Venice. There is recent debate about the exact method of execution, but the superb engravings are often attributed to the workshop of Titian, particularly to his pupil Jan Stephen van Calcar, while the woodcutting is commonly attributed to Francesco Marcolini da Forli. The plates are truly remarkable, not just for their quality, but also for their relation to the text. It was the first time that the illustrations in a medical book related precisely to, and were intended to clarify, the text. They form a sequence from skeletons to the various muscle layers and nerves, and were heavily plagiarised for centuries.

Of Flemish origin, Vesalius studied at the universities of Louvain, Paris and Padua. In 1537 he was appointed lecturer on surgery and anatomy at Padua. The young man swiftly established his own style, performing the dissections himself, contrary to previous practice, and moving away from traditional Galenic theories. He produced four large anatomical charts, based chiefly on dissection and intended as a reference work and memory aid for his students. Vesalius's lectures and demonstrations became extremely popular, and in 1539 he managed to arrange for a regular supply of bodies. For the first time he had sufficient human material to make, and repeat, detailed and comparative dissections. He served the Emperor Charles V as physician to the imperial household and as military surgeon, and died en route to the Holy Land in 1564.

From 1540 Vesalius worked on the explication of his theories in a published form. His book, *De humani corporis fabrica* (commonly known as *De fabrica*), was published in Basel in August 1543, bringing Vesalius great renown and some criticism. Vesalius hoped that by his example in Padua, and by his book, he might persuade the medical world to appreciate anatomy as fundamental to all other aspects of medicine. Although he urged the importance of comparative anatomy by the parallel dissection of animals, Vesalius believed that human anatomy was to be learned only by dissection and investigation of the human body. *De fabrica* was to be one of the most important medical books ever published.

OPPOSITE: A fine woodcut depicting the skeleton, the first stage in Vesalius's sequence of illustrations of the human figure, from the 1555 expanded edition of his *De humani corporis fabrica* (p.203).

LEFT: Secondary muscles of the human figure, from Vesalius's *De humani corporis fabrica*, 1555 (p.174).

Fine early editions of Dante's *La Divina Commedia*

Comento di Christoforo Landino Fiorentino sopra La Commedia di Dante Alighieri, Poeta Fiorentino. Firenze: per Nicolaus Laurentii, Alamanus, 30 August 1481.

Italian. 372 leaves. 2 engravings. 390 × 250 mm.

Provenance: given by Sir Henry Thompson, 1921.

INCUNABULA FOLIO 6b

RIGHT: Pasted-in illustrations in the 1481 printing of the first Florentine edition of Dante's *La Divina Commedia*. Featured is one of the only two illustrations based on the original design by Sandro Botticelli (fol 22v).

OPPOSITE: The beginning of Canto XXIX of the 1491 fully illustrated edition of *La Divina Commedia*, also with Landino's commentary, p.130 (fol. 120).

UCL Library Services is fortunate to possess some of the most splendid early editions of Dante's great work. The first printed edition of *La Commedia* was produced at Foligno in 1472 – a century and a half after the poet's death, but less than a decade after the introduction of printing into Italy. Vendelin de Spira of Venice produced one of the copies now at UCL in 1477, as well as the first Florentine edition of 1481.

The latter has an interesting background to its history and origin. A product of the cultural circle surrounding the Signoria of Florence, Lorenzo de' Medici, it was conceived as a polemical work, directed towards other Italian centres of production – especially those of Venice (the 1477 edition) and Milan (1478). The 1481 edition, featured here, represented the Florentine attempt to reclaim the great poet, whose work had achieved classic status throughout Italy since the 14th century. A manuscript copy was presented to Lorenzo, together with a new commentary by Florentine humanist Christoforo Landino and illustrations by Sandro Botticelli, the city's great contemporary artist. The complete series of illustrations contemplated for this book was never completed, as is shown by the blank spaces left before each canto. Only the first three plates, taken from Botticelli's designs, are ever found printed directly onto the text pages. The remainder are printed on separate slips of paper, subsequently pasted into place. UCL's copy has only two plates, the first cut down.

CANTO.XXIX.DE LA PRIMA CANTICA DE DANTE.

A molta gente: & le diuerse piaghe
hauea le luci mie si iebbiate
che de lo stare a piangere
eron uaghe.

Ma uirgilio mi dixe che pur guate
perche la uista tua pur si suffolge:
laggiu tra lōbre triste & smozighate.

Tu non hai facto si a l altre bolge
pensa se tu annouerar e credi
che migla uentidue la ualle uolge.

Et gia la luna e sotto a nostri piedi
lo tēpo e poco homai che me cōcesso
& altro e da ueder che tu non credi

CHAPOCHIO

¶ Iamo finalmēte ariuati ala decima bolgia nelaquale sono puniti e falsatori. Falsita e la decima specie dela fraude.ne puo esser falsita se non si mostra una cosa punaltra i dāno del pxio:& e generalmēte negare el uero:o fingere che el falso sia uero. Et sono due specie i decti:& q̄sta si chiama bugia & i facti:& chiamasi ppriamēte falsita. Et bēche si falsifica le scripture & altre cose q poni e falsificatori di metalli:che sono alchimisti & falsificatori di moneta.& q̄sto si fa o falsādo la ligha:o falsādo el conio.Pone adūque nel pricipio come lui p stupore & cōpassiōe uo lētieri si fermaua a piagere. Ma uirgilio ladmonisce che lui debba el tēpo d atogli a fare tal uiaggio distri buire in forma che possi fornirlo.Cōcio sia che resti āchora a uedere molte cose & piu horrende. & certa mēte la ragiō supiore quādo ha ueduto le cose i genere uol passare ad altra cognitiōe:pche la sciētia nō e de pticulari.& oltre a q̄sto cōsidera la natura dele cose sāza alchuna passiōe: Ma la iferiore & la sēsuali ta si riuolge ne pticulari:& i quegli nō sta sāza alchūa passiōe:o damore:o dodio:o diuidia:o di cōpassiōe Ilpche biogna ch̄ dāthe sia admōito da Vir.La molta gēte:nō solamēte era molta gēte.ma āchora hauea nō simili:ma diuerse piaghe. HAuean le luci:cioe glocchi. SI iebriate: q̄do locchio nostro dela mente e so brio che nō occupato da alchūa passiōe uede el uero:ma quādo e iebbiato dala cōtagione del corpo seqta uolētieri lappetito:ma uirgilio che e la ragiōe supiore dice che pur guate pche.LA VISTa tua si soffolge. Sappogia & ficca.PEnsa se tu annouerar la credi che migla uētidue la ualle uolge. Allegoricamēte admo nisce la ragiōe supiore la iferiore che nō pda tēpo i uolere hauere cognitiōe de pticulari:pche sono innu merabili.Et p demostrare q̄sto afferma che labito & circuito di q̄lla bogla e uētidue migla:& e piēo dōm bre.Ilpche facilmēte si cōclude che ipossibile sia enūerarle:Et dixe tale abito esser uētidue migla p demo strare che gia sono presso al cētro dela terra:pche nō restaua se nō la decia bolgia & el nono cierchio:elq̄ le i se tiene q̄tro cerchi:& nel q̄rto e el cētro:Ma noi ināzi che itrassemo nellopa dimostrāmo nel sito de lonferno questo circuito di migla.xxii. ET gia la lūa e sotto e nostri piedi:el tēpo cōcesso era un giorno naturale.Adūque gionse al cētro passato la nocte & mezo el giorno.Et laltra meta del di gli torno nocte passato el cētro i forma che da matia arriuo a catone.Ilpche la pria nocte fu itera & el sequēte si fu dal me zo i la nocte.& q̄do al nostro hemispio torno la secōda nocte:lui era gia del cētro salito isino ala supficie dellaltro hemispio:& truououi lalba q̄do qui si faccea nocte:Dimostra adūque che q̄do erono in q̄sta bo glia sappressaua el giorno al nostro hemispio.& pche la lūa era neloppositiōe del sole:gia comiciaua esse re nellaltro hemispio che e sotto e piedi di chi e nel nostro:Alq̄le passato la meta del corpo di lucifero co minciaua a salir adūque eēdo ito la nocte:& pte del di pel nr̄o:& cominciando quādo el di e a noi a salire alaltro trouo noua nocte con laquale dal centro sali isino ala supficie di quello:& giunse alalba. Et altro e da uedere:perche restaua la decima bolgia:& el nono cerchio che nabracciaua quattro.

¶ Ispose dāthe:se tu sapessi la cagiōe p chi mirauo tu mharesti dimesso:cioe pdonato lo stare. PARte
In questo mezo uirgilio ādaua:& dithe seguitādo lo nello ādare seguitaualo similmente nela rispo sta gia comiciata:& soggiugēdo dixe.Io credo che uno spirito di mio sāgue & di mia generatiōe piāga in q̄lla caua douio teneua glocchi si appo sta:cioe fixi.& e trāslatiōe di chi pon la mira al berzaglo. & Virgi lio respose.NON si frāga:nō si rōpa tuo pēsieri sou ello sopra q̄llo.cioe non interrūpere e pēsieri che tu hai dellaltre cose p pēsare a costui attē di a daltre cose:& lui si rim iga.Et sogiūge che lui uide q̄sto spirito: & udi che fu chiam ito geri del bello.Costui fu geri del bello: fratello de misser Cione del bello de glaligeri consorte di dāthe:elq̄le fu molto cismatico:& p tal uitio fu ucci

Setu hauessi risposio apresso
atteso la cagion perchio parlaua
forse mharesti anchor lo star dimesso

Comento di Christoforo Landino Fiorentino sopra La Commedia di Dante Alighieri, Poeta Fiorentino. Vinegia: Petrus de Plasiis, Cremonensis, dictus Veronensis, 18 November 1491.

Italian. 307 leaves. 100 woodcut illustrations; decorated initials. 310 × 210 mm.

Provenance: bequeathed as part of the library of Henry Clark Barlow, 1876.

INCUNABULA QUARTO 5o

The UCL 1491 copy, with Landino's commentary edited by Piero de Figino, was the first completely illustrated edition of *La Divina Commedia*. It features delightful woodcut illustrations and decorated initials at the start of each canto. Formerly owned by Antonius Gallardus (whose inscription appears on the last leaf), it was previously in the possession of the University of Genoa Library, and bears its stamp on the first leaf.

The Dante Collection at UCL owes its origin to Henry Clark Barlow's bequest of his Italian library in 1876. This included his important Dante collection, as well as personal papers and correspondence, travel diaries and sketches. At the same time he endowed the Barlow Memorial Lecture on Dante. The collection was supplemented by editions from the Morris Library, the Mocatta Library (1906) and the Whitley Stokes Collection (1910). A printed catalogue was issued in 1910. Other later editions also came from the Rotton Library in 1926, from Sir Herbert Thompson in 1921 and from the valuable library of Huxley St John Brooks, whose books were purchased by UCL Library Services on his death in 1949.

Born in 1806, Barlow had a lifelong fascination with Italy, first fuelled by early encounters with it as a student at the Royal Academy of Arts. He acquired an interest in geology while studying medicine at Edinburgh and moved to Paris in the late 1830s, which further fanned his enthusiasm. Barlow embarked on his first continental tour to the Low Countries and the Rhine in the summer of 1840, and the following year set out for Italy. Here he was to remain for five years, living the life of an artist and student of art. He compiled his own Italian Grammar and kept a series of notebooks, filled with sketches and notes and places he visited. His observations on the history or painting and continental galleries were often in the form of letters to the *Morning Post*, and they made an appreciable contribution to the development of the National Gallery, which he championed. He discovered Dante while in Pisa during the winter of 1844–5, and the study and illustration of *La Divina Commedia* soon took precedence over all interests. UCL was to benefit from Barlow's deep scholarship and dedication to this field of study.

The collection, now numbering a little under 3,000 volumes, includes 36 editions of the *Divina Commedia* printed before 1600, notably three incunabula: that printed by Wendelin de Spira of Venice in 1477, the 1491 edition of Petrus de Plasiis of Cremona and the first illustrated edition printed by Nicholas di Lorenzo in Florence, 1481 (the latter two featured here). There are also two copies of the first Aldine edition of 1502, together with five later Aldine editions.

OPPOSITE: The beginning of the first Canto of the 1491 printing of Dante's *La Divina Commedia*, from Vinegia, p.11 (fol. 1).

CANTO PRIMO DE LA PRIma cantica o uero comedia del diuino Poeta Fiorentino Dante A
ghieri.   Capitulo.   I.

EL Mezo del
camin di no
stra uita
Mi ritrouai p
una selua ob
scura
Che la diricta
uia era smarri
ta

Quanto adir quale era cosa dura
   esta selua seluaggia aspra & forte
   che nel pensier rinuoua la paura
Tanto era amara che poco e piu morte
   ma per tractar del bē chio ui trouai
   diro dellaltre cose chio uo scorte
I non so ben ridir chomio uentrai
   tātera piē di sonno insu quel pūcto
   che la uerace uia abbandonai
Ma poi chio fui appie dū colle giūto
   la oue terminaua quella ualle
   che mhauea di paura el cor cōpūcto
Guardai in alto & uidi le sue spalle
   uestite gia de raggi del pianeta
   che mena diricto altrui p ogni calle
Alhor fu la paura un pocho queta
   che nellago del cuor mera durata
   la nocte chio passai con tanta pieta

h Abbiamo narrato non solamente la uita del poeta & el titulo del libro & che cosa sia poeta:ma etiā quā to sia uetusta & anticha:quāto nobile & uaria:quāto utile & ioconda tāl doctrina. Quāto sia efficace a muouere lhu mane menti: & quāto dilecti ogni liberale ingegno. Ne giudicammo da tacere quāto i si diuina disciplina sia stata la excellētia dello igegno del nostro poeta . Inche si sono stato piu brieue che forse non si conuerebbe:cōsideri chi legge che lanumerosa & quasi infinita copia delle chose dellequali e necessario tractare misforza non uolēdo chel uolume cresca sopra modo:a inculcare & inuiluppare piu tosto che explicare:& distendere molte chose & maxime quelle lequali quādo bē tacessi non pero ne restera obscu ra la expositione del testo . Verremo adunque a quella Ma perche stimo non esser lectore alcuno ne di si basso i gegno:ne di si pocho giudicio:che hauēdo īteso:quāto sia & la profondita & uarieta della doctrina:& la excellentia

& diuinita dello ingegno del nostro toscano:& fiorētino poeta:non si persuada che questo principio del primo cāto debba per sublimita & grandezza esser pari alla stupēda doctrina delle chose che seguitano: pero con ogni idustria inuestigheremo che allegoricho senso arechi seco questo mezo del camio : & che chosa sia selua.Diche ueggio non piccola differentia essere stata tra glinterpreti & expositori di questa cā tica. Impero che alchuni dicono:che il mezo della uita humana e el sonno mossi:credo dalla sententia da istotile dicēdo lui nellethica nessunna differentia essere tra felici: & miseri nella meta della uita per che le nocti che sono lameta del tempo cinducono sonno:& da quello nasce che ne bene ne male sentir pos siamo. Il perche uogliono questi:che el poeta pongha el mezo della uita per la nocte: & la nocte pel son no:ad notare che questo poema non sia altro che una uisione che gliapparue dormendo per laquale heb be cognitione delle chose da lui descripte ī queste tre comedie. Dicono adūque che lui imita Ioanni euā gelista el quale dormendo sopra el pecto di christo redemptore hebbe uisione delle chose celeste : ouera mēte ponghi la nocte dimostrādo lui hauere comiciato el suo poema di nocte nella quale raccoglēdosi lā nimo in se medesimo & absoluendosi & liberādosi da ogni cura meglio ītēda.Ma ben che tale sententia quadri al poeta: niētedimeno le parole non la dimostrono se non con tanta obscura ambiguita:che non pare degna della elegātia di tāto poeta prima perche non seguita che benche nelle reuolutioni del tēpo tāto spatio occupin le nocti quāto e di:per questo dicēdo io scripsi di nocte sintenda io scripsi nel mezo della mia eta:perche & nel prīcipio & nel fine della eta humana sonno le nocti chome nel mezo & simil mēte e di.Il perche per la medesima ragione si potrebbe fare tale ītrepetatiōe pel di come per la nocte Altri dicono che uole pel mezo del camio ītēdere che nel mezo deleta dette prīcipio al suo poema. ma A non e una medesima opinione del termīe dela nostra eta:perche diuersi scriptori diuersamēte sentono

                                                               B

IL LIBRO DEL CORTEGIANO
DEL CONTE BALDESAR
CASTIGLIONE.

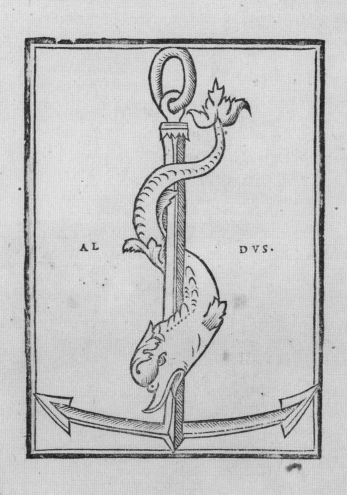

Haffi nel priuilegio, & nella gratia ottenuta dalla Illuftriffima
Signoria che in quefta, ne in niun'altra Citta del fuo
dominio fi poffa imprimere, ne altroue
impreffo uendere quefto libro
del Cortegiano per·x· anni
fotto le pene in effo
contenute ·

A guide to the etiquette of courts and courtiers

Baldassarre Castiglione, *Il Libro del cortegiano del conte Baldesar Castiglione* (*The Book of the Courtier* by Count Baldesar Castiglione). Venetia: Aldus Manutius, 1533.

Italian. 8 pages, 1 leaf, 202 (ie 211) numbered leaves, 1 leaf; 170 × 140 mm. Fine modern binding of full black morocco, with gilt rolled borders on inside edges of boards; edges gilt and gauffred.

Provenance: given by Sir Herbert Thompson, 1921.

S R Castiglione 1533

In early 16th-century Florence Niccolò Machiavelli was reviled for his brutal exposition of human nature in *The Prince* (1513). In contrast Baldassare Castiglione's *Il Libro del cortegiano* (first published 1528) argued for the civilising processes of manners, conversation, dancing and dress – in it the author abhors the idea of princes showing valour, rather than ignorance of warrior skills. Castiglione's work was essentially an etiquette book for courtiers and one of the, if not the most, popular self-help guides of its day. It was used as a political and social manual throughout Renaissance Europe.

UCL possesses one of the most complete collections of editions of Castiglione's work known to exist. The bulk of it was formed from the gift of books made by Sir Herbert Thompson in 1921, which also provided considerable additions to the Dante collection and others, from the collection of Huxley St John Brooks. The Castiglione collection ranges from the Aldine *editio princeps* of 1528 to the translation by L E Opdycke, which appeared in a limited edition in 1902 with a bibliography of the editions of the work.

In addition to the 1528 edition, the other four early editions of Aldus (of 1533, shown here, 1541, 1545 and 1547) are all present. Of the 110 editions listed by Opdycke as appearing before 1640, this collection contains 61. It also features an edition of 1557, published in Paris by E Graulleau, which once belonged to William Lambard and bears his signature; this was not known to Opdyke. The collection now comprises 102 separate editions of this book, of which 70 were published before 1800. They include the first English version translated by Thomas Hoby, printed in London by William Seres in 1561, together with nine other English editions printed before 1640.

OPPOSITE: Title page from the 1533 edition of Castiglione's *Il Libro del cortegiano*, showing the famous Dolphin and Anchor printer's device, of Aldus's printing house.

RIGHT: The final page of the Libro Quarto of *Il Libro del cortegiano*, 'editio princeps' [first edition], 1528. The innovative touch to the layout design of the printed word on the page is typical of the Aldine press for that period.

A rare and unusual late Elizabethan commonplace book

Thomas Trevelyon, manuscript, *c.* 1603.

English. 211 leaves. 390 × 260 mm.

Provenance: purchased as part of the Ogden Library, 1953.

MS OGDEN 24

BELOW: A richly coloured illustration of a compass from Thomas Trevelyon's manuscript volume. The accompanying legend above the image reads, 'The good mariner maye longe for the use of this Instrument: it servethe marveylously his turn' (fol. 20r, detail).

OPPOSITE: A whole page showing the last entry in the work, recording the kings and queens of England and finishing with James I. The date 1602 gives an indication of the creation date of the work (fol. 101r).

The Trevelyon Manuscript is a very rare manuscript volume of the late 16th/early 17th centuries. It was only recently identified as being, in all probability, a previously unknown third and only other copy of the so-called Trevelyon Miscellany of 1608. The most celebrated copy of this work is held in the Folger Shakespeare Library in Washington DC.

This fascinating collection of contemporary textual and illustrative material is thought to have been compiled by Thomas Trevelyon, or Trevilian (born *c.* 1548), a London craftsman of whom little is known. Probably completed in the early 1600s, it consists of richly coloured illustrations and texts reflecting common preoccupations of the late Elizabethan and early Jacobean period. The content ranges from portraits of the kings and queens of England and depictions of biblical scenes to familiar domestic activities, household proverbs and animal husbandry, descriptions of local fairs, representations of Ptolemaic astronomy and popular astrology. These are interleaved with visual interpretations of the Creation myth, and alphabet letters in various floral and Celtic-influenced designs and intricate embroidery patterns.

A highly unusual work, created for the entertainment, education and amusement of close family and friends, the Trevelyon Manuscript offers an intriguing glimpse into the Elizabethan world. It was common for works of this type to have individual leaves taken out so that they could be copied and further shared among such groups before being returned. There is no evidence of this having happened to this volume, however, making it an intact example of its kind.

The Folger manuscript copy is known to many scholars of the period, as is the so-called Trevilian Great Book of 1616. The latter is held in the Wormsley Library in Buckinghamshire, a private collection built up by Sir Paul Getty. When the two known existing manuscripts were edited for publication in 2001 and 2007 respectively, neither editor was aware of the existence of the UCL manuscript. This third copy was identified in 2013 by Heather Wolfe, Curator of Manuscripts at the Folger Library.

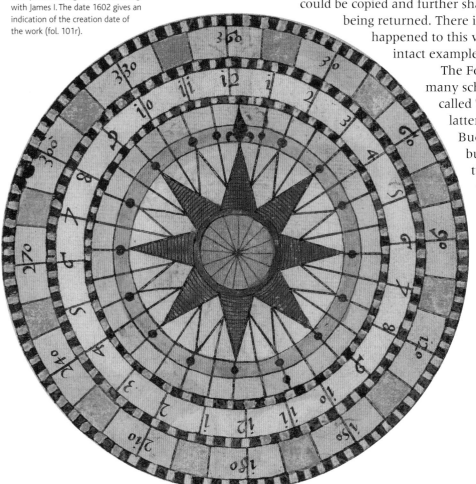

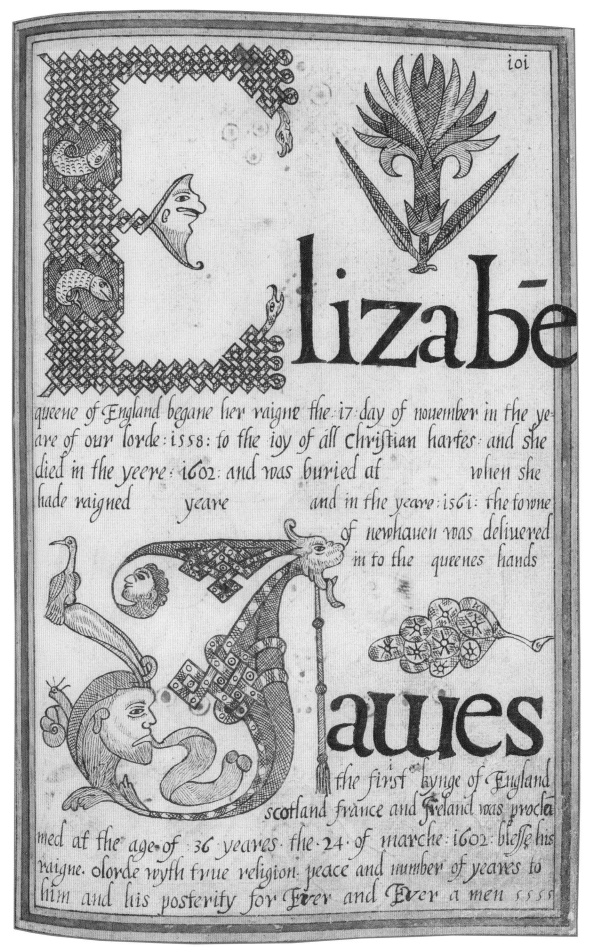

Elizabē

queene of England begane her raigne the 17 day of nouember in the yeare of our lorde: 1558: to the ioy of all christian hartes and she died in the yeere: 1602: and was buried at   when she hade raigned   yeare   and in the yeare: 1561: the towne of newhauen was deliuered in to the queenes hands

Iaues

the first kynge of England scotland france and Ireland was proclamed at the age of 36 yeares the 24 of marche 1602 blesse his raigne. o lorde wyth true religion peace and number of yeares to him and his posterity for Ever and Ever a men ʃʃʃʃ

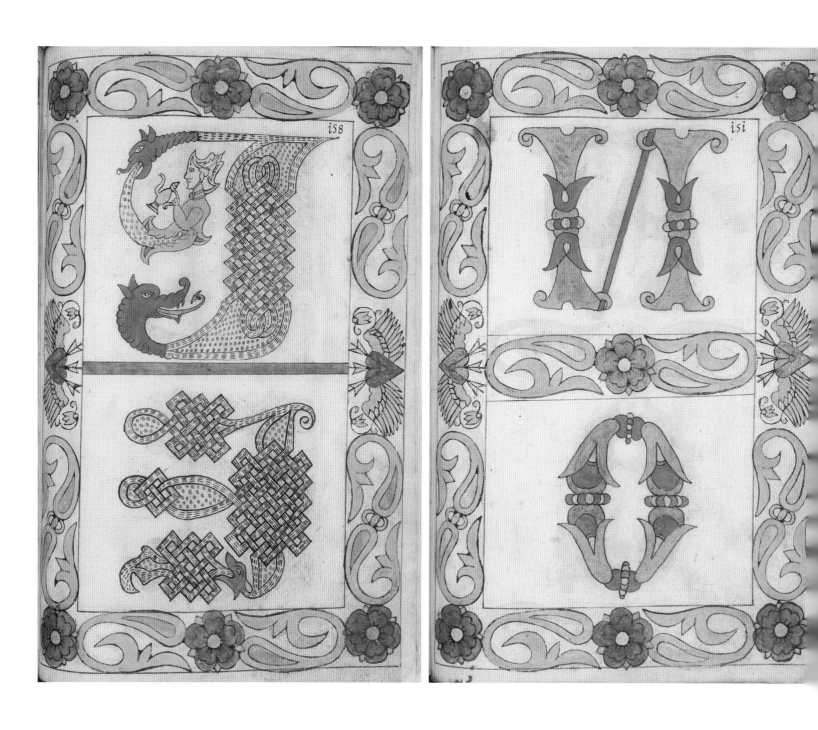

The UCL Trevelyon Manuscript, four examples of illustrated pages (left to right): the Celtic-influenced letter 'J' (fol. 158r); letters 'N' and 'O' (fol. 151r); the Tudor rose, prominently featured (fol. 53r); an imaginative diagram with the title 'A table of all the shyres in England' (fol. 13r).

danger of haye

change of princes

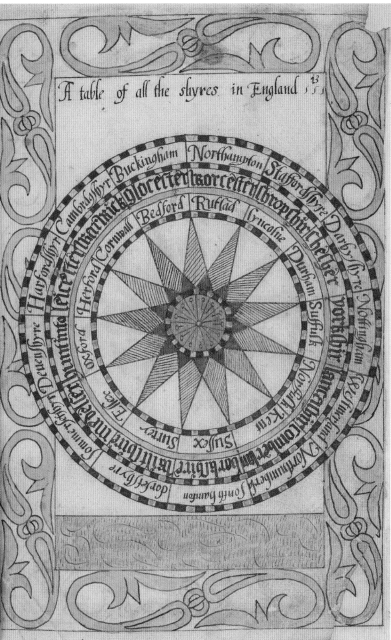

A table of all the shyres in England

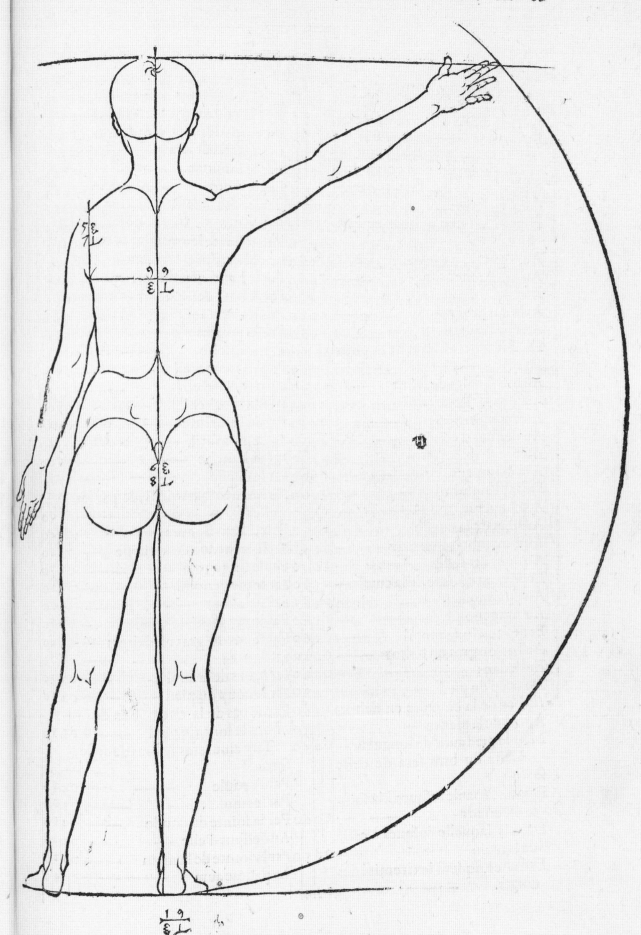

Early mathematical treatise for artists' use

Albrecht Dürer, *Les quatres livres d'Albert Dürer, peinctre & geometrien tres excellent, de la proportion des parties & pourctraits des corps humains. Traduicts par Loys Meigret Lionnois, de langue Latine en Françoise.* Arnheim: Chez Jean Jeansz, 1613. [Originally published under title *'Vier Bücher von menschlichen Proportion'*, Nuremberg, 1528.]

French. [2], 124 leaves; woodcuts; 310 mm.

Provenance: presented by Lady Thane as part of the Collection of Sir George Dancer Thane, 1930.

S R C Quarto 1613 D8

Dürer (1471–1528) was a true 'Renaissance man': a mathematician, painter, goldsmith, engraver and author. Born in Nuremberg, the son of a goldsmith, he learned his father's craft. He became fascinated by the Italian Renaissance in art, visiting Italy in 1494 and 1505–7. He studied mathematics, geometry, proportion and art theory, and became convinced that science must be the basis of all true art.

Dürer produced three major theoretical books. His *Underweysung der Messung mit Zirckel und Richtsceyt in Linien ebnen und gantzen corporem* ['*Treatise on mensuration with the compass and ruler in lines, planes and whole bodies*'] was published in Nuremberg in 1525. It was the first major German mathematics book to be published, intended as a guide for artists. In 1527 Dürer published *Befestigungslehre* ['*Treatise on fortification*'], which contains his major architectural work. This volume was first published posthumously in 1528 as *Vier Bücher von menslicher Proportion* ['*Treatise on proportion*']. It is a synthesis of Dürer's solutions to his own questions and sets forth his formal aesthetic.

Dürer's aesthetic rules are firmly based on the laws of optics. Not strictly a medical work, this was the first attempt to apply anthropometry (the measurement of the size and proportions of the human body) to aesthetics, and influenced many later artists in their representation of human figures. UCL's copy comes from the library of Sir George Dancer Thane (1850–1930) and bears his signature, dated January 1883.

OPPOSITE: A depiction of proportions of the human figure in numbers, from the second 'book' of Albrecht Dürer's *Treatise on Proportion* (p.66).

RIGHT: The human face, as measured and drawn with exquisite artistry by Dürer (p.107, detail).

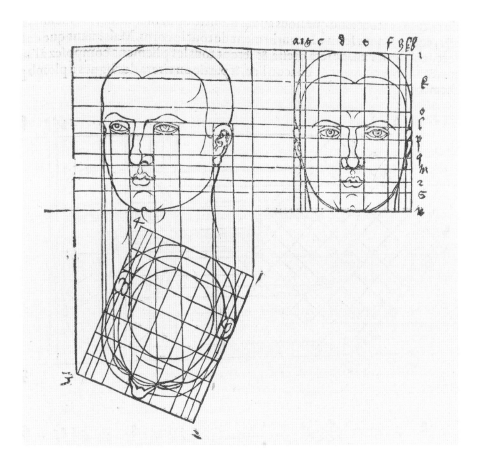

A revolutionary discovery on the circulation of the blood

William Harvey, *Exercitatio anatomica de motu cordis et sanguinis in animalibus.* Frankfurt: Guilielmi Fitzeri, 1628.

Latin. 72 pages, 2 plates. 200 × 160 mm.

Provenance: from the Library of William Sharpey, given 1874.

S R C 1628 H1/1

This has been called the most important book in the history of medicine. In this small, poorly printed book, William Harvey announced his discovery of the circulation of the blood. By this discovery he revolutionised physiological thought, inspired a new generation of anatomists and contributed to the enthusiasm for science that dominated European intellectual life during the second half of the 17th century.

Harvey (1578–1657) studied at Cambridge and received his medical doctorate in 1602 at the University of Padua under Fabrici (Hieronymous Fabricius ab Aquapendente, *c.* 1533–1619), Professor of Anatomy from 1565. Fabrici's most significant work was *De venarum ostiolis* (Padua, 1603) ['*On the valves of the veins*'], for the venous valves were to be crucial for Harvey's demonstration of the blood circulation. Harvey returned to London to practice medicine, and in 1609 was appointed physician to St Bartholomew's Hospital. He was elected a Fellow of the Royal College of Physicians in 1607 and took an active interest in their affairs for the rest of his life, donating money for a library and endowing an annual oration which continues to be held in his honour. In 1618 Harvey was appointed Physician to James I, and he continued his duties under Charles I, attending the king throughout the Civil War, until 1647. He died of a stroke at the age of 79 in 1657.

In *De motu cordis* Harvey proved experimentally that in animals the blood is impelled in a circle by the beat of the heart, passing from arteries to veins through pores (ie the capillaries).

The book itself was published in Frankfurt in 1628. It contained only 68 pages of type, meanly printed on poor paper and featuring many typographical errors. The two engraved plates, which form an essential part of the thesis, clarifying and confirming the text, were copied by Harvey from his teacher Fabrici's *De venarum ostiolis*.

UCL's copy, which belonged to William Sharpey, includes a typed copy of a page from the manuscript of Harvey's lecture of 1616 pasted onto the front fly leaf. A transcript of it by one of the book's former owners, Edward Henry Sieveking (1816–1904), is pasted onto the front endpaper, and a letter from Sieveking to Sharpey, dated 2 March 1877, is inserted.

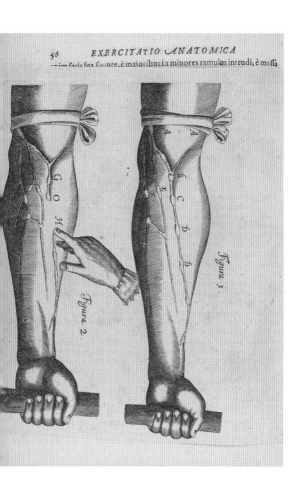

LEFT: Engraved plate from Harvey's *Exercitatio anatomica de motu cordis*, 1628, inserted facing p.56. The illustrations show a man's forearm, indicating the veins and their valves.

OPPOSITE: Title page of Harvey's *De motu cordis*, with an engraving of a device of William Fitzer, publisher of the 1628 first edition, carrying his monogram.

EXERCITATIO
ANATOMICA DE
MOTV CORDIS ET SAN-
GVINIS IN ANIMALI-
BVS,

GVILIELMI HARVEI ANGLI,

*Medici Regii, & Professoris Anatomiæ in Col-
legio Medicorum Londinensi.*

FRANCOFVRTI,
Sumptibus GVILIELMI FITZERI.
ANNO M. DC. XXVIII.

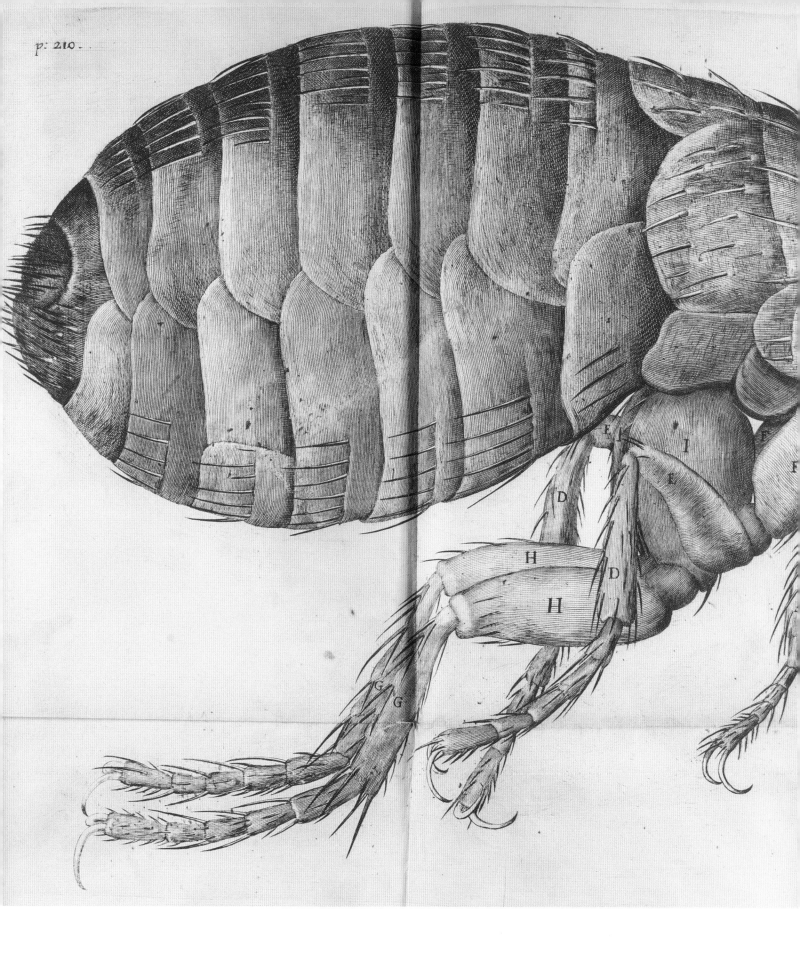

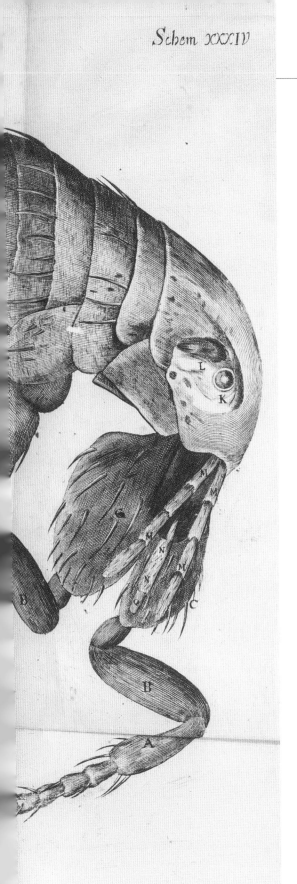

Schem XXXIV

Views of the magnified world

Robert Hooke, *Micrographia: or some physiological descriptions of minute bodies made by magnifying glasses: with observations and inquiries thereupon*. London: printed by Jo. Martyn and Ja. Allestry, 1665.

English. [35], 246, [10] p. I–XV, XVII–XXXVIII leaves of plates (some folded). 300 mm.

Provenance: given as part of the library of William Sharpey, 1869.

S R E Quarto 900 H6(1)

Robert Hooke (1635–1703) was one of the most accomplished experimentalists of 17th-century science. He masterminded the technology behind a string of scientific discoveries at the Royal Society, where he was appointed Curator of Experiments in 1662, only two years after it was founded. Hooke was renowned for his competitiveness and tendency towards intellectual disputes, famously arguing with Isaac Newton over credit for his work on gravitation, the planets and light; but he was also prolifically practical, responding to any scientific problem by inventing a piece of equipment to resolve it.

Hooke provided London's clock- and instrument-makers with a stream of modifications to improve their products, as well as devising new kinds of clock balances and escapements, and superior lenses for telescopes and microscopes. He also designed quadrants for the Greenwich Observatory, and self-levelling compasses for sea voyages. A former research assistant to Robert Boyle, he engineered specific pieces of equipment to test his own and others' theories of atmospheric pressure, motion, combustion and respirations, and constructed one of the most famous of the early compound microscopes.

This work, the *Micrographia,* is the first book on the subject in English. It is the earliest work devoted entirely to an account of microscopical observations, including the first reference to cells, which were revealed for the first time ever by the microscope. Hooke preferred to use a compound microscope which created a distorted and indistinct image. From this he built up a complete picture of his subject through a minute examination of its separate regions, resulting in the vividly accurate illustrations which convey the three-dimensional clarity of the object. Hooke drew the images himself from his own observations and was involved with the preparation of the plates, wanting to produce a series of sensational images that would appeal to a general market. In this he proved spectacularly successful, with the diarist Samuel Pepys describing the *Micrographia* as 'the most ingenious book' that he had ever read. UCL's copy bears the signature of William Sharpey, Professor of Anatomy and Physiology from 1836 to 1874, on the front fly leaf.

Micrographia, 1665: An engraved, fold-out plate depicting the flea, drawn by Hooke from his own observations and minute examination of the subject to create a vividly accurate illustration (pl. XXXIV).

Eleazar Albin, *A natural history of spiders, and other curious Insects: illustrated with fifty-three copper plates, engraven by the best hands.* London: printed John Tilly for R Montagu, J Brindley, O Payne, J Worrall, T Worrall, T Boreman and C Corbett, 1736.

English. 76 pages. 53 leaves of plates, illustrations (some coloured). 290 mm.

Provenance: unknown *A5(4)*.

S R E Quarto 920 A5(4)

Interest in the detailed examination of the natural world continued to flourish, as this delightful work from the early 18th century shows. Albin's principal occupation was as a watercolour painter and teacher of art, but he also produced books on insects and birds, with very fine, hand-coloured illustrations. His daughter Elizabeth helped in his work and produced many of the fine paintings herself. She made history by contributing to the first bird book to use coloured plates, and was among the first successful compilers of the genre of profusely illustrated natural history books for the non-specialist reader.

A German by birth, Eleazar Albin resided in London in the mid-1720s. He cultivated connections with gentleman naturalists, some of whom were patrons of his works, notably Sir Richard Mead (1673–1754), physician to George II. The Duke of Chandos also provided Albin with access to his large collections of exotic birds. Other specimens, which he and Elizabeth were able to paint from life, were often obtained from London's Newgate market, or from sea captains and foreign merchants.

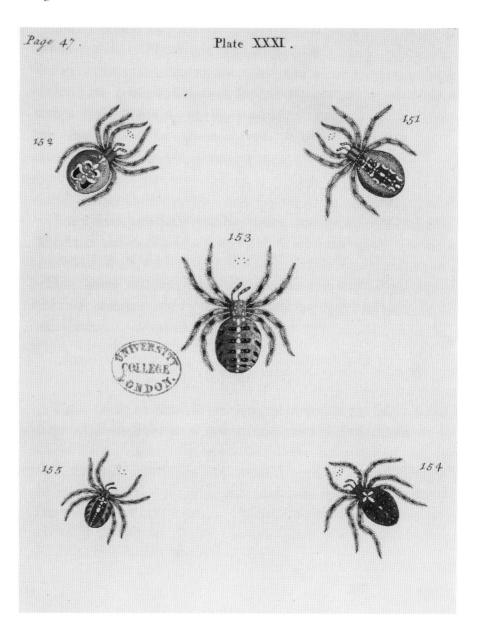

RIGHT: A hand-coloured engraving from Albin's *A natural history of spiders*, 1736. The spider in the centre of this plate (no.153) was apparently taken in a garden in Lambeth, Surrey (p.47, pl. XXXI).

OPPOSITE: An engraving facing the title page of Albin's *A natural history of spiders*, considered one of the most important scientific works of the 18th century.

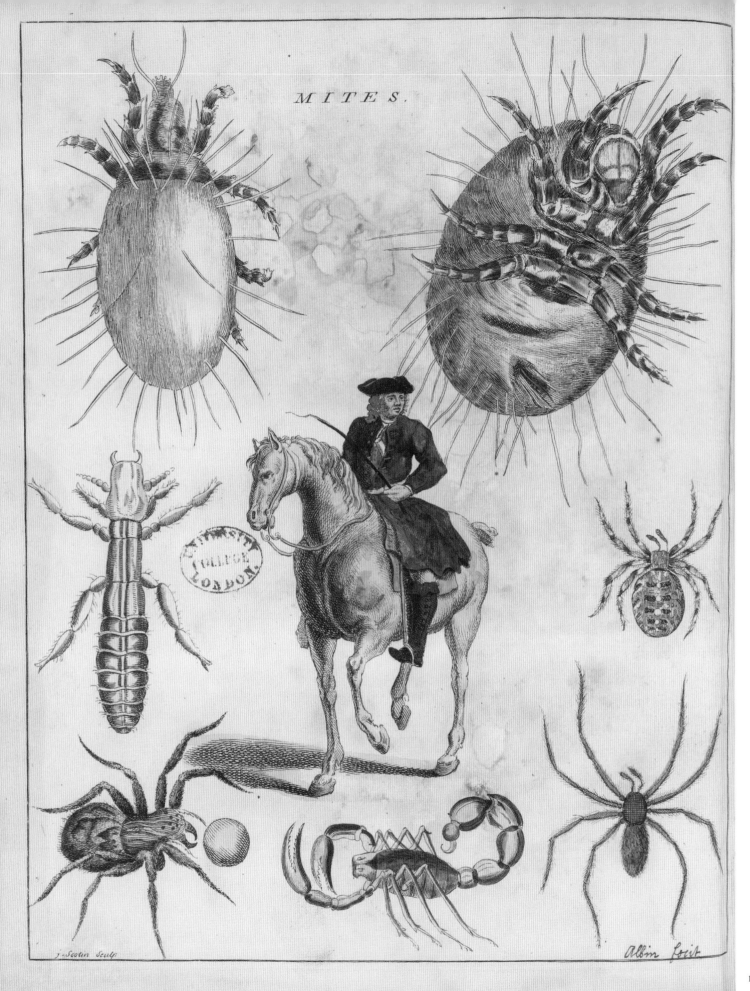

MITES.

j. Scotin Sculp.

Albin fecit

107

The greatest work on exact science

Sir Isaac Newton, *Philosophiae naturalis principia mathematica*. [Mathematical Principles of Natural Philosopy] Londini: Jussu Societatis Regiae ac typis Josephi Streater. 1st edition, 1st issue, 1687.

Latin. [8], 383, 400–510, [1] p: Ill, 1 fold. plate; 250 × 190 mm.

Provenance: bequeathed as part of the Graves Library, 1870

S R E 810 N2 (1)

Sir Isaac Newton's *Philosophiae naturalis principia mathematica*, or *Principia* as it is widely known, was first printed in 1687. The work has been called 'the greatest work on exact science that the human mind has ever conceived', and it established a conception of the universe that remained unchallenged until Einstein.

The subject of the book is the 'mechanics of ponderable bodies', and it sets out the three laws of motion. Two were derived from Galileo and the third was Newton's own, with some help from others.

The nucleus of the work was Newton's series of lectures at Cambridge in the years preceding the publication of the work, but he wrote the entire text in about 18 months. The manuscript is preserved at the Royal Society. The cost of printing was paid for by the astronomer Edmund Halley, who advocated Newton's theories to the Royal Society and saw the book through the press. Only about 250 copies were printed, with a laudatory poem by Halley, and the book quickly became quite scarce. However, the original Latin text was 'more honoured than read'; even Newton himself called it a 'hard book'.

Newton began correcting and enlarging the text almost at once, and his corrections circulated in manuscript for several years. However, a second edition of the work was not seriously proposed until 1708, when Cambridge University Press printed a specimen, of which no copies survive. The type was left standing and the second edition was published in 1713. This text was greatly revised and featured an entirely new section, the 'Scholium generale'. There was a third edition in 1726 and the first edition in English, translated by Andrew Motte, was published in 1729.

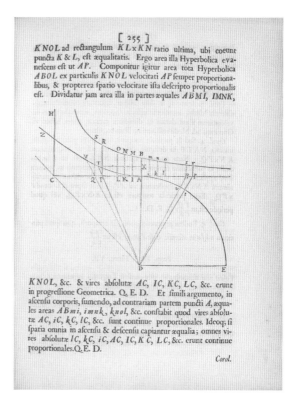

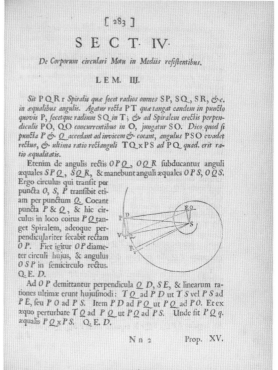

LEFT AND FAR LEFT: Sections from Isaac Newton's *Principia*, first edtion, 1687, heavily illliustrated with diagrammatic figures (p.255 and 283).

OPPOSITE: Title page of the *Principia*, including the beginning of the main text, starting with 'Definitions' (p.1).

PHILOSOPHIÆ
NATURALIS
Principia
MATHEMATICA.

Definitiones.

Def. I.

Quantitas Materiæ est mensura ejusdem orta ex illius Densitate &
Magnitudine conjunctim.

AEr duplo densior in duplo spatio quadruplus est. Idem
intellige de Nive et Pulveribus per compressionem vel lique-
factionem condensatis. Et par est ratio corporum omnium, quæ
per causas quascunq; diversimode condensantur. Medii interea,
si quod fuerit, interstitia partium libere pervadentis, hic nullam ra-
tionem habeo. Hanc autem quantitatem sub nomine corporis vel
Massæ in sequentibus passim intelligo. Innotescit ea per corporis cu-
jusq; pondus. Nam ponderi proportionalem esse reperi per expe-
rimenta pendulorum accuratissime instituta, uti posthac docebi-
tur.

B   Def.

32

A 17th-century manual for mathematical calculations

Rechenbuch, auff der Feder, Johann Best Vater.
Paper manuscript written in Germany, dated 1694.

German and Latin. 66 leaves, 198 × 157 mm.

Provenance: bequeathed as part of the Graves Library, 1870.

MS GERM 3

This delightful rare, possibly unique work is most striking for the numerous intricate and detailed hand-coloured ink drawings it features. Predominantly red and green, all are neatly executed. Bound in pale yellow vellum, the *Rechenbuch* sets out mathematical problems and gives their solutions, often written in verse. These included such calculations as finding the age of the world, the date of Judgement Day and the Golden Number, together with astrological information. One section, the *Regula Millitie* [sic], covers military diagrams, and others are entitled *Regula Radix Quadrate*, *Regula sorti vel societatis*, *Regula Longitudo et Latitudo*, *Regula Cubica* and *Progressio Geometrica*.

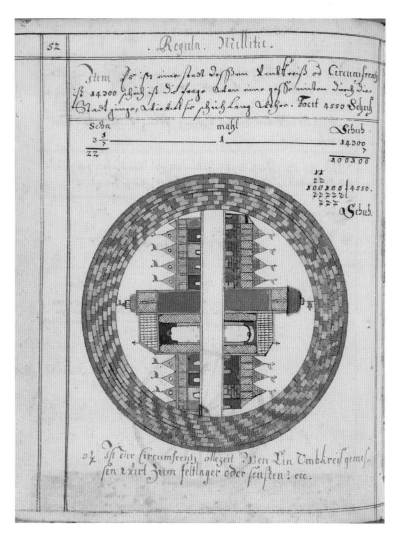
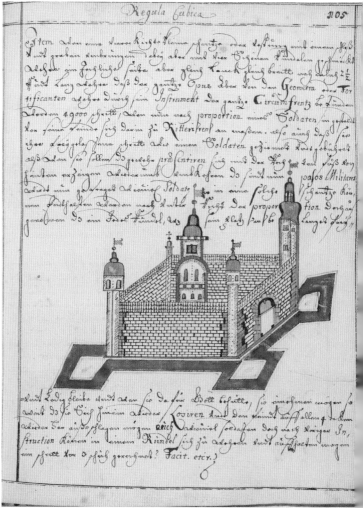

The text is written in German and Latin by the same hand throughout. The script is 17th-century Gothic, very small and neatly written with a fine pen in black ink. Headings are written in a curious ornamental minuscule script, or in roman script, larger than the text. Wording on the title page suggests that the work at one time belonged to a Johann Best, of whom nothing is recorded: he may well be the scribe and artist.

Illustrations from the 1694 manuscript *Rechenbuch* (left to right): from the *Regula Millitie* section (fol. 28v); from the *Regula Cubica* section (fol. 55r); two images illustrating domestic architecture (fol. 16r and fol. 17v).

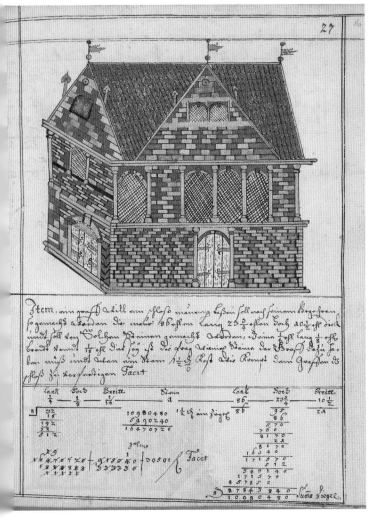

33

The ruins of Rome, seen through 18th-century eyes

Giovanni Battista Piranesi, *Vedute di Roma* ['*Views of Rome*']. '*View of the Flavian Amphitheatre known as the Colosseum*'. Rome: A Rotilj, 1748–62.

Etching on paper, 495 × 718 mm.

Provenance: given by Samuel Angell, *c.* 1858.

S R Piranesi Large Folios

The small collection of works by Piranesi (1720–78) contain some of the finest examples of engraved plates ever executed. They include a complete set of loose plates of the *Carceri* (6 plates, 1751) and the *Vedute di Roma* (44 plates, 1762), originally in a magnificent large red leather box. The 13 large folio bound volumes include the *Antichità d'albano e di Castel Gandalfo* (1764), *Le antichità Roma* (1756), *Diverse maniere d'adornare* (1769) and *Vasi, candelabri, cippi, sarcofagi, tripodi, lucerne et ornamenti antichi* (1778), all in large folio volumes. David Roberts (1796–1864), the painter and Egyptologist, was a former owner of *Le antichità Roma*.

The celebrated series of views of Roman architecture known as the *Vedute di Roma* were published individually or in groups from 1748, continuing throughout the rest of Piranesi's career. All of the views were published in a large-scale format that allowed him to exploit and enhance the spectacular dramatic potential of Roman ruins. An architect, artist, designer, archaeologist and theorist, Piranesi published over 30 volumes on Roman architecture over 35 years; some of the most influential texts and widely disseminated etchings of the 18th century, they found their way into libraries right across Europe. Highly detailed plates contain sections of buildings, foundations and materials as well as monuments – all designed to support his argument of the primacy of Roman architecture against the theories of the Greek Revivalists.

Printed views of cities were produced in Europe from the late 15th century, serving travellers abroad as well as scholars, artists, patricians and merchants. Whereas earlier works, such as the *Nuremberg Chronicle*, were produced to illustrate historical or biblical narratives, by the 18th century this genre had developed into more sophisticated representations based on creativity and imagination, and were commonly employed as a form of armchair tourism. The atmospheric pictorial space Piranesi conjured up in these visions nevertheless contained identifiable real buildings and monuments; it provided the spectator at home with enough information as a guide book, loading the images at the same time with enhanced cultural context and value. This approach did have its drawbacks, however, as the wide dissemination of Piranesi's etched images frequently meant that visitors to the city were disappointed to discover little was as it seemed from his illustrations.

The *View of the Colosseum seen from the Air* (1779), featured here, became one of Piranesi's most famous compositions, serving as a symbol of European civilisation for visitors in the late 18th and 19th centuries and portraying a structure that was more often than not their first port of call. To produce the work Piranesi combined two drawings, one of the façade and one of an aerial view. Cleverly viewing the structure from the west side, so that the taller, more intact façade on the east side is set in the distance, it has the effect of distorting the perspective, giving the impression that the monument was beyond representation.

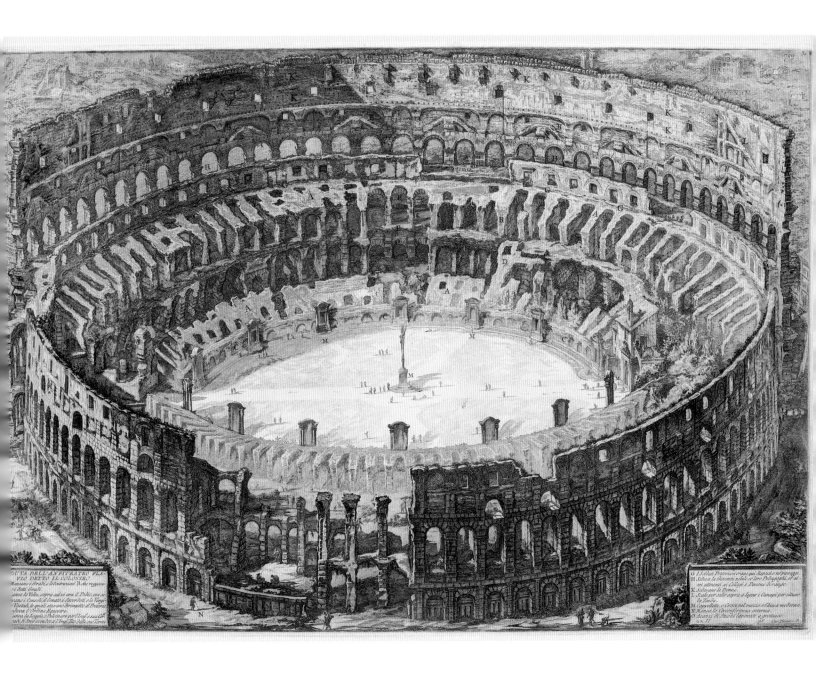

An etching of the *View of the Flavian Amphitheatre known as the Colosseum*, with a key at the left and right base. One of Piranesi's most celebrated compositions, from the mid-18th century.

Breaking new ground: The Johnston-Lavis Collection

Athanasius Kircher, *Athanasii Kircheri e Soc. Jesu Mundus subterraneus in XII libros digestus.........summa rerum varietate exponuntur.* Amsterdam: Joannem Janssonium and Elizeum Weyerstraten, 1665.

Latin. 2 volumes. Illustrations, plates. 410 × 450 mm.

Provenance: from the Johnston-Lavis Collection, transferred to the Library in 1963 from the Geology Department; bequeathed by Henry J Johnston-Lavis, 1914.

S R Johnston Lavis Folio 1665 K4

Dr Henry James Johnston-Lavis was a geologist and volcanologist who studied at UCL in the 1870s. He became a leading expert in volcanology and an internationally recognised authority on Vesuvius and Etna.

Like all geologists, Johnston-Lavis amassed a wide range of specimens. He collected over 600 rare and antique books and an enormous collection of paintings and woodcuts, describing and depicting volcanic eruptions. The volatile and dramatic landscape fascinated and inspired Johnston-Lavis, and it is vividly captured in the woodcuts and paintings. It is easy to understand his fascination with the subject when you take in the glowing and fiery tones of Pietro Fabris's *View of the Great Eruption of Mount Vesuvius* (p.120). This remarkable, hand-coloured drawing manages to convey the awe-inspiring power and beauty within this hostile landscape.

After his death Johnston-Lavis's collection was bequeathed to UCL, and looking through it one gets a sense of his true curiosity and thirst for knowledge. Fellow scientists share not only his desire to learn more about our planet, but also his fascination with how we interpret and respond to the world around us. Curiosity goes much further than just studying a subject in isolation; only by considering how we respond and adapt to the world can we truly see it in perspective. Our understanding of the Earth continues to develop, and these intriguing specimens show how scientists have sought to improve and enlighten us over the ages.

A collection such as this presents an opportunity to reflect not only on the subject, but also upon Dr Johnston-Lavis himself. Like many of the brilliant minds who have been drawn to UCL throughout its history, he was a true polymath. He studied geology and also medicine, literature,

Mount Vesuvius erupting, from the Preface of Athanasius Kircher's *Mundus Subterraneus*, 1665. Kircher included sketches of active volcanoes such as Etna, Vesuvius and Stromboli, described on the basis of first-hand observations (Vol 1, plate 1).

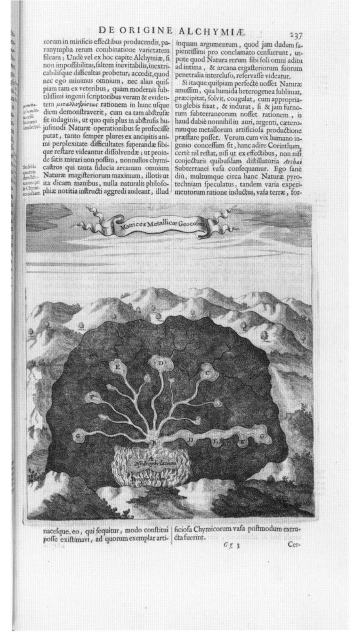

ABOVE: Illustration from the chapter on the nature of mines, '*De fodinarum natura*', from Kircher's fantastical *Mundus Subterraneus*, 1665 (p.191).

ABOVE RIGHT: Illustration showing the presence of 'hydrophylacia' or water-houses – one of the three underground chambers that formed part of Kircher's theory of the Earth's structure (*Mundus Subterraneus*, p.237).

anthropology and seismology. The collection is testimony to the wide-ranging interests and boundless fascination that drew him to Naples.

Highly diverse, it ranges from 'rocks' to an illustrated account of an eruption of Vesuvius in 1538, and from paintings to the *Mundus Subterraneus* – the first encyclopaedic study of geology, earthquakes and volcanoes, dating back to 1665. These scientific accounts provide a revealing insight into early scholars' attempts to record and interpret their world, and the effects of volcanic eruptions on the surrounding landscape and communities. Dr Johnston-Lavis's rich and varied collection has made it possible for past and future generations to appreciate the history of volcanology and place their work within an academic and cultural tradition. DAVID PRICE

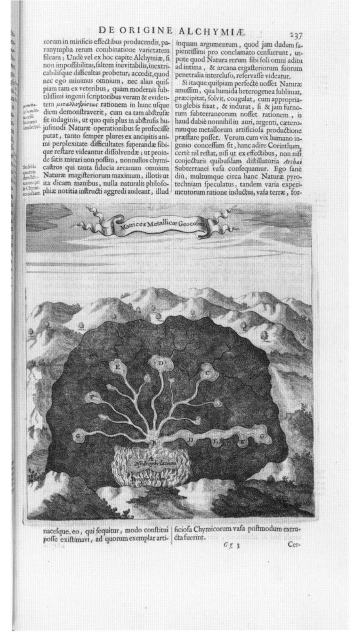

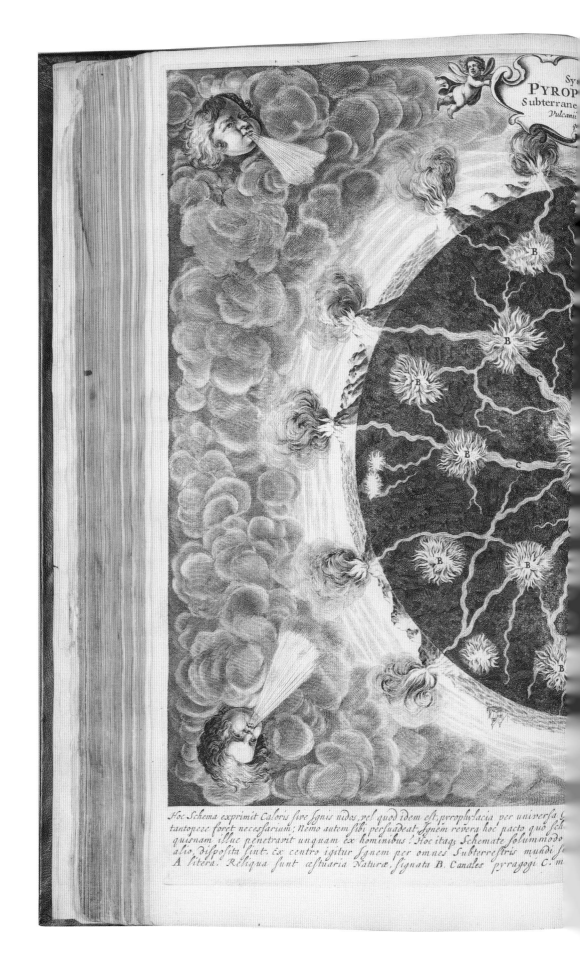

Global section showing the so-called 'pyrophylacia', or fire-houses, from Athanasius Kircher's *Mundus Subterraneus*, 1665. Kircher's theory proposed underground chambers in which fire circulated beneath the earth, eventually venting to the surface through volcanoes. The largest *pyrophylacium* at the centre was hell (Vol 1, pl.180).

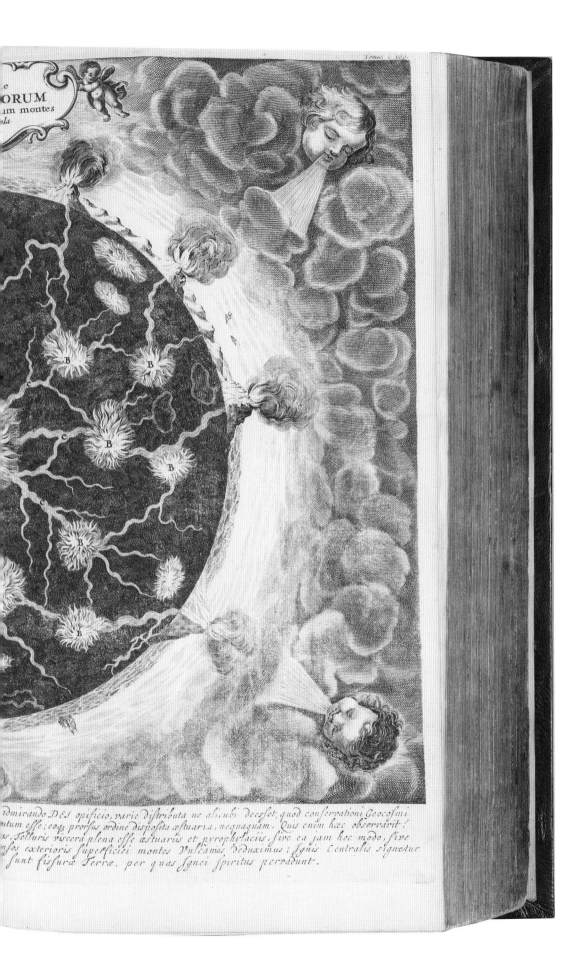

admirando DEI opificio, varie distributa ne alicubi deesset; quod conservationi Geocosmi
ntum esse; eoq; prorsus ordine disposita æstuaria, nequaquam. Quis enim hæc observarit?
ns, Telluris viscera plena esse æstuariis et pyrophylaciis, sive ea jam hoc modo, sive
nsos exterioris superficiei montes Vulcanos deduximus; ignis Centralis signetur
sunt fissuræ Terræ, per quas ignei spiritus pervadunt.

Fiery fields – volcanoes as never seen before

Sir William Hamilton, ed Pietro Fabris, *Campi Phlegraei, Observations on the volcanoes of the two Sicilies, as they have been communicated to the Royal Society*

Naples: s.n. [sine nomine – 'without a name'] 1776–9.

English and French. 2 volumes, plus supplement. 54 plates. 550 × 860 mm.

Provenance: from the Johnston-Lavis Collection, transferred to the Library in 1963 from the Geology Department; bequeathed by Henry J Johnston-Lavis, 1914.

S R Johnston Lavis Folio 1776 H1

Illustration from Sir William Hamilton, *Campi Phlegraei*, portraying a night view of 11 May 1771. Hamilton is seen escorting the King and Queen of the Two Sicilies to a part of Vesuvius where the lava fell down a perpendicular drop before flowing toward the town of Resina (hand-coloured etching by Pietro Fabris, pl.XXXVIII).

The Johnston-Lavis Collection consists of some 600 volumes, of which 129 are pre-1700, and many offprints and periodicals. The majority are concerned with Italian volcanoes and geology, particularly Vesuvius and Etna. The earliest works are by Censorinus, *De die natali* (1503), Beroaldus, *Opusculum de terremotu et pestilentia* (1505) and Elisius, *De balneis* (*c.* 1510). There are several descriptions of Naples, Pozzuoli and the surrounding area, the earliest dating from 1538. No less than 44 books, dated 1632–5, deal with the eruption of Vesuvius in December 1631, the first serious eruption since AD 79.

One particularly interesting early book, featured in the previous entry and here, is Athanasius Kircher's *Mundus Subterraneus* (1665), a huge pioneering work which deals with earthquakes, volcanoes and geology

in general. Kircher (1601?–1680) was a polymath who invented a type of calculating machine, explained a form of symbolic logic, constructed an early *camera obscura* and calculated the speed of a swallow's flight. He published prolifically on many subjects, writing on cryptography, music, phonetics, magnetism and gravity, sundials, hieroglyphs, calendars and bubonic plague, which he attributed to microscopic creatures – the first-ever notion of germs to be introduced. In 1630 Kircher observed the eruption of Mount Etna; he subsequently visited Vesuvius, and published the *Mundus Subterraneus* (overleaf) in 1665.

A century later another fascinating work, Sir William Hamilton's *Campi Phlegraei. Observations on the volcanoes of the two Sicilies* (1776–9), was published in three volumes, with very fine, hand-coloured plates. These volumes, published in Italy and England, and written in French and English, sold very widely and contain the most up-to-date scientific observation of volcanoes of the time. Although expensive to produce, they provided clear, precise, more useful and more detailed explanations of volcanic activity than any previous work.

The *Campi Phlegraei,* or Phlegraeian Fields, is a large complex of craters and fumaroles to the west of Naples, in southern Italy. Here Sir William Hamilton (1730–1806) was British Envoy to the Court of Naples from 1764 to 1779. He saw Vesuvius erupt several times and climbed the volcano himself over 70 times, sometimes at great risk, sending accounts back to the Royal Society in London. Hamilton employed Pietro Fabris, an artist living in Naples, to illustrate his work, and the hand-coloured paintings became very popular for their vividness and drama.

Other works by Sir William Hamilton also feature in the Johnston-Lavis Collection, together with Charles Babbage's *Observations on the temple of Serapis at Pozzuoli* (1847), several books on Naples and Pozzuoli by Andrea di Jorio (1817–35) and George Paulet Scrope's *Consideration on volcanoes* (1825). William Buckland's famous *Geology and mineralogy considered with reference to natural theology* (1837) is also present, as are several works on hot springs by Jacques Etienne Chevalley de Rivaz (1834–59) and a 1912 Baedekker for Southern Italy and Sicily. Early works in the collection include Heneage Finch's extremely scarce *Relation of the late prodigious earthquake and eruption*

Sir William Hamilton, *Campi Phlegraei,* interior view of the crater of Mount Vesuvius prior to the eruption of 1767, hand-coloured etching by Pietro Fabris (pl.IX).

of Mount Aetna (1669), Nathaniel Crouch's *The general history of earthquakes* (1694), works on Vesuvius by Giovanni Maria Della Torre (1755–97) and several early publications of the Accademia del Scienze of Naples (1738–88).

Dr Henry James Johnston-Lavis (1856–1914) became seriously interested in geology while a medical student at UCL, where he was taught for a while by the Professor of Geology, John Morris. He went on to become a world expert on south Italian volcanoes, particularly on Vesuvius, following a move to Naples in 1879. Here he was able to combine his medical profession with his passion for volcanoes, eventually becoming Professor of Volcanology at the Royal University of Naples in 1893; he remained there for 15 years before moving to the south of France. Johnston-Lavis was subsequently appointed secretary by the British Association in order to investigate Vesuvius further, and reported annually from 1886 to 1896.

Over the years he accumulated a magnificent collection. It included not only volcanological specimens, but also books, maps, paintings and engravings, and superb photographs of the late 19th-century Vesuvian eruptions, the latter of which almost cost him his life. The whole collection was bequeathed to UCL; its books were transferred to the Library, and the specimens and other materials to the Department of Geological Sciences (now Earth Sciences). Many of the works in the collection are extremely scarce and not held by the British Library.

Sir William Hamilton, *Campi Phlegraei*, 1776, 'View of the island of Stromboli taken by Mr. Fabris from Sicily with the author', hand-coloured etching by Pietro Fabris (pl.XXXVII).

Showpiece bindings for treasured texts

Solomon ben David de Oliveyra, *Calendario facil y curiozo de las tablas lunares calculadas con las tablas solares. Industria nueva de Selomoh de Olivera para computar los tiempos ... perpetuamente.* Amsterdam: David de Castro Tartaz, 5427 [1667].

Bound with:

Hebrew Bible, Old Testament *(Pentateuch): Seder parashiyyot ve-haftarot ... quinque libri Mosis* ... Amsterdam: David de Castro Tartaz, 5426 [1666].

Portuguese and Hebrew. [2], 446, [2] ff. 16 cm. Engraved title page, hand-coloured. Dutch binding of red morocco, with gilt ornamentation, marbled, gilded and gauffred edges, silk endpapers and hand-painted title page, in a contemporary box.

Provenance: given as part of the library of F D Mocatta, 1906.

Strong Room Mocatta QB 12 TAR

This wonderful object, which comprises an early calendar of the tables of the sun and the moon in Portuguese bound together with an early printed Hebrew Bible, must have been a prized personal possession of its original owner. In all probability it belonged to a wealthy Portuguese Jew, perhaps a merchant. A showpiece of its time, it displays the wonderful craftsmanship to be found in fine bindings of the 17th century. The whole volume has a magnificent Dutch binding of red morocco, elaborately tooled and gilded, with gauffred gilt edges. It features a hand-painted and gilded title page and silk fly leaves; the endpapers are also beautifully tooled and gilded, and the boards edged in rolled gilt. The slipcase in which the work is housed is also a wonderful example of fine gilt-tooled work from the period.

RIGHT: Elaborately tooled bindings of the 1667 *Calendario* and 1666 Hebrew Bible, showing the gauffred top and bottom edges and fore-edge, and the spine, tooled with gold leaf.

OPPOSITE: Front and back covers of the combined Portuguese *Calendario*, 1667, and Hebrew Old Testament Bible (Pentateuch), 1666, gilt-ornamented and bound with red morocco leather.

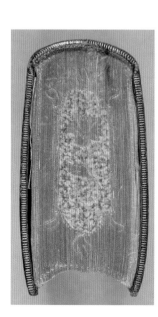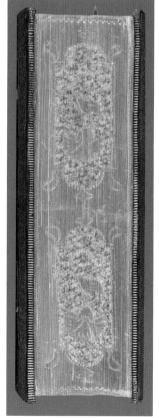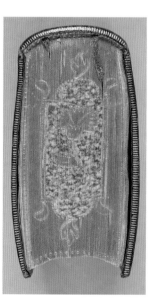

Mír shams al-Dín Faqír Dihlavi, *Masnavi-i Akbar Sultan* ('*Romance of the Sultan Akbar*').

Persian. Paper manuscript [1163 A.H]. 1749. 172 leaves, multi-coloured painted borders. 190 × 120 mm. Bound in lacquered paper on board, decorated with floral designs – mainly in gilt and orange.

Provenance: given as part of the library of Arthur Strong, 1918.

MS PERS 1

This exquisite manuscript is a copy of part of an extensive poem written in Persian by Jalal al-Din Muhammad Rumi (1207–73), the celebrated Persian Sufi saint and poet.

The *Masnavi* is a series of six books of poetry, each of which consists of about 25,000 verses or 50,000 lines. It is a spiritual piece of writing that teaches Sufis how to reach their goal of being in true love with God. One of the best known and most influential works of both Sufism and Persian literature, the poem is often re-copied by later scribes and calligraphers, as here.

OPPOSITE: Back and front cover of the *Masnavi-i Akbar Sultan* manuscript poem, from the mid-18th century. The process of creating the covers involved painting the design on sheets of paper, gluing them on to boards and lacquering over them to produce a luxurious look and feel.

BELOW: Inside back and front covers of the *Masnavi-i Akbar Sultan* manuscript poem, from the mid-18th century. The overall design, using individual flowers in the pattern, is typical of the European-influenced style of the times.

Written in delicate script on very fine paper, the manuscript is not only highly decorated within the text, but also has an exceptionally beautiful binding. The techniques and overall design of the binding and the illuminated text are traditionally Persian. However, the execution of individual flowers, particularly within the medallions and on the interior cover, reflects a European influence, which was prevalent in the 18th century. Intricate patterns woven in a myriad of colours give the whole object the impression of a dazzling, bejewelled box – a magnificent object.

LEFT: The first double-page spread of the *Masnavi-i Akbar Sultan* manuscript poem from 1749. The calligraphy style used throughout the text is Nastaliq, one of the main hands used in the Persian language. A characteristic of this style, when used in poetry, is the frequent occurrence of writing at an angle across the page (fols 1v–2r).

BELOW LEFT: A beautiful example from the early pages in the *Masnavi-i Akbar Sultan* manuscript poem of neatly written Nastaliq script, embellished with gold-leaf borders and floral imagery (fols 3v–4r).

OPPOSITE: The beginning of the *Masnavi-i Akbar Sultan* manuscript poem, elaborately decorated with the addition of blue as well as gold and red, a true masterpiece of Persian calligraphic art (fols 2v–3r).

37

Tortoiseshell binding of the 18th century

Orden de las oraciones cotidianas: por estilo seguido con las de Hanucà, Purim, Ayuno del Solo y las tres Pascuas con sus Parasioth, Aphtarot, Asàarot y muchos cosas mas, en esta impression añadidas. ['Order of the daily prayers: according to custom, followed by those of Hanukkah, Purim, private fasts and the Pilgrim Festivals, with their Parashiyyot, Haftarot, Azharot and many more things, added in this impression'.] Amsterdam: en casa y costs de Selomoh Proops, 1717 (Año. 5477).

Spanish. [16], 535, [13] pages. 160 mm. Bound in tortoiseshell, with gilt clasps and corner; gilt and gauffred edges. Inscribed by F D Mocatta.

Provenance: given as part of the library of F D Mocatta, 1906.

Strong Room Mocatta RP 11/1 PRO

RIGHT: *Orden de las oraciones cotidianas*, 1717, gauffred bottom (above) and fore-edges (below) of the text, with silver gilt clasps.

OPPOSITE: Outer binding and clasps of the *Orden de las oraciones cotidianas*, 1717. They were made of tortoiseshell and silver gilt, a popular luxury covering for a book of this period.

Tortoiseshell has been used and admired as a decorative material for centuries. The type of tortoiseshell used in this next treasured item, another example of individual, custom-made binding, is most likely derived from the hawksbill marine turtle. With its thermoplastic properties tortoiseshell became a favoured luxury book covering for the Jewish community in Amsterdam during the 17th and 18th centuries, also no doubt owing to the shells' abstract patterning. Rabbinic strictures against idolatrous images led to the flowering of imaginative substitutes, highly ornamental as well as practical, for decorating the covers of such books.

This fine example of a tortoiseshell binding was made in Amsterdam in the early 18th century, for a member of the Spanish-speaking Sephardi Jewish community. The tortoiseshell covers are extravagantly embellished with silver gilt clasps and corner pieces, and engraved with foliage and birds. A similar design enriches the gilt, gauffred edges of the text.   FREDERICK BEARMAN

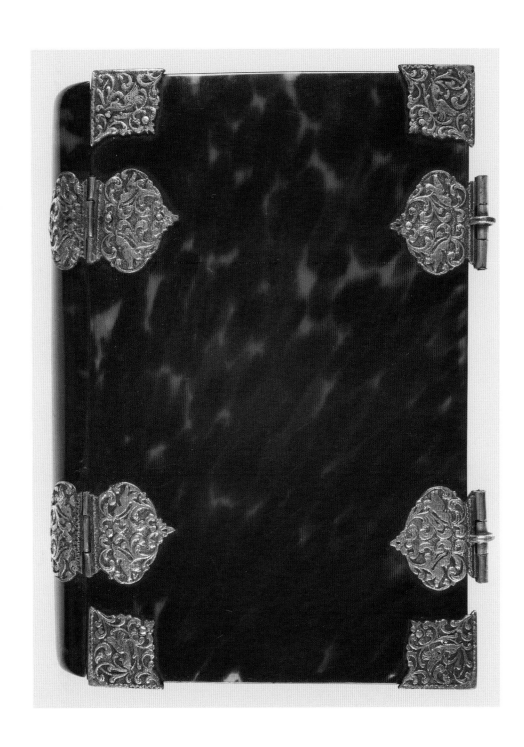

38

A very rare first edition of *Paradise Lost*

John Milton, *Paradise Lost: a poem written in ten books.* London: printed by Samuel Simmons, sold by Peter Parker, Robert Boulter and Matthias Walker, 1667.

1st edition, 1st issue, 1st state of title page. English. 342 pages. 180 mm. Red calf binding with gilt borders on sides, slightly repaired; in cloth folder and morocco solander case.

Provenance: purchased as part of the Ogden Library, 1953.

S R OGDEN A 411

One of the Ogden Library's greatest treasures, this is an extremely rare edition of John Milton's famous work. Over time it became one of the most important books in English ever to be published, though at first it did not sell particularly well. The epic poem tells the story of the Fall of Man, with the principal characters being God, the Son and Satan; the prominence of the last led to Satan being regarded as an anti-hero by the Romantic movement. Milton may have begun his greatest work as early as 1640, but it only took final shape between 1658 and 1663. His work on it was slowed down by blindness, leading to him having to dictate all the lines.

What makes this copy so rare is chiefly the title page. Out of the six title pages that occur with the first edition, it is one of the only two produced that are dated 1667 (the others are dated 1668 and 1669). In addition the author's name appears in large capitals on this copy, known technically as the earliest 'state'. This issue also has many textual variants, for example on folio L3 (at the end of Book 3) the verses are wrongly numbered. The first line is numbered 740, whereas it should be 731. On the same page line 760 reads 'Throw his steep flight with many an Aerie wheele', whereas in later states of the text 'with' is changed to 'in'. These may seem minor details, but they make the book distinctive and extremely rare.

ABOVE: Detail from the end of the Third Book of Milton's *Paradise Lost* 1667 edition. It features line 760, where the word 'with' is clearly distinct; it was substituted for 'in' in later editions (fol. L3).

OPPOSITE: Title page of the first edition, first issue, first state of Milton's *Paradise Lost*, showing the author's name in capitals and the extremely rare 1667 imprint at the bottom of the page.

Paradiſe loſt.

A
POEM

Written in
TEN BOOKS

By *JOHN MILTON*.

Licenſed and Entred according
to Order.

LONDON

Printed, and are to be ſold by *Peter Parker*
under *Creed* Church neer *Aldgate*; And by
Robert Boulter at the *Turks Head* in *Biſhopſgate-ſtreet*;
And *Matthias Walker*, under St. *Dunſtons* Church
in *Fleet-ſtreet*, 1667.

The creation of Dr Johnson's *Dictionary*

Samuel Johnson, *The plan of a dictionary of the English language: addressed to the Right Honourable Philip Dormer, Earl of Chesterfield.* London: Printed for J and P Knapton, T Longman and T Shewell, C Hitch, A Millar and R Dodsley, 1747.

[2], 34 pages. 250 × 190 mm.

Provenance: purchased as part of the Ogden Library, 1953.

S R OGDEN 424

RIGHT: Samuel Johnson's explanation of how he creates definitions for each word in his famous work, *A dictionary of the English language*. Here the word 'arrive' is given as an example (p.22).

OPPOSITE: Samuel Johnson's *Plan of a dictionary of the English language*, 1747, title page. His intended patron's name, Philip Dormer, with whom he later fell out, is prominently featured.

C K Ogden was a scholar of languages as well as a bibliophile. He collected books on all aspects of communication, including unwritten languages, cryptography, shorthand, emblem books, linguistics, phonetics and literature. A sub-genre on which he was particularly keen was dictionaries, vocabularies and word lists, and the works of the first great compiler of an English dictionary, Dr Samuel Johnson, were of course included. Two of the early editions are featured here.

In 1746 Johnson was commissioned by a group of booksellers, headed by Richard Dodsley, to produce a new definitive English dictionary. He signed a contract in June of that year and composed the *Plan* for the intended patron, Philip Dormer, the Earl of Chesterfield. Unfortunately he quarrelled with Chesterfield and this may account for his famous definition of a 'patron' as 'commonly a wretch who supports with insolence, and is paid with flattery'.

The *Dictionary* was published in two folio volumes on 15 April 1755. It was a monumental achievement and became the standard English

[22]

In explaining the general and popular language, it seems necessary to sort the several senses of each word, and to exhibit first its natural and primitive signification, as

To *arrive*, to reach the shore in a voyage. He *arrived* at a safe harbour.

THEN to give its consequential meaning, *to arrive*, to reach any place whether by land or sea; as, he *arrived* at his country seat.

THEN its metaphorical sense, to obtain any thing desired; as, he *arrived* at a peerage.

THEN to mention any observation that arises from the comparison of one meaning with another; as, it may be remarked of the word *arrive*, that in consequence of its original and etymological sense, it cannot be properly applied but to words signifying something desirable; thus, we say a man *arrived* at happiness, but cannot say without a mixture of irony, he *arrived* at misery.

Ground, the earth, generally as opposed to the air or water. He swam till he reached *ground*. The bird fell to the *ground*.

THEN

THE
PLAN
OF A
DICTIONARY
OF THE
ENGLISH LANGUAGE;

Addreſſed to the Right Honourable

PHILIP DORMER,

Earl of *CHESTERFIELD*;

One of His MAJESTY's Principal Secretaries
of State.

LONDON:

Printed for J. and P. KNAPTON, T. LONGMAN and
T. SHEWELL, C. HITCH, A. MILLAR, and
R. DODSLEY.   MDCCXLVII.

Samuel Johnson, *A dictionary of the English language: in which the words are deduced from their originals, explained in their different meanings, and authorized by the names of the writers in whose works they are found. Abstracted from the folio edition … The third edition, carefully revised.* Dublin: W G Jones for Thomas Ewing, 1768.

[952] pages. 220 × 170 mm. Sheepskin binding.

Provenance: purchased as part of the Ogden Library, 1953.

S R OGDEN E 221 J64

dictionary almost at once. The definitions, etymology and illustrative examples are all shot through with Johnson's erudition, wit and personal prejudices. It was printed several times in Johnson's lifetime, with only the fourth edition of 1773 being much revised. After his death several new editions appeared, and many editors abridged or augmented Johnson's work.

The next time a project of any similar significance was undertaken for the English language was Murray's national appeal in England for quotations that illustrated specific senses of specific terms, or lemmas. The result was a multi-volume historical dictionary that took decades to produce and claimed to present the history of the use of each term through illustrations taken from a wide range of printed works, starting with the first surviving use. The dictionary was eventually supported by Oxford University Press and became the Oxford English Dictionary. It was never fully revised until the end of the 20th century, when a revision project began; this is still underway, and has seen the dictionary transferred to an online publication. Besides being the first scholarly historical English dictionary, one of the distinctions of the *OED* is that it is descriptive not prescriptive, although in many countries outside the UK it is nevertheless treated as a prescriptive record of correct usage.

OPPOSITE, BELOW: Samuel Johnson's *A dictionary of the English language*, third edition, 1768, title page and Preface, with a preamble from Johnson about the trials of producing the work.

BELOW: An example of a double-page spread (LIK to LIQ) from Johnson's *A dictionary of the English language*, third edition, 1768. Errors in the page headers often occurred, as here, where the header is 'LIM', but the first word in the entry is LIKE. The first page title does not exactly match the contents.

Designs for a panopticon prison by Jeremy Bentham

Section of an Inspection House, c. 1791

Pencil, pen and ink and watercolour sketch on paper, inscribed with manuscript notes. 1 folio. 202 × 332 mm.

Provenance: given by Sir John Bowring, 1849.

Bentham Papers 119a/119

The three items featured here are from the vast Bentham archive. Jeremy Bentham's name, and indeed his clothed skeleton, are so closely associated with UCL that it is small surprise that the Library houses his corpus of intellectual outpourings. The Bentham manuscripts, which consist of over 60,000 sheets, were given to UCL in 1849 by Sir John Bowring, Bentham's literary executor, closest associate and next-door neighbour. Also editor of the *Westminster Review*, Bowring had inherited the archive on Bentham's death in 1832.

Covering the whole range of Bentham's writings, the manuscripts consist mainly of drafts and notes for published and unpublished works. They reveal so many examples of his remarkable intellect and advanced ideas that a modern reader can only be astonished. To take one example, Bentham was very critical of the planned transportation of convicts to the New South Wales penal colony; in 1791 he worked on its first published financial returns in an effort to demonstrate how uneconomical the practice was. He collected as much relevant information as possible to support his case, among them a moving account of a group of convicts' escape by boat from Botany Bay on 28 March 1791 (some of whom did not survive – the writer, James Martin, was eventually re-captured and sent to Newgate Prison). During 1802–3 Bentham conducted a vigorous campaign against the penal colony. He believed that such establishments, apart from being unconstitutionally run, were inherently incapable of achieving the objectives of a sound policy, following exhaustive analysis of punishment as a means of social control.

Bentham had first written on penal policy during the 1770s, when public interest was high, and he continued to develop his ideas for penal reform. An intrinsic part of them was the 'Panopticon' prison scheme, which was designed to allow a single watchman to observe (-opticon) all (pan-) inmates of an institution – without the latter being able to tell whether they were being watched or not. In 1791 the government announced the establishment of a penal colony at Botany Bay, but transportation had already begun by the time Bentham's proposal for a penitentiary house came before the government.

The Inspection House, as it was also called, was designed for Bentham by his younger brother Samuel, a noted mechanical engineer and naval architect. The design, made when Samuel was in the service of Prince Potemkin, the Russian statesman and favourite of Catherine the Great, was originally intended for a factory in which Russian workers could be efficiently supervised. Samuel made drawings for the proposed panopticon prison, and Bentham later commissioned further designs from the architect Willey Reveley in preparation for the publication of the work. Bentham's schemes eventually foundered on the government's unwillingness to support the principle of private contract management of prisons. He believed this simple architectural idea would mean that the prisoners would modify their behaviour and learn to work and conduct themselves well. Bentham spent many years trying to get the Panopticon built. One of the reasons given to him by the Home Secretary for the eventual abandonment of the scheme was the improved state of the prison colony in New South Wales.

It was not just the architectural design that exercised Bentham. He also designed an internal communication system of 'conversation

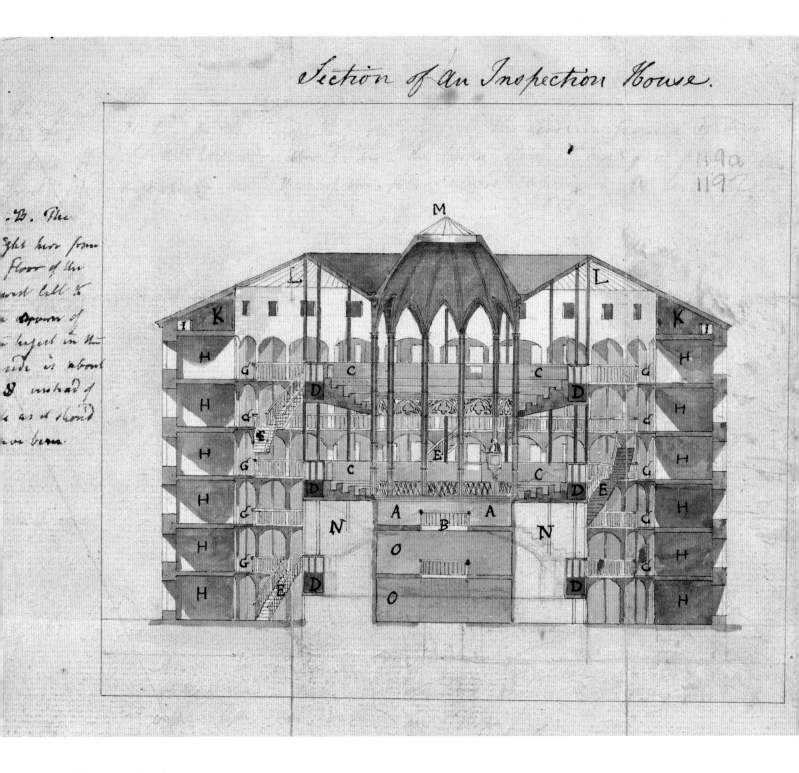

Section of an Inspection House.

Coloured drawing executed by Willey Reveley, based on Jeremy Bentham's design for an Inspection House, or Panopticon, c. 1791. It shows a cross-section with the cells (H) on the circumference of the building and a 'great annular light' (M) above, to provide a source of light as well as ventilation (fol. 119).

... ference ... tion.

Are as far as H the same as in the plan excepting
only F which does not appear.

I Annular cistern for water to supply every cell. &c or for keeping provi--sions tools materials &c to ventilate the whole building when opened.

K Rooms serving for lodging the taskmasters, inspector L Large annular skylight, serving M Skylight to the Chapel.
N. O Parts not yet applied to any use.

Plan of House of Inspection

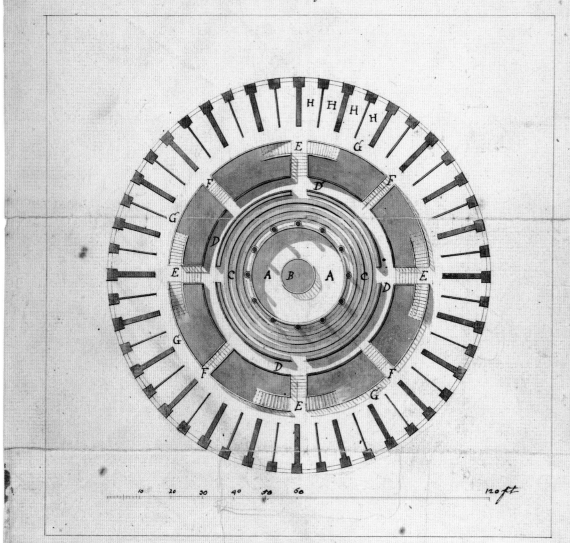

10   20   30   40   50   60   120 ft

References on this Plan.

A ~

A Chapel.

B Circular opening to light the Story underneath.

C Gallery of the chapel.

D Inspector's Gallery

E Four staircases leading from bottom to top of the building, & from

one story of the cells to the inspectors gallery.

F Communications from the same to the other story of cells

G Gallery of general com--munication for the Cells.

H Cells, two of which may be laid into one.

tubes' for his panopticon prison. At first the device was to run between the inspection lodge and each cell, enabling the governor to instruct and admonish each inmate; in later proposed plans the system was expanded to connect the lodge and the inspection galleries. Bentham delighted in the novel technique of these tubes – tools for constantly enforcing a clockwork regularity on the administration of the prison.

Such was Bentham's blind faith in his tubes' efficacy over long distances that he suggested to the Home Office that his prison could be the nerve-centre of a far greater network, stretching for hundreds of miles underground and forming a national system of intelligence and defence. Another example of the more unexpected materials in the collection, and of the inventions in which he was involved, is the 'frigidarium'. Here Bentham envisaged a large underground 'ice house', in which foods and other grains could be stored for long periods of time using vapours and salts. This foray into the science of food preservation illustrates the fine detail of Bentham's concern for his prison building.

The manuscripts arrived at UCL from Bowring in bundles. Still inside the wooden boxes in which Bentham had stored them, they were left undisturbed in the cellars below the main buildings for 43 years. In 1892 John Power Hicks, a Life Governor of the College, placed the sum of £100 at the disposal of the Council to investigate the collection. Under the supervision of Professors W P Ker and George Croom Robertson, the investigator Thomas Whittaker recommended a new arrangement to replace the 'chaotic' condition in which he found them. A new catalogue, organised by subject and compiled by A Taylor Milne, was published in 1937. It was reprinted in 1962 and is still in use today.

OPPOSITE: Elevation plan of the Houses of Inspection, or Panopticon, drawn by Willey Reveley after designs by Bentham, with an alphabetical key to the different spaces (fol. 121).

RIGHT: Cross-section of a panopticon prison showing the prison cells (K) around the circumference of the building. Prisoners could be watched from the inspection galleries (D), and were able to participate in chapel services from galleries (C) (fol. 122).

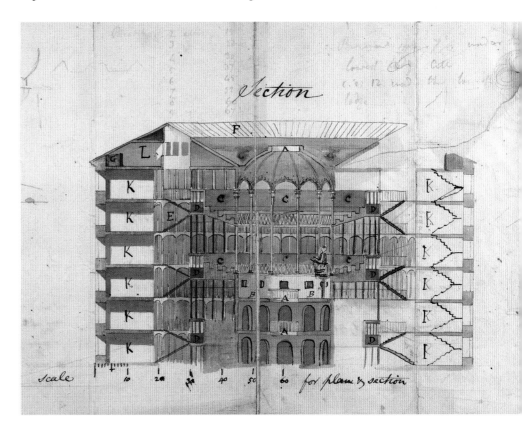

41

An unusual manuscript poem of Lord Byron

Samuel Rogers, *The pleasures of memory: with other poems*, with a handwritten poem by George Gordon Byron, 6th Baron Byron. London: printed for T Cadell and W Davies by T Bensley, 1810.

English, with manuscript poem on front fly leaf and annotations. [8], 167, [1] p. Wood engravings. 160 mm.

Provenance: given by Mrs Helga Hacker, 1950.

S R E 221 R6

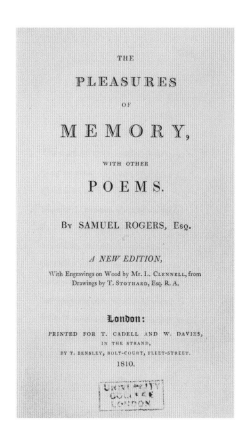

Samuel Rogers (1763–1855) was a rich patron of the arts and a minor poet. He established a London literary salon in 1793, where he entertained writers, artists, actors and politicians. *The pleasures of memory* was his most noted work; published in 1792, it went through 15 editions before 1806. Rogers liked to present inscribed copies of his work to his friends, one of whom was the poet Lord Byron. UCL's copy is inscribed to 'The Right Hon.ble The Lord Byron, from his obliged & faithful friend The Author'.

However, this is not the most remarkable feature of this little volume, for it revealed something far more newsworthy when it was recatalogued in 2009. Beneath the dedication inscription is another in a different hand: 'Afterwards returned by Lord Byron to Mr Rogers with the lines written on the other side', and on the other side of the page is a 12-line poem beginning 'Absent or present still to thee'. Written in Byron's own hand, it is signed in Greek characters and dated 19 April 1812. Up until this point in the history of Byron's manuscripts, it was assumed the manuscript of the poem had been lost.

Byron had returned the gift with an added surprise to his friend, in appreciation of the book. He is known to have praised the work highly in a letter to Thomas Moore in 1813, writing 'His elegance is really wonderful – there is no such thing as a vulgar line in the book'. The poem talks of friendship and memory, the same themes as Rogers' work, and it seems likely that Byron was directly inspired by his reading of *The pleasures of memory* to compose his own poem, which appeared in print in 1816 in a volume of collected poems.

The history of the former ownership of this finely bound item is unique to UCL. The donor, Helga Sharpe Hacker, was herself related to Samuel Rogers through her father Karl Pearson, a Professor of Applied Mathematics and Mechanics at UCL in 1884. He later became Galton Professor of Eugenics from 1911 and of Statistics from 1935 until his retirement in the 1970s. (Samuel Rogers' sister Maria married Sutton Sharpe, whose granddaughter married Pearson.) Their three children, Helga, Sigrid and Egon (the last also a professor at UCL for many years), presented a large quantity of family books and papers to UCL in the 1950s. Also interesting are the wood engravings by Luke Clennell (1781–1840) from drawings by Thomas Stothard RA (1755–1834) on pages 83 and 84, and manuscript annotations by Rogers.

LEFT: Title page of *The pleasures of memory: with other poems* by Samuel Rogers, 1810.

OPPOSITE: Manuscript poem by Lord Byron, 19 April 1812, dedicated to Rogers, in *The pleasures of memory: with other poems*. Byron's signature is shown bottom right of the front fly-leaf, written in Greek.

Absent or present still to thee
  My friend, what magic spells belong!
As all can tell, who share, like me,
  In turn thy converse, and thy song,
But when the dreaded hour shall come
  By Friendship ever deemed too nigh,
And "Memory" o'er her Druid's tomb
  Shall weep that aught of thee can die,
How fondly will She then repay
  Thy homage offered at her shrine
And blend, while Ages roll away
  Her name immortally with thine.

Moosphor

April 19th 1812

42

A musical note

Ludwig van Beethoven, handwritten note

Black ink on paper manuscript, written in Germany, 1824. 1 folio. 155 × 230 mm.

Provenance: given as part of the Lord Odo Russell collection, unknown date.

MS ADD 254/B1

Collecting autographs, either as a signed letter or a signed name, has always been popular. This gem is a good example of the genre, and a prize for UCL. It was a very unexpected find, as the correspondents in the rest of the collection are mainly European scientists of the late 18th or early 19th century, including Nikolaus Joseph and his son Joseph Franz, Freiherr von Jacquin, both of whom were at different times Professor of Chemistry and Botany at Vienna University. Other names include the zoologist Leopold Fitzsinger and the botanist Istvan Laszlo Endlicher. Topics of discussion range from natural sciences, medical sciences, physical sciences, the arts, theology and politics.

Beethoven's note is a strange inclusion in this largely scientific community, although the German writer and statesman Goethe also features among the correspondents. This curious item was found in the Department of Electronic and Electrical Engineering at UCL in 1976 in the collection of autograph letters amassed by Lord Odo Russell, 1st Baron Ampthill (1829–84). He was a descendant of John Russell, 6th Duke of Bedford (brother of the 1st Earl Russell, twice Prime Minister of the UK), whose family estate encompassed much of Bloomsbury in the 19th century. Written in 1824 on what looks like a throw-away scrap of paper, it deals with the mundane request from Beethoven to his neighbour, the 'kitchen procurator' in the address line, to fetch him a piece of pike for his lunch. An ephemeral piece perhaps, but all the more vivid and touching for its close association with the musician's domestic environment, only three years before his death in 1827.

OPPOSITE: Detail of a note written in Beethoven's hand to Herr von Holz, his neighbour, 1824.

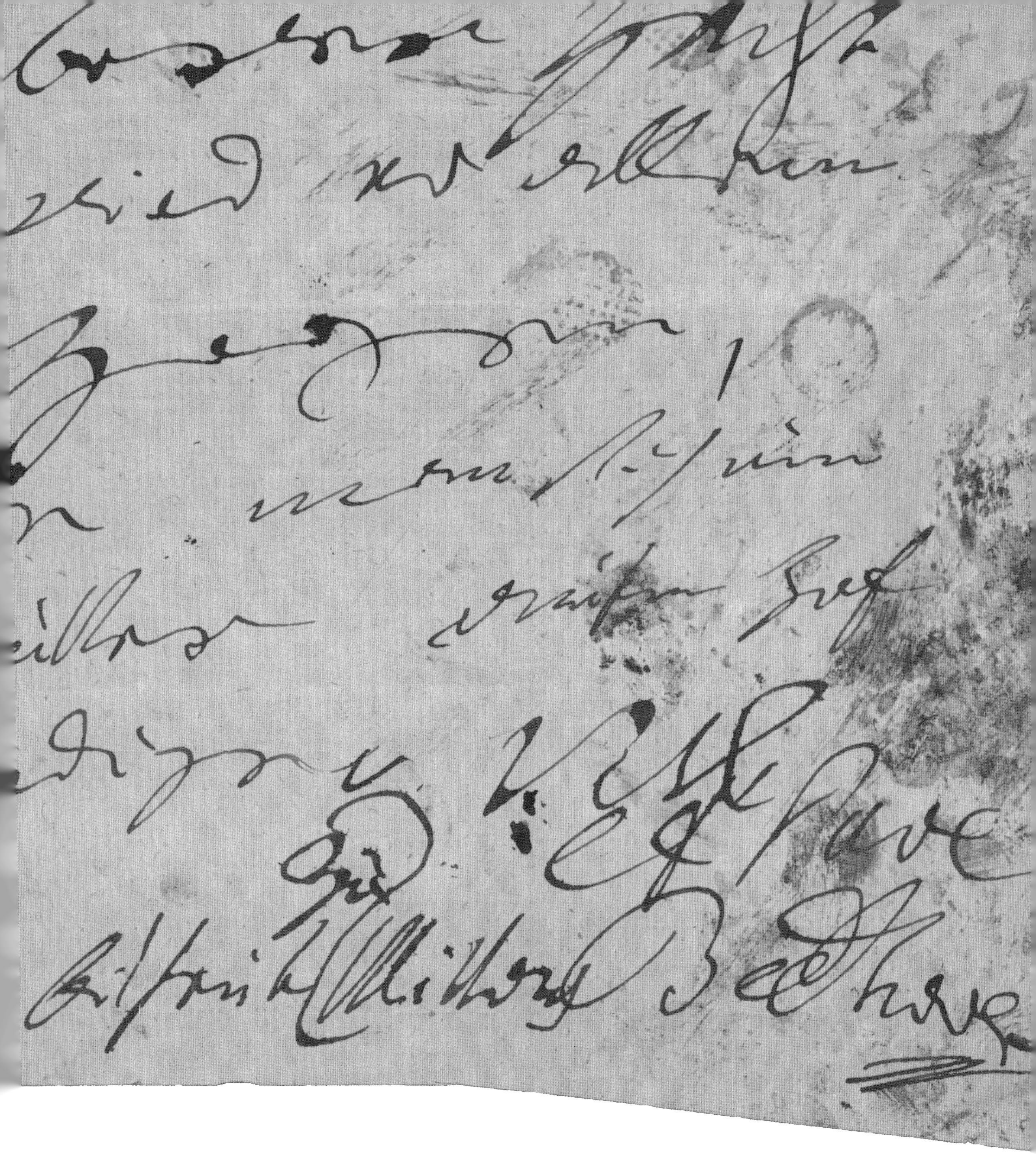

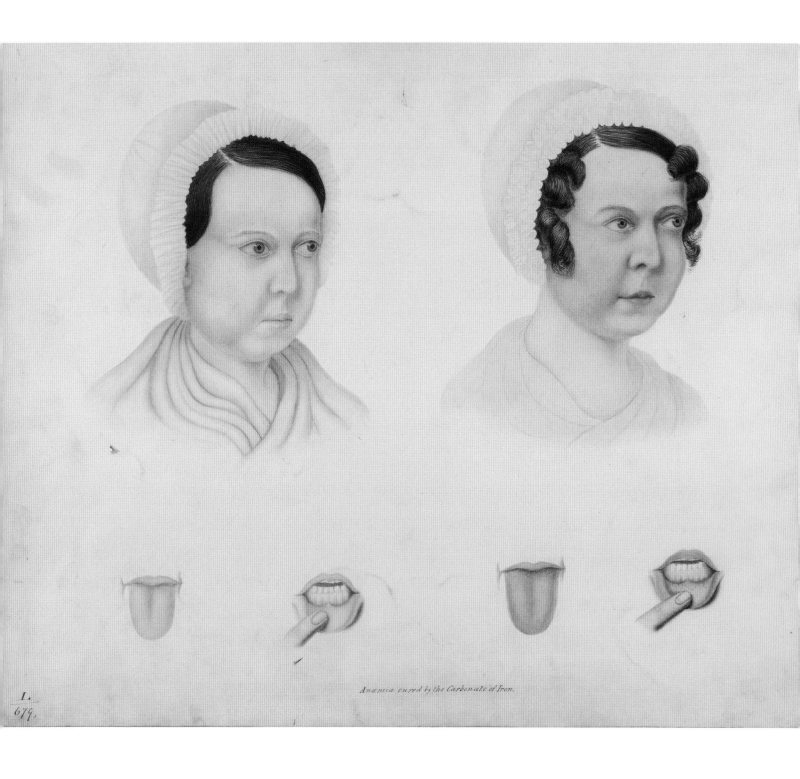

Anæmia cured by the Carbonate of Iron.

Watercolour sketch of the patient
Eliza Newman, in March and April 1837,
before and after successful treatment for
anaemia, a major medical landmark of
the 19th century (Carswell L679).

Art for medicine's sake: Carswell collection of drawings of pathological conditions

Sir Robert Carswell, *Anaemia cured by the Carbonate of Iron*, London, March 1837. [Dr Elliotson's Case, Eliza Newman at 23, admitted 23 March 1837; discharged cured 8 April 1837.]

Watercolour on paper, 440 × 560 mm, with manuscript notes.

Provenance: transferred as part of the Medical School archives.

UCL/MED/MHMS/UNOF/1/L679

Born in Paisley in 1793, Carswell studied medicine at the University of Glasgow. Here he was distinguished for his skill in drawing, and employed by Dr John Thompson of Edinburgh to make a collection of drawings illustrating morbid anatomy. To pursue this work, he went to France in 1822, working in hospitals in Paris and Lyon for two years. He then returned to Scotland and took his MD at Marischal College, Aberdeen in 1826, before returning to Paris. In about 1828 he was nominated by the Council of University College London (then known as the University of London) to be Professor of Pathological Anatomy there. Before starting teaching duties, however, Carswell was commissioned to prepare a collection of pathological drawings, to be used as basic teaching tools for medical students of the time. He remained in Paris until 1831 when he had completed a series of two thousand watercolour drawings of diseased structures.

Carswell then came to London and undertook the duties of his professorship. Soon afterwards he was also appointed physician to University College Hospital; he never practised, however, and embarked on preparing his great book on pathological anatomy. He later returned to Paris, then a centre of excellence for pathological research, to resume his studies in morbid anatomy. Later in life he became unwell, and in 1840 he resigned his professorship and accepted the appointment of physician to the Belgian king. He spent the remainder of his life in Belgium, occupying himself with official duties and charitable medical attendance on the poor. He was knighted in 1850 by Queen Victoria, and died in 1857.

Carswell was a superb draughtsman and an accurate observer, and his drawings are extremely beautiful as works of art. They are also widely recognised as some of the most important works of their kind.

The reverse side of the sketch of Eliza Newman, with the legend 'Doctor Elliotson's Case, Eliza Newman, at 25. See case page 140'. The UCH case records, to which this reference refers, are still in existence for this period (see also p.154).

Sir Robert Carswell, *Heart with hydatid* [cyst] *in walls of left ventricle.* London, November 1834. [From Richard Quain, Esq, 'Sudden Death'.]

Watercolour on paper, 260 × 220 mm, with manuscript notes.

Provenance: transferred as part of the Medical School archives.

UCL/MED/MHMS/UNOF/1/A918

In 1832 the *Anatomy Act* was passed, legalising the use of cadavers in the event of the body being unclaimed. This allowed medical schools access to a good supply of corpses for dissection. The discipline thus finally gained respectability after many years of being blighted by the practice of resurrectionists (also known as body snatchers), commonly employed by anatomists in the United Kingdom during the 18th and 19th centuries to disinter the bodies of those recently deceased for anatomical research. The Carswell drawings, taken from recently deceased bodies as well as live subjects, form a unique collection of groundbreaking work and a valuable resource for researchers of medical history. The collection offers a fascinating contemporary perspective on medicine in the early 19th century, a significant period in the development of anatomy. During this time the subject began to flourish as a new scientific discipline, and it became clear that it should form an essential part of medical training.

The collection contains many items of historical significance, notably the first illustrations of the pathology in Hodgkin's Disease, the first portrayal of the lesions on the spinal cord in multiple sclerosis and the first depictions of iron deficiency anaemia (featured here). It comprises over a thousand finely drafted watercolour and ink drawings of various dimensions, depicting diseased structures divided into groups by subject. They were published in 1837 in *Illustrations of the Elementary Forms of Disease*, Carswell's great work on pathological anatomy. This fine folio contains remarkably well-executed plates which were furnished from his large store of drawings. The UCL collection also includes some manuscript notes, contained in four volumes bound in hard covers, and one box of partly bound loose sheets in Carswell's hand.

OPPOSITE: A vividly accurate depiction of the human heart damaged by a cyst, by Robert Carswell, 1834.

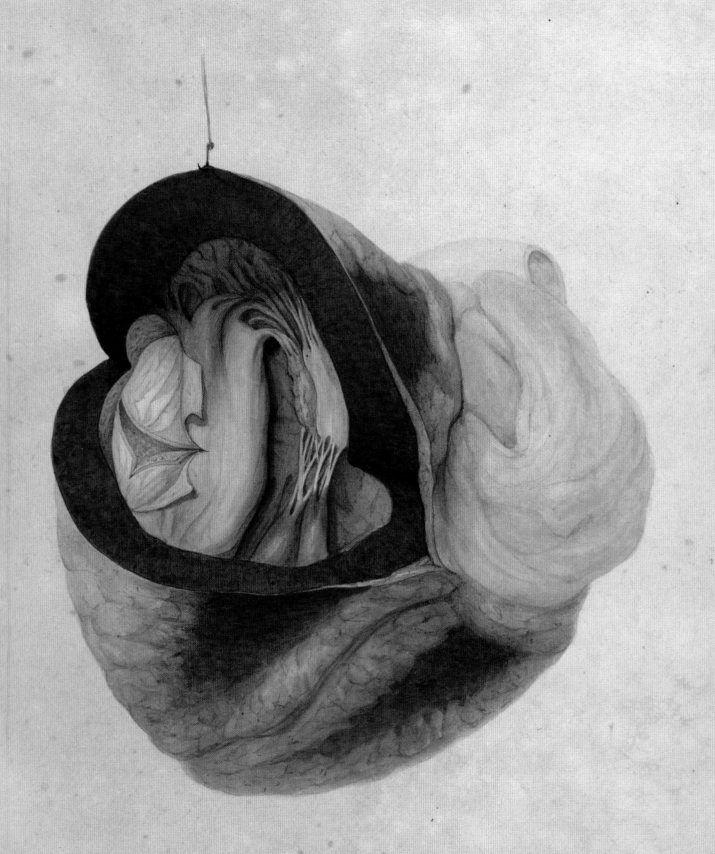

A Cyst in the parietes of the Left Ventricle and in one of the
columnæ carneæ, containing an-hydatid? — (Sudden Death.)

Illustrations by Edward Lear and 'the Bird Man'

John Gould, FLS, *A century of birds from the Himalaya Mountains*. London: published by the author, 1831.

6 pages, 72 leaves, 80 hand-coloured lithographic plates. 550 mm.

Provenance: unknown.

S R E Folio 920 G6/1–4

John Gould, FLS, *A monograph of the Ramphastidae: or family of toucans*. London: published by the author, 1834. Lithographs by Edward Lear and by John and Elizabeth Gould. Printed by C Hullmandel.

47 leaves, 34 lithographic plates (33 coloured). 570 mm.

Provenance: unknown.

S R E Folio 920 G6.1/1–3

The plates contained in these two works, among the finest natural history images of the 19th century, constitute a high point of illustrative technique. Gould was not directly responsible for the illustrations himself, although he supervised their production closely. His talent lay in drawing rough sketches, having an uncanny eye for capturing the characteristics and differences of each species. A keen observer, he had an extraordinary faculty for quickly recording in a rough sketch the characteristics of any bird that he saw. It was from these sketches that his artists made the beautiful finished drawings. These were re-drawn on stone to create lithographs, which were then hand-coloured by his chosen artists, bringing the depictions of exotic birds vividly to life.

Some of the original illustrations were by Edward Lear, best known as a poet but also, as we see in the plate featured here, a very accomplished artist. The last four pages of the *Ramphastidae* contain a piece by the naturalist Richard Owen (1804–92), titled *Observations on the Anatomy of the Toucan*, and an anatomical plate by the artist George Scharf (1788–1860).

Gould was born in Dorset in 1804. His father was a gardener in the royal gardens at Windsor and the young John helped him in his work there, developing a particular interest in birds. By 1827 he was working for the Zoological Society, where he looked after their ornithological collections. In 1829 he married Elizabeth Coxon, an accomplished artist, and together they created these wonderful books, publishing seven major works with nearly 700 coloured plates. Edward Lear assisted with two of them, contributing nearly 150 plates. Elizabeth died in 1841, but John continued to produce beautifully illustrated works on birds and other animals. A shrewd businessman, he published his works himself, amassing a considerable fortune. He died in 1881, desiring his own epitaph to be 'John Gould, the Bird Man'.

OPPOSITE: Hand-coloured lithographic plate from *A monograph of the Ramphastidae: or family of toucans* by John Gould and Edward Lear, dated 1833. It shows the species *Ramphastos Toco* (the Toco Toucan).

RAMPHASTOS TOCÖ, (Linn:)

Toco Toucan.

C. Lear del.
1833.

OTUS BENGALENSIS.

MUSCIPETA PRINCEPS.

OPPOSITE: Hand-coloured lithographic plate of the *Otus Bengalensis* (Bengal Owl), from John Gould's *A century of birds from the Himalaya Mountains*, 1831.

RIGHT: Hand-coloured lithographic plate of the *Muscipeta princeps* (fly-catcher) from John Gould's *A century of birds from the Himalaya Mountains*, 1831.

45

The cult of the autograph – and a Bloomsbury literary connection

Autograph book of Mary Talfourd. London, 1840–50s.

Manuscript signatures, sketches and notes in various hands and inks, on thick paper bound in a single volume. 38 leaves. 92 × 75 mm. Housed in two-part box, covered in green morocco leather with gilt lettering. 110 × 90 mm.

Provenance: purchased as part of the Ogden Library, 1953.

MS OGDEN 92

Like many of the items from the Ogden collection, this little gem has UCL historical connections as well as shining a spotlight on Victorian society. The signatures were collected by Mary Talfourd (1828–1901), daughter of the author and judge Sir Thomas Noon Talfourd, who hosted famous dinner parties with his wife at their Bloomsbury home. The signatures in this book, often accompanied by sketches and written dedications, belong to a number of well-known people who frequented the house at 56 Russell Square, a stone's throw from the site of the new London University (now UCL). Talfourd's regular guests included Robert Browning, Charles Dickens, Leigh Hunt, William Makepeace Thackeray, Wordsworth, Landseer, David Roberts and other artists and writers, all of whom are represented in the volume.

Sir Thomas Talfourd (1795–1854) had consulted two founder members of the new university, Henry Brougham and Henry Crabb Robinson, about his future, and on their advice embarked on a legal career. In 1833 he accepted the rank of serjeant-at-law and was soon to become the most respected member of the Oxford circuit and a popular figure in London society. In the early 1830s Talfourd became famous for dinner parties, remembered for their informality, conviviality, swarming children and numerous cats. He became a close friend of Charles Dickens, who dedicated *The Pickwick Papers* to him. Mary often wrote to Dickens, and her brother and sister feature as Frank and Kate in *Nicholas Nickleby*. Talfourd himself is thought to have been the model for the idealistic Tommy Traddles in *David Copperfield*. Dickens later wrote of him:

RIGHT: Ink sketch of the Sphinx, with dated signature of David Roberts, from Mary Talfourd's autograph book (fol. 15).

OPPOSITE, RIGHT: Spine of Mary Talfourd's autograph book, and the custom-made, gilt-tooled 'spine' of the two-parted box in green leather in which it was housed.

OPPOSITE, FAR RIGHT: Signature of Charles Dickens, December 1844 (fol. 5).

'If there ever was a house … where every art was honoured for its own sake, and where every visitor was received for his own claims and merits, that house was his … Rendering all legitimate deference to rank and riches, there never was a man more composedly, unaffectedly, quietly, immovable by such considerations … On the other hand, nothing would have astonished him so much as the suggestion that he was anyone's patron.'

Dickens and his family lived in and around Bloomsbury for many years. He would almost certainly have witnessed the building of UCL on his frequent walks around London, perhaps on his travels to visit Thomas Talfourd. Mary would no doubt have been delighted to acquire his signature which, according to the date, was written in December 1844. The entry for the Egyptologist David Roberts (1796–1864) is particularly arresting for its depiction of the sphinx (folio 15, featured here, dated 1845). Other pictorial compositions include musical annotations from John Parry, the Welsh composer and musician (1776–1851), dated 1 August 1846 (folio 8). The poet Leigh Hunt (1784–1859) writes an especially touching dedication: 'for little Mary – with an imaginary kiss' (folio 4). Whether or not Mary continued with the collecting in later years is not known, but it makes it all the more evocative if this is her only surviving personal item.

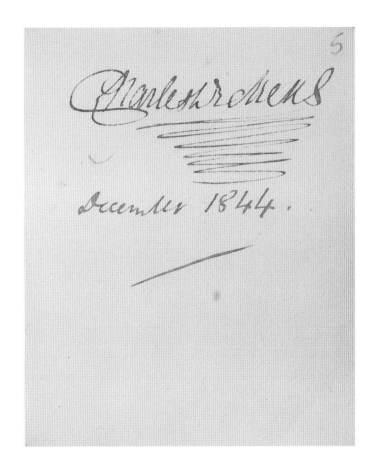

46

The first operation under ether in Europe

Robert Liston, Patient case register, University College Hospital, December 1846.

Manuscript on paper, written in black ink. Bound in contemporary parchment cover, 263 folios, 380 × 240 mm.

Provenance: transferred from the UCL Medical School, 1988.

UCH/MED/H/MR/1/1846

The handwritten notes in this volume from the archives of University College Hospital Medical School are a poignant reminder of the first experiment on a patient under ether in England, which took place on 21 December 1846. This was also the first operation under anaesthetic conducted in Europe, and it represents one of the greatest-ever medical breakthroughs – eliminating the suffering of patients undergoing painful amputations and other severely traumatic procedures. The discovery of the use of anaesthetics during surgical operations also put a welcome end to the somewhat distasteful sense of theatre and glamour that surrounded the performance of some surgeons, renowned first and foremost for their speed.

Robert Liston (1794–1847) was one of the most dextrous and resourceful surgeons of his day. He had a reputation as one of the fastest

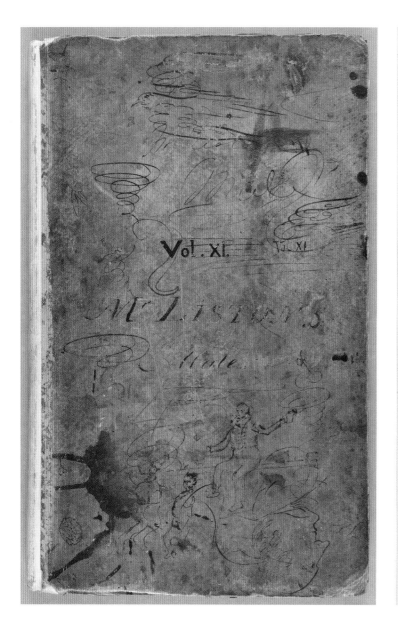

surgeons in the business, once removing a leg in under two minutes! In 1847 James Simpson, Professor of Midwifery at Edinburgh University, discovered chloroform, which acted faster than ether and had fewer side effects. Many people still distrusted surgeons, and many religious fundamentalists resisted the idea of easing pain in other situations, such as childbirth. After Queen Victoria took chloroform for the birth of her eighth child in 1853, however, it became wholly respectable.

The historic occasion of 1846 was recorded here, noting the condition of Frederick Churchill, the patient, throughout the procedure and after. Liston had heard of the use of ether by a dentist two months previously at the Massachusetts General Hospital. The glass used for administering the ether during the leg amputation was devised by William Squire, a 21-year-old medical student. Liston's operation was a complete success and the patient survived, heralding a new era of modern surgery.

The classic description of the struggle for life

Charles Darwin, *On the Origin of Species by Means of Natural Selection, or, The Preservation of Favoured Races in the Struggle for Life,* first edition, first issue. London: John Murray, 1859.

English. [ix] 502 [32] pages.
200 × 125 mm.

Provenance: presented by the author to Sir Francis Galton, bequeathed in 1911.

GALTON/1/5/2

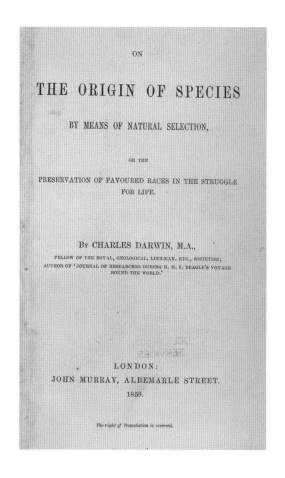

If ever a scientific work deserved to be called a landmark book, this must surely be it. Charles Darwin (1809–82) served as a naturalist on the voyages of HMS *Beagle* across the Atlantic Ocean to South America from 1831 to 1836. Inspired by what he saw during the expedition, Darwin began collecting facts about different species, culminating in the publication of this book some 20 years later. While others, notably the Australian naturalist Alfred Russell Wallace, had also started thinking along the same lines, *On the Origin of Species* was both ground-breaking and highly controversial at the time. The work became the foundation of modern evolutionary studies by providing a scientific explanation or theory of how species change and adapt through time. Darwin elaborated a proposition that species slowly evolve from common ancestors through the mechanism of natural selection. As he himself anticipated, his theory became, and in some circles continues to be, the object of intense controversy. Darwin continued to write on botany, geology and zoology until his death in 1882.

This highly prized copy came into the collections with the Galton Bequest in 1911, believed to have been presented to Francis Galton by his half-cousin Darwin (Erasmus Darwin was their common grandfather). It is clearly Galton's personal copy and features his handwritten marginalia, notably on pages 64 and 227, the former being a charming note showing approximate calculations explaining the probable minimum rate of natural increase in the population of elephants. An initial 1,250 copies were printed and the run was soon oversubscribed. Darwin's publisher, John Murray, did not immediately reprint it, but gave him a chance to read the work through for small corrections. A new printing with corrections was issued in 1860, and a further six editions had appeared by 1872. The second printing of the sixth edition in 1878 contained Darwin's final corrections. In addition to the 1859 first edition with its significant provenance, UCL is fortunate to have not one but two copies of the 1860 printing in UCL Special Collections.

LEFT: Title page of Charles Darwin's presentation copy of the first edition of *On the Origin of Species*, 1859. It was given to his half-cousin Francis Galton.

OPPOSITE: Page 64 of Francis Galton's copy of *On the Origin of Species*, showing his manuscript annotations on the projected rate of the elephant population's natural increase.

be now increasing, more or less rapidly, in numbers, all cannot do so, for the world would not hold them.

There is no exception to the rule that every organic being naturally increases at so high a rate, that if not destroyed, the earth would soon be covered by the progeny of a single pair. Even slow-breeding man has doubled in twenty-five years, and at this rate, in a few thousand years, there would literally not be standing room for his progeny. Linnæus has calculated that if an annual plant produced only two seeds—and there is no plant so unproductive as this—and their seedlings next year produced two, and so on, then in twenty years there would be a million plants. The elephant is reckoned to be the slowest breeder of all known animals, and I have taken some pains to estimate its probable minimum rate of natural increase: it will be under the mark to assume that it breeds when thirty years old, and goes on breeding till ninety years old, bringing forth three pair of young in this interval; if this be so, at the end of the fifth century there would be alive fifteen million elephants, descended from the first pair.

But we have better evidence on this subject than mere theoretical calculations, namely, the numerous recorded cases of the astonishingly rapid increase of various animals in a state of nature, when circumstances have been favourable to them during two or three following seasons. Still more striking is the evidence from our domestic animals of many kinds which have run wild in several parts of the world: if the statements of the rate of increase of slow-breeding cattle and horses in South-America, and latterly in Australia, had not been well authenticated, they would have been quite incredible. So it is with plants: cases could be given of introduced plants which have become common throughout whole islands in a period of less than ten years. Several

Charles Darwin, manuscript drafts of *On the Origin of Species* and *The Descent of Man*

1 folio (folio 226 of the *Origin of Species* manuscript, *c.* 1850s; 4 folios from *The Descent of Man, and Selection in Relation to Sex, c.* 1870s. Ink on paper, 330 × 210 mm.

Provenance: given by Egon Pearson, 1967.

PEARSON/10/2–3

Darwin did not keep the manuscript of his most famous work, *On the Origin of Species*, and what has survived of it is widely dispersed. He started work on it in July 1858 and it was accepted for publication by John Murray in April 1859, on sight of the first three chapters. By early September it was in corrected proof, apart from the index, and publication day was 24 November. This single sheet is a fair copy in brown ink on blue paper. It corresponds closely, with minor changes in proof, to the printed text, which is in Chapter VI, page 203. The sheet was given by Darwin's daughter Henrietta, later Mrs R B Litchfield, to Karl Pearson in 1923; he was Egon Pearson's father.

The other four manuscript sheets which make up this set are all early drafts from *The Descent of Man* (published 1871). They consist of the following:

1   Chapter 6: folio 2 in the manuscript, with eight lines in the hand of Emma Wedgwood, Darwin's wife, at the bottom of the folio (Chapter VIII, pp.214–15 of the 1871 edition).
2   Chapter 1: folio 16 in the manuscript, with Darwin's signature (Chapter I, p.45 of the 1871 published edition).
3   Chapter 5: folio 1 in the manuscript (Chapter VI, p.185 of the 1871 published edition).
4   Chapter 6: folio 1 in the manuscript (Chapter VII, p.214 of the 1871 published edition).

The Descent of Man was the first time Darwin had addressed human evolution, in a work that also considered sexual selection and the comparative characteristics of animal, birds and other species. These manuscript folios were kept by Horace Darwin, Charles Darwin's son, and were also acquired by Karl Pearson in 1923. A delightful note written by Horace Darwin, dated 3 January 1923, begins: 'When we were children, we often used the blank sides of my father's M.S.S. [*sic*] when returned from the printers as scribbling papers. These sheets were kept by me…'.

UCL also holds an important collection of letters from Darwin to his half-cousin Francis Galton. The Galton Papers contains over 40 letters, probably representing almost their entire correspondence, which continued until Darwin's death in 1882. His hand is notoriously difficult to read. At its best accurate transcription needs practice; at its worst Darwin himself sometimes admitted to finding it difficult to read. His wife Emma, or one of his sons, especially George or Francis, took his letters from dictation, and he only signed them.

RIGHT: Detail from a note written by Horace, Charles Darwin's son, in 1923, explaining how the manuscript sheets from *The Descent of Man* came to be in his possession.

OPPOSITE: A page from Charles Darwin's manuscript draft of *On the Origin of Species*, *c.* 1850s, which closely corresponds with the printed version, Chapter VI, p.203.

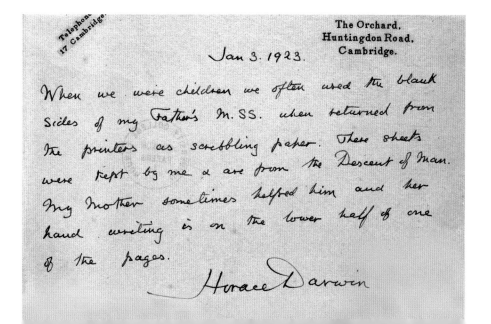

undoubted[ly] this is for the good of the community; & material loss or molested [...] though fortunately most rare, is all the same to the inexorable principle of natural selection. If we admire the most ingenious contrivances by which the orchids [...] are fertilised through insects agency; can we consider an equally perfect [...] the destruction of [...]

[...] if on [...] bees that a few grains of pollen in order that a [...] breeze on the [...] may be wasted if a [...] on the [...]?

<u>Summary of chapter.</u> — We have in this chapter considered some of the difficulties & objections which may be urged against our theory. Many of them are very good; but I think that, here or there, light has been thrown on them & [...] that, here or there, light has been thrown — on large classes of facts, which, on the theory of separate acts of creation, are utterly obscure. We have seen that species are not infinitely numerous & are not linked together by a multitude of intermediate gradations, partly because the process of natural selection must be very slow & will act at any one time only on a very few forms;

Paris, le 27 janv. 66

Mon cher ami,

Je ne t'oublie pas, seulement
je suis tellement occupé que
j'ai remis à quelques jours toutes
lettres et toutes visites.

Je quitte la librairie mercredi;
chaque heure que je dois encore
y passer a son travail marqué.

Donne moi jusqu'à la fin
de la semaine prochaine, et
j'irai te serrer la main à ton
restaurant, ou bien je t'écrirai
pour te donner un rendez-vous.

à toi

Emile Zola

Paris literary and theatre life in the 1860s

Manuscript letters of Emile Zola

French. 67 letters dated from 1864 to 1885, bound in one volume. 221 × 170 mm.

Provenance: purchased as part of the Ogden Library, 1953.

MS OGDEN 95

Born in Paris in 1840, Emile Zola rose to become one of France's most respected and revered novelists, publishing many novels, short stories and essays in his lifetime. In 1862 he was employed by Hachette and Co, and he later worked on the *L'Evénement* newspaper. This neat volume of handwritten correspondence gives a fascinating and important snapshot of a 20-year period of Zola's literary career.

The letters provide a colourful backdrop to the author's everyday life. All are from Zola to his friend Marius Roux, who collaborated with him in the play *Les Mystères de Marseilles*. A number of letters refer to the presentation of this play given at Marseilles that he and Roux worked on, and the difficulties they encountered, as illustrated by the only telegram in the volume, featured here. The drama was performed only four times and never appeared in print. Zola's wording in the telegram he sent on 6 October 1867 is somewhat ambiguous, referring to '*applaudissements et sifflets*' (applause and whistles), followed by '*succès incertain*'.

The volume contains many items of interest, including mentions of contemporary figures, such as Edouard Manet and Paul Cézanne, and of *Nana*, *Germinal* and other works. One of Zola's main features as a writer was his great interest in heredity and atavism, and there are possibly early musings in the letter of 6 June 1863 on the idea which became his *magnum opus*. *Les Rougon-Macquart*, the epic story following a French family across the generations, was published in a cycle of 20 novels between 1871 and 1893.

OPPOSITE: Letter dated 27 January 1866, from a volume of correspondence of Emile Zola with his friend and collaborator Marius Roux (MS OGDEN 95).

BELOW AND BELOW RIGHT: Front and back of a telegram by Emile Zola. It carries a slightly ambiguous report on the audience reception for his and Roux's play, *Les Mystères de Marseilles*, and was sent shortly after the first perfomamce on 6 October 1867.

A British entrepreneur in 19th-century South America

José Manuel Groot, *Portrait of Joseph Brown*, 1830s.

Watercolour on thick card, 250 × 170 mm.

Provenance: given by Miss F E Hunter, 1984.

MS ADD 302/6/11

BELOW: A certificate from the family scrapbook, issued by the British Legation in Bogota, 15 March 1831, attesting to Joseph Brown's British citizenship. The document allowed him safe passage when travelling through Colombia.

OPPOSITE: A portrait of the merchant Joseph Brown, wearing the traditonal Colombian sporting attire, 1830s. The poncho-style garment, called a *ruana*, is now housed in the British Museum.

LEGACION DE S. M. BRITANICA.

El infrascrito, enviado estraordinario y ministro plenipotenciario de S. M. B. cerca de la repùblica de Colombia, certifica que el portador de esta boleta *Señr Brown* es un súbdito de su Majestad, y como tal, autorizado á reclamar los privilejios, anexado à aquel caràcter.

Bogotà *15 de Marzo* de 1831.

In this arresting portrait of British merchant Joseph Brown, rather self-consciously sporting Colombian riding dress, we have an extraordinarily rich visual source. It captures a good deal about the manners and mores informing Britain's relations with Latin America during the early 19th century. Britain was then the main imperial presence in the region, facing some competition from France but not yet from the United States. Many British entrepreneurs, engineers and speculators of various kinds went to try their luck at creating wealth in the newly-independent former colonies of Portugal and Spain. Some got badly burned and returned home in disillusionment, but others stayed, coming to know and appreciate the countries where they sought to do business, and even playing a small part in their history.

Brown (1802–74) was born in London. He became a merchant like his father, who bore the same Christian name, and worked for the Levant Company in Turkey and Naples. In 1826 he went to Colombia and stayed until 1841. Brown later returned to South America in 1866 as manager of the Lima branch of the London Bank of Mexico and South America. UCL also holds the diary of his time there.

The picture was painted in Bogotá by the Colombian artist José Manuel Groot during the 1830s.

Groot (1800–78) was a polymath, in the manner of a significant minority among the well-educated sons of the Latin American landed elites. He was acclaimed as a historian, journalist and educator as well as a painter. Groot came from a family of wealthy merchants, and the fact that he painted Brown's portrait is eloquent testimony to the Englishman's level of acceptance among the most prestigious social circles in Bogotá. This is also readily revealed by the visiting cards and invitations pasted into the family scrapbook, another delightful item among the Brown Family Papers held at UCL.

Brown was himself a talented amateur painter. He produced a series of charming and characterful paintings (mostly watercolour or ink) of people and places he saw on a journey through parts of Colombia during the 1830s. Together, these paintings represent the first substantial collection of scenes of Colombian rural life. They are a prelude to the *costumbrista* movement (about local customs), which featured in the art and literature of many Latin American countries later in the 19th century.

In the portrait Brown wears a poncho-style garment, known as a *ruana* in Colombia. Believed to be the oldest such garment surviving, it used to be held at the Museum of Mankind, now absorbed into the British Museum, along with a pair of his *alpargatas* (shoes made of rope). Brown's own paintings, most of which are held by the Royal Geographical Society, have been reproduced in a beautiful volume, with bi-lingual commentary, by Malcolm Deas, Efraín Sánchez and Aída Martínez: *Tipos y costumbres de la Nueva Granada: la colección de pinturas formada en Colombia por Joseph Brown entre 1825 y 1841 y El Diario a su excursion a Girón, 1834*, Fondo Cultural Cafetero, Bogotá, 1989. NICOLA MILLER

50

A gallery fit for sculpture models

Decoration of the Flaxman Gallery, University College, Gower Street. Carried out by Messrs Green & Abbott, Oxford Street. From the Design by Prof F M Simpson, FRIBA.

Colour photographic print, *c.* 1922.

Provenance: part of the College Archives.

College Archives Photographs/Interiors/ Flaxman Gallery

An attractive feature of UCL today is its renowned Flaxman Gallery, a domed gallery of the sculpture models of John Flaxman (1755–1826). Having worked in the English Department from 1974 to 2012, I passed through the gallery almost daily on my way to the Library. In 2007 leading a research project on reforming institutions in 19th-century Bloomsbury disclosed to me more of the story behind the acquisition of Flaxman's models for the university. In particular it revealed the heroic role performed by one of the institution's early supporters on its foundation as the University of London in 1826–8.

Henry Crabb Robinson (1775–1867) was one of the most active figures in the history of UCL and of two other reforming institutions in Bloomsbury – the Ladies' College (later Bedford College), founded in Bedford Square in 1849 by Crabb Robinson's friend Elisabeth Reid, and University Hall, built on Gordon Square, also in 1849, as a hall of residence for the young men of University College. Both Crabb Robinson and Mrs Reid were Unitarians, as were several other supporters of UCL, established to allow young men of non-Anglican backgrounds to take the degrees from which they were barred at Oxford and Cambridge. Crabb Robinson served for several years on the Senate of UCL, on the board at University Hall (now Dr Williams's Library, which houses the country's foremost collection of Dissenting publications) and as a supporter of Mrs Reid in her venture to bring higher education to women for the first time.

Crabb Robinson lived in bachelor comfort in a large house on Russell Square. He spent his days attending meetings of the three institutions in which he had an interest, doing the rounds of Gower Street, Gordon Square and Bedford Square. He is best known to posterity as a leisured giver of breakfasts to writers and public men, and as the friend, particularly in his younger days, of men of genius, including Wordsworth, Coleridge, Southey and Lamb. A prodigious diarist whose journals – 62 manuscript volumes from 1811 until his death in 1867, aged 91 – are lodged, appropriately, in Dr Williams's Library, Crabb Robinson occupies a unique position as a recorder of the cultural life of the 19th century. He also single-handedly performed the difficult, long-drawn-out feat of securing the Flaxman sculptures for UCL.

Though Flaxman had acquired an international reputation, he left his sister-in-law and adopted daughter Maria Denman only debts on his death in 1826. A group of admirers, including Crabb Robinson, saved some of his pieces from his creditors, raising money to build a gallery to exhibit the casts. Crabb Robinson led the project, patiently persuading the reluctant Miss Denman over several years to allow UCL to house them in the splendid gallery specially built to the design of Thomas Donaldson (1795–1885), UCL's first Professor of Architecture. The building opened to a fanfare in 1851.

The Gallery has since undergone many changes. One occurred in 1922, when this colour design was produced. It featured in *The Times*, who reported on 17 April 1923 that 'The Flaxman Gallery at University College, Gower-street has recently been redecorated at a cost of £1,600'. This redecoration had been planned for more than a decade, and Professor Simpson (Frederick Moore Simpson, Professor of Architecture at UCL from 1903 until 1919) prepared his scheme in collaboration with the then Slade Professor of Fine Art, Henry Tonks. In the central panel of the design a

DECORATION OF FLAXMAN GALLERY, UNIVERSITY COLLEGE
GOWER STREET.
CARRIED OUT BY MESS*ʳˢ· GREEN AND ABBOTT, OXFORD ST.
FROM THE DESIGN BY PROF. F. M. SIMPSON, F.R.I.B.A.

ABOVE: Photograph taken in the early 20th century showing the statue of St Michael overpowering Satan, by John Flaxman. The work graces the centre of the Flaxman Gallery (College Archives, Photographs, Interiors, Flaxman Gallery).

ABOVE RIGHT: Photographic print of the 1922 colour design for redecoration of the Gallery. It displays casts and reliefs by the artist, created and endowed by Henry Crabb Robinson in 1851.

mural can just be seen. Executed by Tonks for UCL's 1926 centenary year, it depicts an imaginary meeting of four principal figures involved in the university's founding. The architect William Wilkins presents his plans to Jeremy Bentham and Thomas Campbell, who first conceived of the idea of a London university, flanked by Henry Brougham and Henry Crabb Robinson. The work was fixed in the central panel on the West side of the Gallery, with a plan to add later companion paintings at each side of it, although this never happened.   ROSEMARY ASHTON

Pioneers in science and medical science who shaped 20th-century life

Sir Victor Horsley, physiologist and surgeon, First World War field operations notebook, Gallipoli, July 1915.

Manuscript in ink and pencil on paper in bound notebook, with sketches. 190 × 130 mm.

HORSLEY PAPERS B29

Provenance: given by Lady Robinson, 1976.

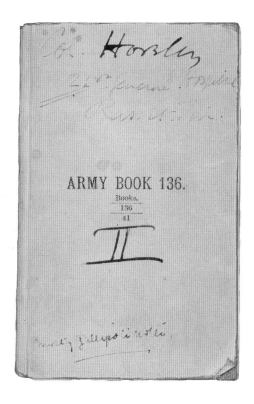

Out of the numerous individuals whose papers are held in UCL Special Collections, several scientists stand out in their own fields. Each has in some way forged new paths and received many accolades, including Nobel Prize awards and Royal Society fellowships. Their work represents the important link between academic research and innovation in the world outside academia, be it in industry or medicine. UCL is pre-eminent among university libraries in the UK in having its history reflected through the acquisition of many personal as well as research papers. These provide invaluable resources, not only for the study of each particular field and its development from the 19th century into the 20th, but also as a window into the cultural, political and social scenes of the day.

Four of these pioneers are featured here. Victor Horsley, Professor of Clinical Surgery from 1900 to 1907, played a pivotal role in shaping the face of standard neurosurgical practice. William Ramsay, Professor of General Chemistry 1887 to 1912, was the discoverer of rare gases, while Ambrose Fleming, Professor of Electrical Technology from 1884 to 1926, invented the thermionic valve. Kathleen Lonsdale, Professor of Chemistry 1949 to 1968 and later Emeritus Professor, specialised in X-ray crystallography. She confirmed the cyclic nature of benzene, one of the basic building blocks of life.

Victor Horsley (1857–16) studied medicine at UCL under John Burdon Sanderson and G D Thane. In 1880 he was appointed House Surgeon at University College Hospital, where he experimented with anaesthetics, before studying at postgraduate level in Berlin in 1881. He was appointed Surgical Registrar at UCH in 1882 and admitted to the Royal College of Surgeons a year later. Horsley was appointed Assistant Surgeon at University College Hospital in 1885, and elected to the Royal Society the following year. In 1886 he also became Surgeon to the National Hospital for the Paralysed and Epileptic, Queen Square, emerging as a leading cerebral surgeon of his time. In June 1887 Horsley removed a tumour from a spinal cord, the first operation of this kind ever performed.

Horsley wrote hundreds of papers and was knighted for his contribution to medicine in 1902. He was also awarded a Royal Society gold medal for his 'investigations relating to the physiology of the nervous system, and of the thyroid gland, and to their applications to the treatment of disease'. One of his later papers to the Royal Society was about the brain of Charles Babbage, which he had examined and described in great detail.

Horsley studied the effects of death from intra-cranial pressure for several years. In 1894 he presented a paper to the Royal Society about the effects of bullet wounds on the brain, an area of work he expanded upon over the next 20 years. He published much more on the subject during the First World War. Horsley died of heat exhaustion and intestinal infection in 1916, while serving with the Mediterranean Expeditionary Force near Baghdad.

This notebook, one of a series used while serving as a frontline colonel in the Gallipoli campaign in 1915, is a vivid reminder of the immediacy of the perils and challenges faced by surgeons working in the battlefield, as well as of the traumas suffered by soldiers. Horsley's success in this arena greatly contributed to his reputation as a practitioner who pushed the boundaries of 20th-century military surgery to a new level.

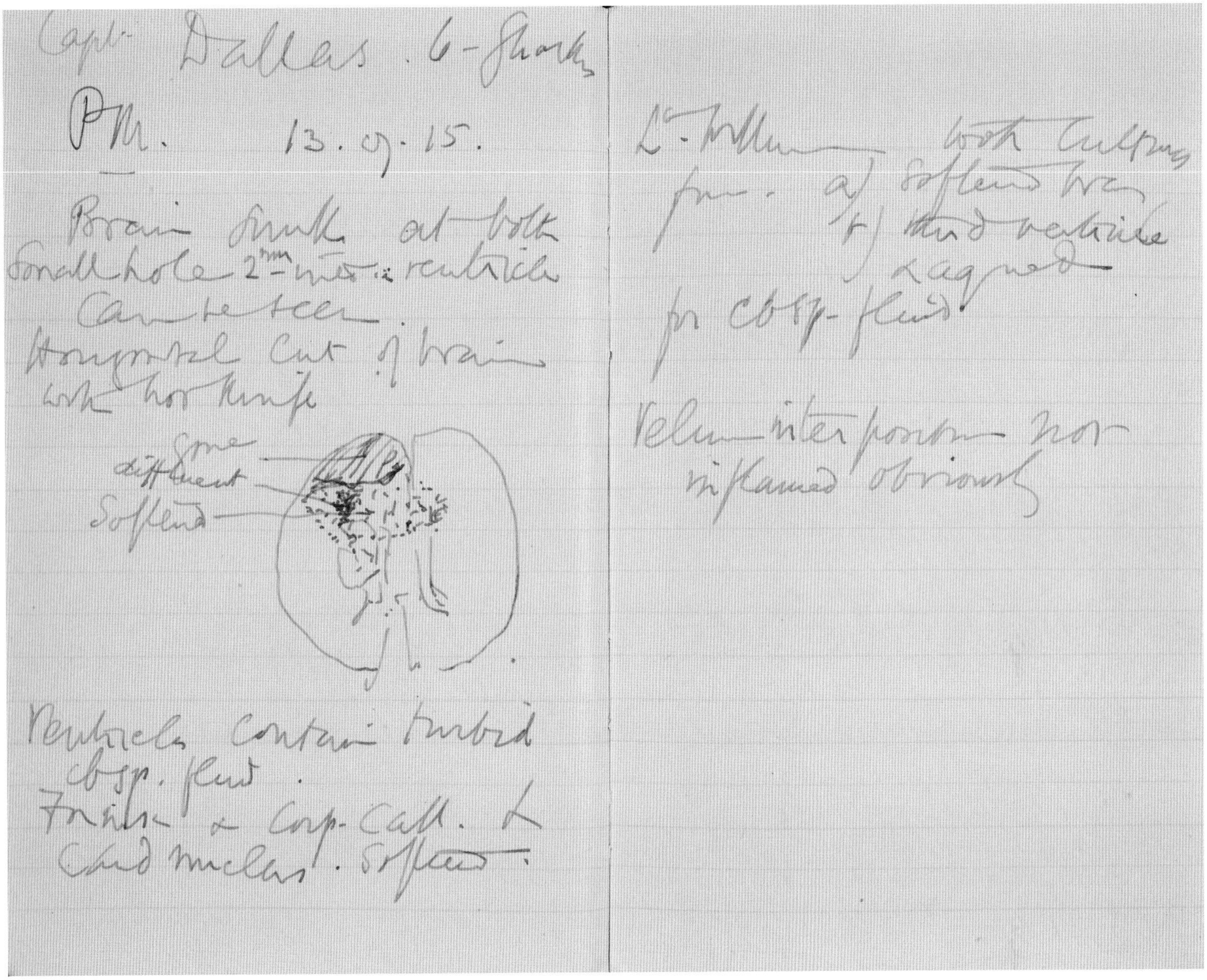

Capt. Dallas. 6—Sharks

P.M.   13. 07. 15.

Brain [illegible] at both
[illegible] hole 2mm into a ventricle
Can se[illegible].
Horizontal Cut of brain
with hot knife

diffluent
Softened

Ventricles contain turbid
cbsp. fluid.
Fornix & Corp. Call.
Caud nuclei. Softened.

Dr. Williams both culture
from. a] softened brain
b] third ventricle
ragged
for cbsp. fluid

Velum interpositum not
inflamed obviously

Sir William Ramsay, discoverer of argon, helium, krypton and other gases, laboratory notebook, UCL, 1894.

Manuscript in ink on paper, with diagrams 225 × 180 mm.

Provenance: given by Lady Tidy and Morris W Travers, 1957.

RAMSAY PAPERS 23

William Ramsay (1852–1916) made one of the most important scientific discoveries of the late 19th/early 20th centuries. The gas argon was his first discovery in 1894, followed by helium in 1895 and krypton, neon and xenon (with one of his students, Morris W Travers) in 1898. The series of laboratory notebooks contained in the papers chart the day-to-day experiments of this research, providing a detailed insight into the process.

From 1866 to 1869 William Ramsay studied at Glasgow University. In 1870 he went to Heidelberg, intending to study under R W von Bunsen, and went in early 1871 to Rudolf Fittig's laboratory in Tübingen. There he was awarded a PhD for research on toluic and nitro-toluic acids. In 1872 Ramsay returned to Glasgow as an Assistant in Young's laboratory of technical chemistry. He became Professor of Chemistry at University College Bristol in 1880, and was made Principal of the Unversity the following year. In 1887 Ramsay succeeded Alexander William Williamson in the Chair of General Chemistry at UCL, a post he held until his retirement in 1912.

This notebook dates from the early period of experimentation which made his name. He continued to work with the rare gases after the turn of the century, collaborating with Dr Frederick Soddy on radium in 1903 and with Robert Whytlaw-Gray on radon from 1909 to 1912.

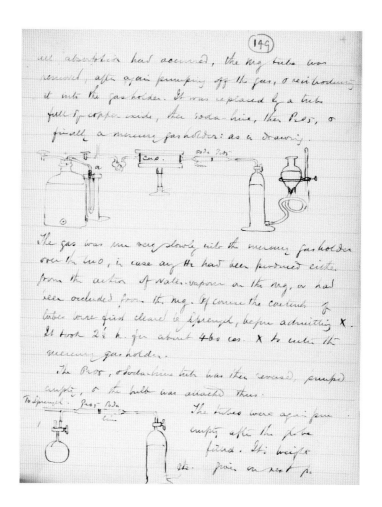

Sir William Ramsay's notes recording the experiments which led to the discovery of the rare gases in his UCL laboratory (fol. 149r).

Sir Ambrose Fleming, inventor of the thermionic valve, laboratory notebook on telegraphy, UCL, 1901.

Manuscript in ink on paper. 92 × 160 mm.

Provenance: bequeathed by Sir Ambrose Fleming, 1945.

MS ADD 122/49

John Ambrose Fleming (1849–1945) was appointed in 1885 to the first Chair of Electrical Engineering at UCL, a post he continued to hold until 1926. His lifelong interest in engineering science and innovative thinking began at the age of 11; he set up a workshop at home, made models of ships and engines, and experimented with photography. Fleming registered as a student at UCL, but gave it up due to financial difficulties in 1868, later studying chemistry at the Royal College of Chemistry. A bursary enabled Fleming to study Natural Sciences at St John's College, Cambridge, where he received first-class honours in 1880. The following year he was appointed Professor of Mathematics and Physics at University College Nottingham.

In 1884 Fleming was invited to give a course of lectures on electro-technology at UCL, and was appointed a year later to the first Professorship of Electrical Technology there. In 1899 Fleming became scientific adviser to Guglielmo Marconi's Wireless Telegraph Company. He helped to scale up Marconi's apparatus to allow for communications to travel across the Atlantic, resulting in the installation of the world's first long-distance wireless station at Poldhu in Cornwall in 1901. From here signals were sent over 1800 miles to Newfoundland at the end of that year, marking the beginning of the electronic age.

The Fleming archive at UCL is extensive, consisting of over 500 volumes and boxes. It includes this notebook, which dates from the time Fleming carried out experiments in radiotelegraphy in his laboratory, a practice he pursued over many years. In 1904 Fleming patented his thermionic valve. This device detected high-frequency electromagnetic waves, and was the first electronic device to lead directly to modern electronic media. Fleming became Emeritus Professor when he retired in 1926, and he continued to write and lecture almost until his death in 1945, aged 95. During his career he published over a hundred important papers and made significant contributions to the teaching of Electrical Engineering in universities.

A diagram by Sir Ambrose Fleming illustrating the detailed process involved in sending the first signals across the Atlantic, dated 12 December 1901.

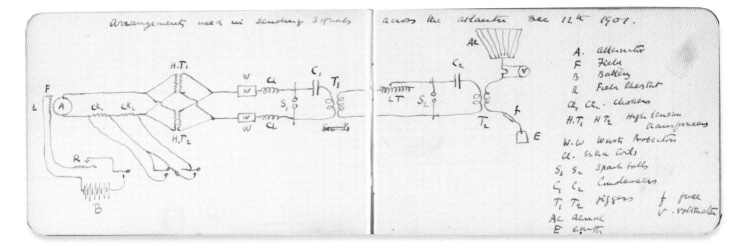

DAVY FARADAY RESEARCH
LABORATORY.

DIRECTOR: SIR WILLIAM BRAGG.

TELEPHONE:
REGENT 0669.

THE ROYAL INSTITUTION,
21, ALBEMARLE STREET,
LONDON, W.1.

25. 2. 1943.

The Governor,
H.M.P. Holloway,
London N 7.

Dear Dr. Matheson,

I am writing to thank you for your kindness in allowing me to have my scientific papers, etc for use while I was in prison. I did manage to spend about seven hours each day in really concentrated scientific work, besides doing my prison work in the officers' quarters and my cell tasks. I am afraid that this means that other prisoners had a good deal of empty time on their hands.

You asked me to let you know my opinion of the illumination in the cells, especially when the bottom cover was put on to the shade. I tested this on several occasions. With the conical shade only, and without the additional "lid", the illumination was very good; in my opinion it was more than sufficient for reading or sewing. Perhaps I was fortunate, but it seemed to me that a lamp of lower candle-power would have still provided ample light. With the lid, however, there was only a space on the table about 8" x 12" in area which was well enough lit for reading, and the illumination was definitely not sufficient for dark sewing. I think the hole in the lid could be considerably enlarged without impairing the blackout, and I would also like to point out that my

Kathleen Lonsdale, crystallographer, letter to Dr Matheson, Governor of HMP Holloway, 25 February 1943 (draft).

Manuscript in ink on paper, 3 folios. 225 × 180 mm.

Provenance: given by Judith Milledge, 1998.

LONSDALE PAPERS A.49

Kathleen Lonsdale was born in 1903 in Newbridge in what is now the Republic of Ireland, the youngest of ten children of the local postmaster and his wife. In 1908 her mother, concerned about Irish unrest, moved with the children to the small town of Seven Kings in Essex. Lonsdale won a scholarship to the County High School for Girls in Ilford in 1914, and two years later became the first girl to attend classes in Physics, Chemistry and Higher Mathematics at the County High School for Boys (no such subjects were offered at the girls' school). At the age of 16 she decided to leave school, despite hopes of her getting into Cambridge after phenomenal success in her scholarship exams. Lonsdale was able to enter Bedford College, however, where she studied first mathematics and then physics, achieving the highest score for the latter subject in the entire University of London at the age of 19. One of her University of London examiners was the Nobel prizewinner William H Bragg, and he invited Lonsdale to join his research team, studying X-Ray crystallography at UCL.

Kathleen Lonsdale was one of the first people to use X-rays to study crystals to determine their size, shape and structure. Throughout her career she studied many different crystals, including sodium nitrate, but she had a particular interest in diamonds, and her work in this area contributed greatly to knowledge on the subject.

In 1945 Lonsdale and the biologist Marjory Stephenson became the first women elected into the Fellowship of the Royal Society of London. She was made a Dame of the British Empire in 1956 and a year later received the Royal Society's Davy Medal – the first female recipient of the award since it was bestowed on Marie and Pierre Curie in 1903. During 1960–1 she was Vice-President of the Royal Society, realising yet another first in 1967 when elected the first female president of the British Association for the Advancement of Science. Lonsdale travelled widely as an academic, but also to carry out her peace and prison work. She continued to commute to her laboratory from home in Sussex up until her death in University College Hospital in 1971.

Political and religious commitments can feature strongly in the lives of scientists in the the 20th century, as they have over the last 500 years. Lonsdale became a pacifist after witnessing the effects of Zeppelin raids on London and the surrounding area during the First World War; she also became a Quaker in 1935. During the Second World War she was imprisoned in Holloway for refusing to register for civil defence duties. Throughout her month of incarceration she was sent papers and instruments by colleagues, enabling her to continue with her scientific work.

This draft of a letter sent to the then Governor is a snapshot example of how war affected everyone's daily lives. Lonsdale's experience affected her greatly. She became a prison visitor after her release, wrote about her experiences and worked hard for the reform of penal institutions for the rest of her life.

OPPOSITE: First page of draft letter from Kathleen Lonsdale to the Governor of Holloway Prison, 25 February 1943. In it she thanks him for allowing her to carry on her scientific work during her stay (she was imprisoned for a month), and comments on the insufficient light in the cells.

An early supporter of women's rights

Leonora Tyson, ed, *An Anti-Suffrage Alphabet*. London: The Women's Press for The Women's Social and Political Union, 1911.

Designed by Laurence Housman, with stencils by Alice B Woodward, Pamela C Smith, Ada P Ridley and others. Thick paper cover. 37 leaves, unnumbered. 280 × 380 mm.

Provenance: part of the library of Ian Kenyur-Hodgkins, purchased in 1978.

Housman Collection 347

OPPOSITE: Cover and pages from *An Anti-Suffrage Alphabet*, created for The Women's Social and Political Union by Laurence Housman, 1911. The work was brilliantly designed, with clever use of stencilled tableaux and accompanying text providing perfect counters to the sexist attitudes of the time.

These delightful items are part of the collection amassed and largely produced or created by Laurence Housman (1865–1959). He was an extremely versatile artist and book illustrator, writer and social reformer, whose output covered all kinds of literature, from socialist and pacifist pamphlets to children's stories. Brother of the better known poet and scholar A E Housman, who was Professor of Latin at UCL from 1892 to 1911, Laurence Housman was himself a committed socialist and pacifist.

The collection at UCL houses many of Housman's prose and fiction works as well as non-fiction, totalling 620 individual items. It contains books of verse, poems in anthologies, magazines and journals, including, for example, poems in 15 issues of the *Pall Mall Magazine* between 1901 and 1912. The collection contains numerous first editions, such as the 1902 publication of a Nativity play, *Bethlehem* (together with Joseph Moorat's music scores for the play), *Prunella, or, Love in a Dutch garden* (1906) and *The Little Plays of St. Francis* (1922), each of which features a scene design by Laurence Housman.

Housman wrote articles on religion, justice, social subjects, literature and art, many of which can be found in the collection. A note of satire pervaded much of his writing in varying degrees. His artistic fearlessness was echoed in his public commitment to underprivileged sections of society, and to controversial campaigns. He supported the women's suffrage movement, becoming a founder member of the Men's League for Women's Suffrage, and published advice on strategies for protesting in the *Women's Freedom League* newspaper. Housman was also an indefatigable public speaker and writer of pamphlets and articles on women's issues.

The publication *An Anti-Suffrage Alphabet*, featured here, was designed by Housman with contributions by women. The work must have caused quite a stir when it was first published in 1911. Its pointed sarcastic snipes at the prevalent attitudes towards women as second-class citizens appeared in alphabet form, strikingly encapsulated in large, thick, paper-covered book format, cleverly designed by Housman. Other non-fiction works in the collection which reflect his Suffragette sympathies include introductory poems by Housman in works published by the Women's Press, and a series of the newspapers entitled *Votes for Women*, also featured here, to which Housman regularly contributed. Works on peace include a first edition of 14 essays entitled *The preparation of peace* (1941).

Housman made numerous contributions to the journal *The album: a journal of photographs of men, women and events of the day* in 1895, under the rubric *The world of art* or *Our art supplement*. Among them were *An evening with Sir Joshua Reynolds* (Issue No.39, 28 October 1895) and *Mr Baxter gives his views upon Dutch art* (Issue No.38, 21 October 1895). 'Mr Baxter' was Housman's fictitious practising artist friend, used by him as a mouthpiece for the academic point of view. As well as containing contributions by Housman, the aforementioned journal, *The album*, is a vivid snapshot of late 19th-century life. It includes colourful pictorial covers, numerous photographs of well-known contemporary politicians, actors, musicians, singers, sportspeople and authors, together with articles on travel, gardening, animals, fashion, sport, music and home improvement.

In the 1920s and 1930s he regularly contributed poems, stories and articles on religious matters to *St Martin's Review*, the church magazine of St Martin's-in-the-Fields, Trafalgar Square. This was a church known for its

"Votes for Women," December 31, 1909.   Registered at the G.P.O. as a Newspaper.

Lawrence Hausman   4161

VOTES FOR WOMEN

EDITED BY FREDERICK AND EMMELINE PETHICK LAWRENCE.

VOL. III. (New Series), No. 95.   FRIDAY, DECEMBER 31, 1909.   Price 1d. Weekly. (Post Free, 1½d.)

THE POT CALLING THE KETTLE SMUTTY.

Mr. POT: "Kettle, you black, unrepresentative rogue, how dare you touch the Budget? Don't you know taxation without representation is legalised robbery?"

SERVANT: "Now then, Pot, you're blacker than he. You've been taxing women for years, and you refuse to consult them at all. It's you that want cleaning, and I'm going to do it with this brush."

Front cover of issue No.95 of *Votes for Women*, Vol III, New Series, 1909, published on New Year's Eve. Caricatures and cartoons were common currency in such publications.

Frederick and Emmeline Pethick Lawrence, eds, *Votes for Women* newspaper, Vol III (New Series), No.95, dated Friday December 31, 1909.

2 single leaves of printed paper, illustrated. 330 × 215 mm.

Provenance: part of the library of Ian Kenyur-Hodgkins, purchased in 1978.

Housman Collection 461

Frederick and Emmeline Pethick Lawrence, eds, *Votes for Women* newspaper, Vol III (New Series), No.65 [21 December 1909].

This issue of *Votes for Women* highlights the more serious side of campaigning for women's suffrage in an article about the physical abuse of women prisoners. Housman was a regular contributor (Vol III, New Series, No.65, December 1909).

active role in wider social, humanitarian and international issues. Among Housman's writings on sexual subjects is *The immoral effects of ignorance in sexual relations* (a lecture given in 1911 and published by the Women's Freedom League). Many of these works contain Housman's inscriptions, and some were donated by Housman to the dramatist and critic Harley Granville-Barker, with whom Housman collaborated.

Housman's first works were fairy tales, legends and poems which he illustrated himself. First editions of prose fiction include the novel *An Englishwoman's love-letters* (1900), which gained notoriety as a daring work when it was first published anonymously, and *A doorway in fairyland* (1922), which includes a frontispiece and 14 illustrations by Housman. His children's poems and stories were also published in a wide range of children's magazines, journals and annuals, among them *Little folks: a magazine for young people* (in 1898 and 1900) and many issues of *Joy Street: a medley of prose and verse for boys and girls* (between 1923 and 1936).

Housman later turned to playwriting, encouraged by Granville-Barker, and it is perhaps in this field that he is best known. *Prunella, or, Love in a Dutch garden* (1906) was co-authored with Granville-Barker and produced at the Royal Court Theatre in London. Later plays featured public figures, heroes and role models. The collection of *The Little Plays of St Francis* (1922) gave a voice to his pacifist leanings, while *Victoria Regina* (1934) was a satirical take on the life of Queen Victoria and Prince Albert. The author's depictions of biblical characters and members of the Royal Family were considered scandalous at the time, and many of his plays had to be produced privately because of censorship. *Victoria Regina*, for instance, was performed with great success on Broadway before it was granted a licence in England in 1937 at the Lyric Theatre.

Housman was a member of the No Conscription Fellowship, formed to support those who objected to taking up arms in the First World War, and whose members later became known as conscientious objectors. In 1919 he joined the Independent Labour Party, and prison reform and international peace became pressing issues for him. He was also an active member of both the British Society for the Study of Sex Psychology, which had as its aim sex education and promoting sexual freedoms, and the Order of Chaerorea, a society for the cultivation of a homosexual moral, ethical, cultural and spiritual ethos. In 1945 he opened Housmans Bookshop in Shaftesbury Avenue, London (later located at 5 Caledonian Road), founded in his honour by the Peace Pledge Union, of which he was a sponsor. Another of his legacies springs from the proceeds from productions of *The Little Plays of St Francis* at UCL, which supported the Franciscan Society – with the result that the latter's library is now deposited in UCL.

53

Contemporary literature of the First World War

Francisco de Sancha y Longo [F Sancha],
Aesop's Fables Up to Date, 1915–16

Six colour postcards, designed by F Sancha.
London: Raphael Tuck and Sons.
140 × 80 mm.

Provenance: bequeathed by Leonard
A Magnus as part of the 1914–18
Collection, 1925.

1914–18 COLLECTION/POSTCARDS/
SANCHA

The 1914–18 Collection is an unexpected archive to discover in UCL Library Services, bequeathed by a former student. To describe it in plain terms as a collection of contemporary publications relating to the First World War does not do justice to the fascinating, visually stunning range of material it covers. At its heart is a 24-volume series of the *Daily Review of the Foreign Express*, chronicling the events as they unfolded in the countries engaged in the campaigns and were reported by European media. Allied propaganda from the United States is also included, and the views of neutral countries are not left out. Bulgarian territorial claims, military aspects of the projected Channel Tunnel, British campaigns in the Middle East and the role of women are just a few of the diverse reports of the times that are recorded – in a range of languages, including English, German, Italian, French, Flemish, Portuguese and Spanish. The material dates from 1914 to the early 1920s, the majority being from 1916–18.

Over 300 books and around 1500 pamphlets complete the bulk of the collection. Titles are both serious and light in tone, examples being *The Fight for Right Pocket Book, Munition Lasses, Truth and the War, Some Frightful War Pictures* and *Nursery Rhymes for Fighting Times*. However, the stars of the collection have to be the series of six propaganda postcards which depict the players and action on the main stage in the form of the fables of Aesop (with striking results). The fables covered by these colourful postcards comprise 'The Dog and the Shadow', 'The Fox and the Grapes', 'The Hen that laid the Golden Egg', 'The Hare and the Tortoise', 'The Wolf and the Stork' and 'The Tortoise and the Eagle'.

The 'Dog and the Shadow' (below) illustration shows a wooden dog in a Kaiser-style helmet labelled 'Made in Germany' dropping a sausage labelled 'Prosperity' into water, in which is reflected a sausage labeled 'World Dominion'. The explanation on the card reads: 'Germany has lost the prosperity she had so laboriously acquired, in the vain endeavour to obtain the mastery of the world'. The series is accompanied by rare posters, broadsheets, maps and postcard photographs of leading soldiers, military and naval equipment.

FAR LEFT: 'The Hare and the Tortoise' from the series of postcards entitled *Aesop's Fables Up to Date*, with original artwork by Francisco de Sancha y Longo. Colourful imagery provides a contemporary take on Aesop's fables during the First World War.

LEFT: A postcard illustration by Francisco de Sancha y Longo for 'The Dog and the Shadow', updated 1915. It depicts the dog in a Kaiser-style helmet, symbolising Germany.

OPPOSITE: An illustration for the fable of 'The Wolf and the Stork', showing the wolf with the unmistakable helmet of Russian troops in 1916. The original narrative tells of a crane who rescues a wolf by dislodging a bone from its throat.

54

A modern classic with notoriety

James Joyce, *Ulysses*, first edition. Paris: Shakespeare and Company, 1922.

Number 307 of 750 copies on hand-made paper. [vii] 732 pages, 250 mm. Bound in morocco with gilt decorations by J May, London, in slipcase with original wrappers.

Provenance: this copy, no.307, was originally sent by the publishers to Mr George M Crowther of Bradford. No subsequent provenance information is available.

JOYCE XB 70 [1922]

This is a copy of the first edition of a modern classic. *Ulysses* was first published in book form in a limited edition of 1,000 copies, printed for Sylvia Beach, under the imprint Shakespeare & Company in Paris, by Maurice Darantière in Dijon. Of these, 100 signed copies were printed on Dutch hand-made paper and numbered from 1 to 100; 150 copies were printed on 'vergé d'Arches' (a high-quality, air-dried paper from Lorraine) and numbered from 101 to 250; and 750 copies on hand-made paper numbered from 251 to 1000.

Ulysses appeared in print on Joyce's 40th birthday, 2 February 1922, and sold out almost immediately. In October of the same year a second edition appeared under the imprint of the Egoist Press in London (which UCL also holds); 500 copies were seized by UK Customs under obscenity laws, but were reprinted. Several hundred more copies were seized and suppressed by the US customs throughout the 1920s, after a trial in 1921 declared as obscene a magazine *(The Little Review)* in which passages from the work had been published from 1918 to 1920. These early editions of *Ulysses* are notoriously full of errors (warranting a plea by the publisher to the reader, reproduced here): the Egoist Press edition contains seven pages of errata alone. This reflects the publisher's eagerness to publish this book despite its errors.

The publisher asks the reader's indulgence for typographical errors unavoidable in the exceptional circumstances.

S. B.

A publisher's note on the front fly-leaf in the 1922 first edition of James Joyce's *Ulysses*, which first came out in Paris. It was so full of typographical errors that Sylvia Beach ('S.B.'), Joyce's publisher and champion, felt compelled to remark on the fact.

ULYSSES

by

JAMES JOYCE

SHAKESPEARE AND COMPANY

12, Rue de l'Odéon, 12

PARIS

1922

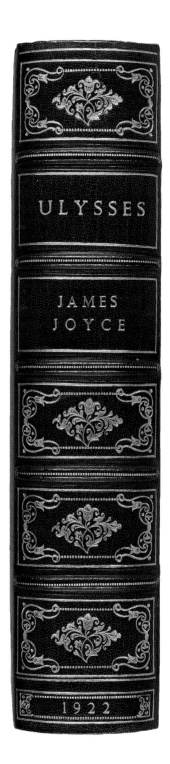

ABOVE LEFT: The title page of the first
edition of James Joyce's *Ulysses*.
It is one of only 750 copies printed
on hand-made paper. Altogether 1000
copies of this edition were printed on
different qualities of similar paper.

ABOVE: A gilt-tooled leather spine of
the first edition of *Ulysses*, 1922.

55

Henry James and George Orwell

Henry James, *The Turn of the Screw*; *The Aspern Papers*. Everyman's Library. Fiction no.912, editor Ernest Rhys, 1935. London: J M Dent & Sons Ltd, first edition.

ix, 299 pages. 180 mm.

Provenance: purchased from the library of Sir Richard Rees Bt, 1960.

Orwell Collection L10 JAM 1

INTRODUCTORY NOTE

THE two stories by Henry James in this volume show him in his characteristic personal manner of tale-telling, but to entirely different effect, the one leading to tragedy, the other to subtle and delicate comedy. The scene of the first, *The Turn of the Screw*, is laid in an English country house, and the characters are two tragic children, two intermediary grown-ups (one the narrator of the tale), and two ghosts. We must remember that Henry James, like his master Balzac, had a taste for mystery and the macabre which he did not often indulge so cruelly. The second story, *The Aspern Papers*, has its scene in Venice, that Venice to which he often returned in his real and fictive European wanderings. One may recall a letter of his, dated from Palazzo Barbaro, Venice, 23rd June 1907, in which he wrote: '. . . For myself, in this paradise of great household spaces, I kind of feel that even the bribe of the Canal Grande and a *giardinetto* together wouldn't quite reconcile me to the purgatory of a very small, *really* (and not merely relatively) small house. . . .' The fact is, he had every inclination to be housed in a palace, if not one quite so forlorn as that of *The Aspern Papers*. The chief characters there, the two derelict American ladies, and their very alert fellow-countryman with 'the literary heart' who wants to get hold of Jasper Aspern's relics, are perfectly conceived to suit the purpose or plot of the story and educe the other character—the old palace itself! For James was a master in depicting the power, or, if you will, the spirit, of place. Places to him were as significant as the people who lived in them; he was an epicure in old cities, in palaces, and in American, English, or foreign vistas.

In the year when *The Aspern Papers* was written, James was writing a series of critical appreciations of his favourite novelists and tale-tellers, especially the

vii

These days 'lab rats' rarely visit libraries: the scientific literature arrives online. Indeed the UCL electronic subscription list is now so comprehensive that I cannot remember the last time I had to go to the UCL Science Library. When invited to write a short piece about an item from the UCL Special Collections I was on holiday, and had just finished reading *Roderick Hudson* by Henry James – a memorable day, as I had been carrying a battered copy around for at least three years, with many false starts. A perusal of the UCL Special Collections revealed that they held ten Henry James books, all of which had belonged to George Orwell. The idea of the direct Orwell reading the elliptical James intrigued me.

When I saw the volumes in Special Collections, it turned out that the books had belonged to Orwell at the time of his death, in 1950 from TB, in University College Hospital. He had married his second wife Sonia in UCH in 1949. The books passed to his literary executor Sir Richard Rees, who later sold them to UCL Library Services. They are a motley set of editions, in line with Orwell's policy of buying secondhand books (see Orwell's *Books v. Cigarettes* essay published by Penguin Books in 1946) and comprise short stories and short-ish works such as *The Aspern Papers* and *The Turn of the Screw*. No James door-stopping tomes for him. For a magic space of time in a busy week I was allowed to look through them for margin notes in Orwell's handwriting. On crisp, white, proper paper, with hand-coloured illustrations and italic printing, this volume was the most remarkable book, *qua* book, that I had ever handled.

Orwell expressed little sympathy for James. His life was one of action and urgency. He declared that 'no one, now, could devote himself to literature as single-mindedly as Joyce or Henry James ('Writers and Leviathan' in George Orwell *Politics and Letters*, 1948), but I think that he also persevered in hope. When asked by *Horizon* for favourite books of 1947 he supplied: 'I enjoyed especially, ie among books I had not read before: *Under Western Eyes*, Joseph Conrad; *The Aspern Papers*, Henry James; *Framley Parsonage*, Anthony Trollope' (*It is what I think: 1947–1948, Complete Works of George Orwell*, 1998, no.3311).

In 1948 he was in hospital in Scotland. From here he wrote in a letter to Mrs Jessica Marshall, 'I have been making one of my periodical attacks on Henry James, but I never can really get to care for him' (*Complete Works of George Orwell*, 1998, no.3401A). However, in those pre-Internet days, he nevertheless took time that year to chase down Edmund Wilson's Freudian interpretation of *The Turn of the Screw*, in an essay published in 1934. He eventually found it in a volume entitled 'American Harvest', but he disagreed with Wilson's thesis. For much of 1949 Orwell lived in a spartan chalet at the Cotswold Sanatorium at Cranham, a few miles from spectacular views to the Malvern Hills. During this year he was more seriously ill, but still managed to read 140 books, including Dorothy L Sayers and Agatha Christie. On 1 June he wrote to Sir Richard Rees: 'I'm trying to read Henry James's *The Spoils of Poynton*, but it bores me unbearably' (*Our job is to make life worth living: 1949–1950 Complete Works of George Orwell*, 1998, no.3638).

One of my favourite Orwell essays is 'What is Science?' (George Orwell, *Tribune*, London, 26 October 1945). In this piece he expresses the view that experts in the 'exact sciences' are not especially qualified to comment on issues outside their own expertise. I would agree: the 'Laureates for World Peace' agenda has always struck me as absurd. Please forgive me, then, for writing about books. MARY COLLINS

VII

I got hold of Mrs. Grose as soon after this as I could; and I can give no intelligible account of how I fought out the interval. Yet I still hear myself cry as I fairly threw myself into her arms: 'They *know*—it's too monstrous: they know, they know!'

'And what on earth——?' I felt her incredulity as she held me.

'Why, all that *we* know—and heaven knows what more besides!' Then as she released me I made it out to her, made it out perhaps only now with full coherency even to myself. 'Two hours ago, in the garden'—I could scarce articulate—'Flora *saw*!'

Mrs. Grose took it as she might have taken a blow in the stomach. 'She has told you?' she panted.

'Not a word—that's the horror. She kept it to herself! The child of eight, *that* child!' Unutterable still for me was the stupefaction of it.

Mrs. Grose of course could only gape the wider. 'Then how do you know?'

'I was there—I saw with my eyes: saw she was perfectly aware.'

'Do you mean aware of *him*?'

'No—of *her*.' I was conscious as I spoke that I looked prodigious things, for I got the slow reflection of them in my companion's face. 'Another person —this time; but a figure of quite as unmistakable

56

horror and evil: a woman in black, pale and dreadful —with such an air also, and such a face!—on the other side of the lake. I was there with the child— quiet for the hour; and in the midst of it she came.'

'Came how—from where?'

'From where they come from! She just appeared and stood there—but not so near.'

'And without coming nearer?'

'Oh, for the effect and the feeling she might have been as close as you!'

My friend, with an odd impulse, fell back a step. 'Was she someone you've never seen?'

'Never. But someone the child has. Someone *you* have.' Then to show how I had thought it all out: 'My predecessor—the one who died.'

'Miss Jessel?'

'Miss Jessel. You don't believe me?' I pressed.

She turned right and left in her distress. 'How can you be sure?'

This drew from me, in the state of my nerves, a flash of impatience. 'Then ask Flora—*she's* sure!' But I had no sooner spoken than I caught myself up. 'No, for God's sake, *don't*. She'll say she isn't—she'll lie!'

Mrs. Grose was not too bewildered instinctively to protest. 'Ah, how *can* you?'

'Because I'm clear. Flora doesn't want me to know.'

'It's only then to spare you.'

'No, no—there are depths, depths! The more I go over it the more I see in it, and the more I see in it the more I fear. I don't know what I *don't* see —what I *don't* fear!'

OPPOSITE: Opening section of the editor's introduction to the volume containing *The Turn of the Screw; the Aspern Papers* by Henry James, 1935. Orwell regularly bought secondhand books, and in a 1947 magazine interview he said *The Aspern Papers* was one of the works he particularly enjoyed.

ABOVE: An extract from the Everyman's Library edition of Henry James' *The Turn of the Screw*, bound in the same volume with *The Aspern Papers*, also by James, from 1935 (pp.56–7). Orwell was not a great fan of James, but he was intrigued by the psychology behind the story line of *The Turn of the Screw*.

George Orwell: a timeless voice

George Orwell (born Eric Blair), literary notebook, 1939/40–1946/47.

Manuscript on paper, in Orwell's hand, written in blue-black, and red ink, also blue biro. 55 folios. 225 × 180 mm.

Provenance: presented by Sonia Orwell, 1972.

ORWELL B/1

When Sonia Orwell, Orwell's second wife, approached David Astor, the proprietor of the *Observer* newspaper, for help in finding a suitable home for the residue of the writer's papers, he turned for advice to Sir Ifor Evans, one of his circle of friends. Evans was then Provost of UCL and former Professor of English Language and Literature. UCL had already established a reputation for forward-thinking collecting policies in the field of literature (having acquired, for example, the Ogden Library, James Joyce collection, Poetry Store and Little Magazines collections), and it was a natural choice for her to make, creating a centre for Orwell Studies through the George Orwell Archive Trust. Two outstanding items are featured here – one of the series of literary notebooks, containing the synopsis for a draft of Orwell's apocalyptic novel *Nineteen Eighty-Four*, and an item of personal interest: his subscription card for the National Union of Journalists, which bears the now famous image of Orwell at the peak of his writing career (shown overleaf).

It is difficult to give a precise date for this outline of *Nineteen Eighty-Four*, though Orwell wrote to his publisher Fredric Warburg in August 1948 that he first thought of the idea in 1943. The notebook seems to have been used by Orwell over a period of years (the ink used here also appears in his 1942 wartime diary) and includes phrases to be brought into the work, at various stages entitled *The quick and the dead* and *The last man in Europe*. Here we see the main structure, themes, notes and phrases jotted down, incuding the slogan 'War is Peace', IngSoc, Newspeak and the Two Minutes Hate. He started work on the first draft of the novel in 1946, and completed the second draft by November 1948. Even then, Orwell was still hesitating between possible titles. The book was published by Secker and Warburg in June 1949 and has been a best-seller ever since, translated into more than 30 languages.

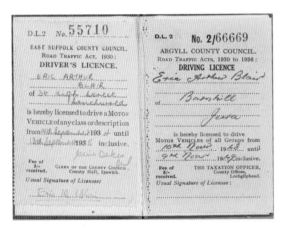

OPPOSITE: Manuscript notes for a novel by George Orwell, written probably some time in 1944. Many elements of the book, published in 1949 with the title *Nineteen Eighty-Four*, appear already conceived and noted down (ORWELL B/1, fol.35r).

ABOVE: The inside of Orwell's driving licence, featuring addresses in both Southwold, Suffolk (his parents' house) and Barnhill, Jura, where the novel *Nineteen Eighty-Four* was completed in 1948 (ORWELL J/7).

RIGHT: Orwell's notebook contains a general layout of *Nineteen Eighty-Four*, shown here. At the end of the notebook are other examples of 'Newspeak', written in Biro, so it is possible to date these to the post-war period (ORWELL B/1, fol. 36r).

George Orwell (born Eric Blair), National Union of Journalists membership card, 1943 to 1946.

Printed on paper, with handwritten entries, and black and white portrait photograph of Orwell pasted in, mounted on card, with blue cover. 2 leaves, 90 × 55 mm.

Provenance: deposited by the George Orwell Archive Trust on behalf of Sonia Orwell and the Orwell Estate, 1960.

ORWELL J/26

Orwell's National Union of Journalists photograph may well be the most famous picture of him that exists. He was 39 when it was taken, already the veteran author of a number of well-received novels and essays, though *Animal Farm* and *Nineteen Eighty-Four* were still to come. Orwell relished imagining the faces of writers, as he acknowledged in his seminal essay on Dickens: 'When one reads any strongly individual piece of writing, one has the impression of seeing a face somewhere behind the page ... What one sees is the face that the writer *ought* to have. Well, in the case of Dickens I see ... the face of a man who is always fighting against something, but who fights in the open and is not frightened, the face of a man who is *generously angry* – in other words, of a nineteenth-century liberal, a free intelligence, a type hated with equal hatred by all the smelly little orthodoxies which are now contending for our souls.'

Orwell entered the lists to contend 'for our souls' from the other side of orthodoxy, in the process changing forever who we are. He took Dickens to task for a social critique that was ultimately ineffectual, because it was predicated on the social and moral platitude that if people were more decent, then the world would be a better place. Nevertheless, Orwell turned into as fervent a moralist as Dickens, with the difference that the targets of his critique were intensely relevant to the age he lived in. Chief among them was the death penalty, which he viewed with abhorrence. In arguably his greatest essay, *The Lion and the Unicorn*, written during an air raid, Orwell deplored the fact 'the gentleness of English civilization is mixed up with barbarities and anachronisms ... Over against the Nazi Storm Trooper you have got to set that typically English figure, the hanging judge, some gouty old bully with his mind rooted in the nineteenth century, handing out savage sentences'.

Orwell knew all about the unconscionable awfulness of judicial killings. His essay 'A Hanging', from his days in the Burmese imperial police, remains a searing act of bearing witness. As the guards march the condemned man to the gallows, he sidesteps a puddle. 'When I saw the prisoner step aside to avoid the puddle, I saw the mystery, the unspeakable wrongness, of cutting a life short when it is in full tide. This man was not dying, he was alive just as we were alive ... He and we were a party of men walking together, seeing, hearing, feeling, understanding the same world; and in two minutes, with a sudden snap, one of us would be gone – one mind less, one world less.'

Orwell died aged 46 in University College Hospital, not far from my office at UCL. His was a profoundly civilised, unforgettable, timeless voice that has lived with me since my early teens. It should, and will, inspire generations to come.   RENÉ WEIS

OPPOSITE, ABOVE: Photograph of George Orwell taken in 1942 for his National Union of Journalists membership card, 1943–6. This famous image shows him at the age of 39.

OPPOSITE, LEFT: Cover of Orwell's NUJ membership card for 1943–6, in which the above photograph was used.

OPPOSITE, RIGHT: Cover of Orwell's NUJ membership card for 1947–8, notably unsigned.

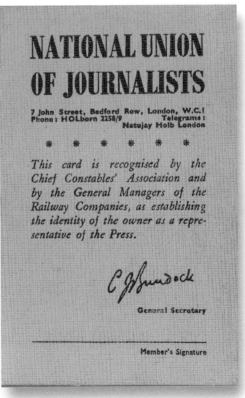

NATIONAL
UNION OF JOURNALISTS

MEMBERSHIP CARD

NATIONAL UNION OF JOURNALISTS

7 John Street, Bedford Row, London, W.C.1
Phone: HOLborn 2258/9   Telegrams:
                              Natujay Holb London

* * * * * *

This card is recognised by the
Chief Constables' Association and
by the General Managers of the
Railway Companies, as establishing
the identity of the owner as a repre-
sentative of the Press.

C. J. Bundock

General Secretary

_____
Member's Signature

Glossary

Aldine: material produced by the printing press started by Aldus Manutius in 1494 in Venice. This press introduced italics as a typeface and became the first to issue printed books in the small, portable octavo size. See also **Printer's device.**

Alum-tawed: material that has undergone 'tawing', an ancient process of treating prepared hide or skin with aluminium salts (hence the term 'alum') and other materials, such as egg yolk and flour. The process improves the skin's thickness and stability, making it easier to stretch and giving it a white-creamy colour.

Blind-tooled: a method of decorating a book in which impressions are made in the covering material, usually leather or tawed skin, by means of heated tools, pallets, rolls, fillets or combinations of one or more of these. It does not entail the use of leaf metal, foil or any other colouring material, with the possible exception of carbon, sometimes used to darken the impressions.

Breviary: a book containing the Latin liturgical rites of the Catholic Church. It includes all the daily psalms, hymns, prayers and blessings necessary for reciting the office.

Chemise: a textile or leather cover made with extended flaps at the head, fore-edge and tail of a binding. The tail flap was often used to attach the book to a belt or girdle, or as a convenient way to carry the book.

Folio: a single leaf of a book. It is also a book size, resulting from folding a sheet once to form leaves half the size of the sheet. The standard measurements for a folio-sized book are 382 x 305mm.

Fore-edge: the edge of a book opposite the spine.

Gauffred: (sometimes 'gauffered'): the term applied to the edges of a book, usually gilded, which have been decorated further by means of heated finishing tools or rolls that indent small repeating patterns.

Gouache: a type of opaque paint consisting of pigment and a binding agent, usually gum arabic.

Grotesque: a style of decorative art characterised by fanciful or fantastic human and animal forms. These are often interwoven with foliage or similar figures that may distort the natural into absurdity, ugliness or caricature.

Hagiographical: an adjective describing the life, or lives, of a saint, or saints.

Historiated: a term used to describe initials, capitals or borders in manuscripts and early books decorated with figures of men or animals (rather than simple floral or formal designs).

Illumination: a general term meaning decorated in gold and/or silver and /or coloured paint. It is applied to initial letters, single words, first lines or the opening pages of books.

Incunabula: a term used for books and other material printed from moveable metal type which can be dated before the year 1501. The cut-off date for incunabula was first adopted in 1643 by Johann Saubert in his history of the Nurnberg library (*Historia Bibliothecae Noribergensis*), which includes the first known catalogue of a collection of incunabula. The word derives from the Latin *cunae* ('cradle') and refers to books produced in the infancy of printing.

Micrographic: an adjective describing a drawn or photographed object as viewed through a microscope.

Minuscule: a form of small or lower-case lettering (ie not capitals), mainly used to describe all small writing forms.

Palimpsest: a manuscript consisting of a later writing superimposed upon the original text, which has been removed, from the Greek *palimpsesto*s ('scraped again'). A double palimpsest is a manuscript that carries two subsequent pieces of text, and has therefore undergone two removals.

Printer's device: from the earliest days of printing, a 'printer's device' or 'mark' was used as the printer's 'trade mark'. Printer's devices can be found at the end of books printed before 1500–1510; after this date, they more usually appear on the title page. Aldus's *Dolphin and Anchor* is one of the most famous devices.

Roundel: a picture, pattern or symbol contained in a circle.

Rubricated: initial capitals, headings and/or paragraph marks in a manuscript or printed book that have been written by hand or painted in red.

Solander box: a book or document box invented by Dr Daniel Charles Solander, a botanist, during his tenure at the British Museum (1773–82). The solander box is generally of a 'drop-back' or 'clamshell' construction, in which the spine remains attached to the lid once opened. These boxes can be made in elaborate or simple style.

Uncial: a majuscule script, written entirely in capital letters. It was commonly used by scribes from the 4th to the 8th centuries AD to write Greek and Latin.

Select Bibliography

Numbers in brackets refer to related entry.

Ashton, Rosemary, *Victorian Bloomsbury.* London: Yale University Press, 2012.   (no.50)

Ayris, P, *A Transcription and Critical Edition of Thomas Cranmer's archiepiscopal Register,* forthcoming.   (no.11)

Bearman, F, 'The Origins and Significance of Two Late Medieval Textile Chemise Bookbindings in the Walters Art Gallery', *Journal of the Walters Art Gallery,* 54, Essays in Honour of Lilian M C Randall, 1996, pp.163–87.   (no.4)

Chabas, Jose and Roca, Antoni, 'Early Printing of Astronomy: The Lunari of Bernat de Granollachs', *Centaurus,* vol.40, 1998, pp.124–34.   (no. 17)

Cooper, Tarnya and Hawker, Daisy, *Paper Cities: Topography and Imagination in Urban Europe c.1490–1780.* London: University College London, 2003.   (no. 33)

Coveney, Dorothy K, *A descriptive Catalogue of Manuscripts in the Library of University College London.* London: printed for University of London, University College, 1935.

Cranmer, Primate of all England: a catalogue of a quincentenary exhibition at the British Library, 27 October 1989–21 January 1990, compiled by Paul Ayris and edited, with an introduction and chronology, by Peter Newman Brooks. London: The British Library, 1989.   (no.11)

Deas, Malcolm, Efraín Sánchez and Aída Martínez, *Tipos y costumbres de la Nueva Granada: la colección de pinturas formada en Colombia por Joseph Brown entre 1825 y 1841 y El Diario a su excursion a Girón, 1834.* Fondo Cultural Cafetero, Bogotá, 1989.   (no. 49)

Eichard, Sian (ed), *A companion to Gower.* Cambridge: D S Brewer, 2004.   (no.9)

Febvre, Lucien and Henri-Jean, Martin, *The Coming of the Book: Impact of Printing, 1450–1800,* trans. David Gerard. London and New York: Verso, Modern Classic Series, 1997 (first published in French as *L'apparition du livre,* 1958).

Fletcher, H G *et al, The Wormsley Library: a personal selection by Sir Paul Getty, KBE.* London: published for the Wormsley Library by Maggs Bros. in co-operation with The Pierpont Morgan Library, New York, 1999, pp.8–10, 26–7.   (no.4)

Foot, Mirjam M, *The Henry Davis Gift, A Collection of Bookbindings,* vol.II. London: British Library, 1983, p.270.   (no. 37)

Freeman, R B, *Darwin and Gower Street, An Exhibition in the Flaxman Gallery of the Library.* London: University College London, 1982.   (no. 47)

Fuller, Catherine (ed), *The Old Radical: Representations of Jeremy Bentham.* London: University College London, 1998.

Furlong, G and Percival, J, *Exhibition: George Orwell 1903–1950,* exhibition catalogue. London: The Library, University College London, 1984.   (nos.55 and 56)

Furlong, G, 'UCL's Manuscripts and Rare Books', *UCL OSA News 1993,* University College London Old Students' Association, pp.8–14.

Keynes, Geoffrey, *A Bibliography of The Writings of Dr William Harvey 1578–1657,* 2nd edition. Cambridge: Cambridge University Press, 1953.   (no. 29)

Ker, N R, *Medieval Manuscripts in British Libraries: I, London.* Oxford: Oxford University Press, 1969, pp.331–65, 434.

McAdam, E L and Milne, George, *Johnson's Dictionary, A Modern Selection.* London: Victor Gollancz, 1963.   (no. 39)

MacCulloch, D, *Thomas Cranmer: A Life.* New Haven & London: Yale University Press, 1996.   (no. 11)

Pearson, David, *Books as History: The importance of books beyond their text.* London: British Library & Oak Knoll Press, 2008.

Robinson, P, *Catalogue of Dated and Dateable Manuscripts c. 888–1600 in London Libraries.* London: British Library, 2003, vol.1, pp.70–5.

Scott, J W, 'The Library of University College London' in *The Libraries of London.* London: The Library Association, 1961.

Stead, S, *Adventure and Art: Examples of Early Printed Books from University College London Library,* exhibition guide, May 2000 (unpublished work).

Vidler, K, 'Conservation of a Tortoiseshell Book Cover', *The New Bookbinder, Journal of Designer Bookbinders.* London: Designer Bookbinders, vol.26, 2006, pp.26–8.   (no. 37)

Acknowledgements

This book has been produced with the assistance and support of the following individuals:

Dr Paul Ayris, Director of UCL Library Services & UCL Copyright Officer, Chief Executive, UCL Press; Martin Moyle, Assistant Director (Support Services), UCL Library Services; Lara Speicher, Publishing Manager, UCL Press; Catherine Bradley, text editor; the named individual contributors (page 9); Mary Hinkley, UCL Media Services; Drusilla Calvert, indexer; Steve Wright, Special Collections, UCL Library Services; Frederick Bearman, Preservation Librarian, UCL Library Services; Tabitha Tuckett, Rare Books Librarian, UCL Library Services; David Cotterill, freelance journalist and author; Vanessa Freedman, Hebrew and Jewish Studies Librarian, UCL Library Services; Katy Makin, Project Archivist, Special Collections, UCL Library Services; Dan Mitchell, Mandy Wise and Rafa Corrales Siodor, from the Special Collections Readers' Services Team, UCL Library Services; Angel Warren Thomas, Warren Thomas Conservation.

Index

Note: *Italics* denote image